THE COMPLETE INDOOR/ OUTDOOR GRILL

175 DELICIOUS RECIPES WITH VARIATIONS BASED ON WHERE YOU COOK

D1370119

DONNA RODNITZKY

PRIMA PUBLISHING

*To my husband, Bob,
my companion for over thirty years,
who has been a constant source of
support, guidance, and pride;
and my children, David, Adam, and Laura,
who through their own achievements
have been an inspiration for me.*

Interior Illustrations by Lisa Cooper

On the cover: Barbecued Baby Back Pork Ribs (page 224), Grilled New Potatoes (page 342), Grilled Artichokes (page 332), and Grilled Fruit Kebabs (page 341).

PRIMA PUBLISHING and colophon are registered trademarks of Prima Communications, Inc.

Library of Congress Cataloging-in-Publication Data
Rodnitzky, Donna.
    The complete indoor/outdoor grill : 175 delicious recipes with variations based on where you cook / Donna Rodnitzky.
        p.   cm.
    Includes index.
    ISBN 0-7615-1233-0
    1. Barbecue Cookery.   I. Title.
TX840.B3R617 1998
641.7′6—dc21   97-39139
                                                         CIP

98 99 00 01 DD 10 9 8 7 6 5 4 3 2 1
Printed in the United States of America

HOW TO ORDER

Single copies may be ordered from Prima Publishing, P.O. Box 1260BK, Rocklin, CA 95677; telephone (916) 632-4400. Quantity discounts are also available. On your letterhead, include information concerning the intended use of the books and the number of books you wish to purchase.

Visit us online at http://www.primapublishing.com

Contents

Acknowledgments

*T*his cookbook might never have been written without the encouragement of Susan Silva, acquisitions editor for Prima Publishing. Her enthusiastic and gracious style persuaded me to take on this project, and I am grateful and honored by her confidence in me. I would also like to thank my project editor, Jennifer Fox, cover designer, Linda Dunlavey, food stylist, Bunny Martin, and those at Prima Publishing for their constant support and exceptional professionalism in creating and guiding this book to publication.

A special thanks goes to so many of my friends who shared their special recipes with me. They are Connie Brothers, Joyce Corbett, Sonia Ettinger, Mary Gantz, Valda Gebhart, Shelagh Hayreh, Mary Kathol, Mary Lea Kruse, Joanne Madsen, Sugar Mark, Pat McCormick, Kathy Moyers, Judy Neiman, Susan and Mike Wall, Trudy Ward, Jo Gail Wenzel, and Patti Yamada. David Klose, owner of Klose Custom BBQ Pits, provided a very interesting overview of the art of barbecuing and grilling and several fabulous recipes. Steve Strauss enlightened me about the history of the Vienna hot dog. The staff at Fareway's meat department were a consistent and reliable resource on how to select and grill meats, and the New Pioneer Co-op's seafood department provided similar expert guidance for choosing and grilling denizens of the sea.

Preface

The art of grilling food was discovered while our ancestors were still living in caves and dodging woolly mammoths. Over 100,000 years ago, early man believed he had perfected the technique of grilling by spearing meats on long sticks and cooking them over a fire. This desire for grilled food has remained with us through the millennia, and we have continued to strive for grilling perfection by replacing the simple fire with a variety of progressively more sophisticated and efficient grills, tools, and fuels. But in the midst of all this progress, we've paused to learn one important lesson from our Neanderthal forebears: It's just as easy to grill inside your cave as outside.

Grilling today has become more than just a great way to prepare foods—it has become a showcase for culinary creativity, both inside and outside the home. To watch a neighborhood chef at the grill is like observing an artist carefully mixing different colors and textures on the palette and then lifting a brush to the canvas to create a masterpiece. Poised as artists, wrapped in an apron and with barbecue tongs and tools in hand, we can create a culinary master-piece with a simple stroke of the basting brush or a gentle sprinkling of fresh herbs.

In this cookbook, you will learn how to combine an array of fla-vorful spices, herbs, and sauces and transform them into savory marinades featuring the flavors of one of many exotic international cuisines or the many delicious regional cuisines of the United States. Even if you are occasionally daunted by a recipe that includes less-familiar ingredients, take heart. Like the artist mixing colors on the palette, you can combine, substitute, or eliminate individual ingre-dients in a recipe and consider the result a new creation. In a recipe that calls for ketjap manis, for example, try substituting soy sauce; although I suggest using Sriracha hot chili sauce in many recipes, you can use any of your favorite hot pepper sauces in place of it. Cooking on a grill is a creative process, and the recipes in this book are important aids; but keep in mind that they should be considered guidelines and an inspiration and not your destiny.

As the name of this cookbook implies, *The Complete Indoor/Outdoor Grill* is not only for outdoor grill lovers. It is also designed for those who have discovered one of the most appealing trends of the 1990s: indoor grilling. The sheer number of indoor grill-ranges on the market today speaks volumes for the popularity of grilling in the kitchen, as does the proliferation of grill pans and tools that can be used to grill on an ordinary range. Indoor grilling has become most attractive to aspiring grillmeisters who do not have easy access to an outdoor grill or who live where it can get very cold during the winter months. Although many of us (including me) would not always let freezing temperatures or torrential rains pre-vent us from venturing out to the patio to grill, I have come to appre-ciate the versatility and convenience of using an indoor grill-range. While the food may be prepared indoors, friends and family can still share in the ritual of gathering around good food to enjoy the unique aromas and flavors that can only emanate from a grill.

Now is the time to expand your grilling horizons. Whether you prefer grilling in the kitchen or on the patio or, better yet, enjoy both, I invite you to discover the excitement of creating a sizzling masterpiece on the grill. Leave any culinary inhibitions you may have behind, and don't hesitate to experiment with novel ingredients and new techniques. You'll be delighted with the creative spirit you have unleashed.

Introduction

Eighty-four percent of all American families own at least one kind of grill. With such widespread enthusiasm for grilling, it is not surprising that there is such an extensive array of indoor and outdoor grills from which to choose. Each type has its own unique characteristics, and among the great variety of grills, there is one suitable for almost every personal lifestyle.

While charcoal grills are still most popular for outdoor use, gas grills have gained in popularity, including state-of-the-art stainless steel models equipped with side burners that will allow you to simmer a béarnaise sauce at the same time you are grilling a steak. The grill-range, initially popularized by Jenn-Air and now produced by several other manufacturers as well, is definitely in vogue for indoor grilling. It enables you to enjoy the wonderful flavors previously possible only with outdoor cooking in your own kitchen, year-round. For those lacking the space or the budget for an indoor grill-range, a wide array of indoor grilling equipment is available that can fit directly over your existing range, under the broiler, or even freestanding on a countertop. Most of the recipes I tested outdoors for this book were prepared on a Weber Charcoal Kettle grill or on a gas grill, and those done indoors were on a Jenn-Air grill-range; by following some simple guidelines, however, comparable results can be obtained with any of the popular grills I will describe.

OUTDOOR GRILLS

Outdoor grills come in an extensive assortment of styles and sizes, and there is one to fit almost every budget. While each type allows you to commune with nature and waft wonderful aromas into your neighbor's backyard, the technique required for each style of grill is slightly different, as is the time required to cook and the intensity of smoke flavor. You will be able to choose the type of grill that serves you best by determining whether it must be portable or relatively stationary, whether you most often grill fast and sear your food or cook slowly with indirect heat, and whether your preferred fuel is gas or charcoal.

KETTLE GRILL

The kettle grill's hood and base are rounded so that heat is evenly reflected off all surfaces and back onto the food. This makes for shorter cooking time and locks in the natural flavors and juices of foods. Although the hood is removable, it is usually advisable to cook with it on. This limits the oxygen supply and prevents flare-ups, thereby eliminating the need for water bottles and reducing the possibility of burning the food. Regulation of heat is controlled by vents on the base and hood, which should be in the open position when starting the charcoal and while cooking. However, if the heat from the coals becomes too great, the vents on the base can be closed. Make sure to use insulated barbecue mitts when adjusting the vents, because they will be hot to the touch. When you are finished grilling and the coals are cool, it is necessary to remove any accumulated ashes from the vents at the bottom of the grill to allow for proper ventilation with your next use.

Kettle grills come in a variety of sizes. Some are large enough to cook turkeys or platters of meat, while smaller models may fit perfectly on a small deck or balcony. If going to the mountains or spending a day at the beach is your favorite way to spend a Sunday afternoon, you can still enjoy the thrill of grilled foods by choosing from the wide assortment of portable kettle grills that are available. For those who prefer the taste of charcoal grilling but the convenience of gas, there are kettle grills equipped with all the features of the charcoal kettle grill, with the added feature of a special gas ignition system that lights the briquettes with just a push of a button.

BRAZIER OR OPEN GRILL

These open grills are usually most often made without a hood. They are round in shape, have a single cooking rack, and are supported on long legs. Some models are made with a half hood or windscreen. The brazier is an inexpensive way to grill, but its use should be limited to those foods that do not take a long time to prepare, because the coals burn down to ashes very quickly. With this type of grill, it is useful to keep a water bottle nearby to extinguish any flare-ups that may occur when fat drips onto the coals.

HOODED GRILL

Hooded grills resemble kettle grills, except they are square or rectangular and the hood is hinged onto the base. Food can be cooked either with the hood open, as on a brazier, or with it closed, allowing more smoke to accumulate and generating greater heat so that the food cooks faster.

SMOKER

A smoker is an elongated, cylindrical grill. In addition to having a fuel grate and a cooking rack, a smoker has a pan positioned between them. Water is added to this pan, and when the liquid gets hot, it produces steam. Soaked smoking wood chips of your choice are sprinkled on top of the hot coals. The combination of the steam from the hot water, cooking the food at a very low temperature, and smoke from the wood chips allows the food to acquire a very intense, smoky flavor and at the same time remain moist and juicy. It may be necessary to add additional coals every fifty to sixty minutes, but avoid opening the lid unnecessarily, as it may prolong the cooking time.

GAS AND ELECTRIC GRILLS

Gas and electric grills are very similar in design to a kettle or hooded grill. However, they use permanent lava rocks or ceramic briquette-shaped rocks instead of charcoal. These rocks are heated by an underlying gas burner or electric heating element. The major advantage of these grills is that they get hot quickly and the briquettes do not have to be replaced since they do not burn down to ashes. A gas grill requires a gas canister or a natural gas hookup, and an electric grill requires a nearby electrical outlet. Both of these grills impart a smoky flavor when drippings from the food fall onto the hot briquettes and vaporize; however, the flavors are not nearly as intense as when charcoal is used.

HIGH-TECH GRILL

In recent years, there has been a growing demand for state-of-the-art, deluxe cooking systems that are virtually a complete outdoor kitchen. The market response to this has been the production of very high-tech gas grills that come packaged in heavy-gauge all-stainless-steel carts with a wide range of options, such as a rotisserie, wok and griddle plates, warming racks, food storage and preparation areas, and infrared burners. Although these gas grills are very pricey, they are the ultimate in convenience and versatility and their elegance makes a certain statement—that is to say, they are the Maserati of grills.

LIGHTING COALS

The terms *barbecuing* and *grilling* are frequently confused and used interchangeably. However, there is a distinct difference between the two. Food that is barbecued is cooked slowly at temperatures ranging from 180 to 250 degrees, while food that is grilled is seared quickly over high heat to seal in its natural juices. Because grilling correctly requires the proper intensity of heat, learning the techniques of building a proper fire will pay enormous dividends.

When using a grill that requires charcoal, it is important to get all of the briquettes equally hot so that the food is uniformly cooked. The best way to accomplish this is to stack twenty to thirty coals in a pyramid before starting them on fire. There are several effective techniques to start the coals on fire, as discussed below. After burning for twenty-five to thirty minutes, the coals should all be ashen gray on the outside, and within the pyramid there should be a red glow. Using barbecue tongs, spread the coals out so they cover an area a little wider than the food to be cooked. The coals will remain hot enough to cook foods for forty-five minutes to one hour. If the cooking continues beyond this time, additional coals can be added; however, you will have to allow at least fifteen minutes for the new coals to get hot.

FIRE STARTERS

A host of techniques and equipment are available for creating a fire that will provide a uniformly hot charcoal bed. Some starters light fires in a relatively short amount of time, others are safer to use, while a few are popular because they do not impart chemical odors to the food that is being prepared. Some techniques require little more than a match, while others are dependent on specialized tools or equipment. No matter which techniques or apparatus fits your budget and your grilling timetable, the following discussion contains useful suggestions that can help decrease the chemical odors of some and explains how to use others more safely.

Chimney Starter   The chimney starter (or flue starter) is used to quickly get enough coals hot to start the remaining coals needed. It is a metal cylinder with holes on the sides to allow for ventilation. It may have a wooden or a heat-proof handle. The best way to use a chimney is to place some crumbled newspaper in the bottom of it and place coals on top. Open all the vents and set fire to the newspaper. In a very short time, the air will draw the flames up through the chimney and heat the coals. Wearing insulated barbecue mitts to grasp the handle (even if it is heat-proof), transfer the hot coals from the chimney onto the fuel grate and add the remaining coals.

Kindling   Take pieces of newspaper and roll them diagonally into a long, narrow cylinder. Grasp the ends and tie them into a knot. Place the knots on the fuel grate and cover them with pieces of dry twigs or wood scraps. Loosely mound six to seven coals on top of the pile. Carefully ignite the newspaper knots. As coals ignite, add more coals to the mound, continuing this process until all the coals have been added. Using tongs, carefully spread out the coals over the fuel grate once they have become hot.

Electric Charcoal Starter   The electric charcoal starter consists of a heating element attached to an extended handle with a cord that plugs into a regular 120-volt electrical outlet. The element is placed among the coals, and when it is plugged in, it gets hot enough to ignite the coals resting on it. The hot coals ignite others, and after about eight minutes, all of the coals will have become hot. Although this starter is very easy to use, a major concern is that it remains hot for a while, even after it is unplugged and removed from the coals. If you have children or pets, be certain to find a safe area where it can cool down.

Block Starter   Two to three of these small chemically treated cubes are placed among the coals and ignited with a match. They do not affect the taste of the food and are very easy to use.

Liquid Starter   Liquid starters are a very popular way to light coals. However, the chemicals in the starter are absorbed by the coals and can impart an unpleasant taste to your food. The best way to avoid this potential problem is to place only a few coals on the fuel grate and sprinkle them with starter. Add the remaining coals and ignite the treated coals. Using this technique, the majority of the coals are untreated and cannot generate a chemical taste. Never add additional starter if any of the coals are still burning, as this practice is a serious fire hazard.

BRIQUETTES AND WOOD CHIPS

Two of the most important considerations when grilling are creating a hot fire, so that the food is cooked uniformly and quickly, and producing adequate aromatic smoke to flavor the grilled food. The type of fuel you burn and the additional combustible materials you include in the fire, such as wood chips, will help determine how these two goals are met.

Charcoal Briquettes   Charcoal briquettes are made of carbonized scraps of wood combined with a filler and compressed into the shape of a briquette. Often, chemicals are added that allow the coals to light more quickly. However, food cooked over coals containing these additives can have an unpleasant taste. To minimize this problem, make sure all of the coals are uniformly ashen gray, which indicates that the chemicals have largely burned away and are no longer a source of fumes.

Hardwood Charcoal   Hardwood charcoal is made of wood without the addition of fillers or chemical additives and therefore does not impart an unpleasant taste to grilled food. It burns hotter than ordinary charcoal briquettes. Charcoal of this type is frequently made of hickory, maple, oak, cherry, or mesquite.

Smoking Chips or Chunks   Smoking chips or chunks are used to impart a unique flavor to the food rather than to act as a fuel. They are made of wood from nut- and fruit-bearing trees, such as mesquite, cherry, pecan, alder, ash, maple, hickory, oak, walnut, or apple, each having its own distinctive smoke aroma and flavor. Wood chips or chunks will generate the most smoke when allowed to sit in water (try beer or wine for an interesting change) for at least thirty minutes before they are scattered onto the hot coals, just before grilling the food. If you have any grape vines, they can also be used in the same way.

   If you plan to use smoking chips or chunks with a gas grill, you might consider buying a metal smoking box. These are small, vented boxes for holding the chips and are placed directly over the heat. This will prevent the gas fuel ports from getting clogged by wood particles.

Instant Charcoal   This is really the sanitized way to build a fire! Your hands never have to touch the charcoal. The charcoal comes premeasured, enough for one cookout, in a simple bag that is placed on the grate. With just a touch of a match to the bag, the charcoal ignites.

TECHNIQUES

When cooking with an outdoor grill, there are only two basic methods available. Food is cooked either directly over the coals or indirectly, receiving reflected heat from coals that are not immediately under the food.

DIRECT METHOD

The direct method is most frequently used when the food to be grilled can be cooked in thirty minutes or less. Using this technique, the food is placed on the cooking rack over the coals and is exposed directly to their heat.

INDIRECT METHOD

The indirect method is used when the food to be grilled will take longer than thirty minutes to cook and when it is necessary to prevent the food from getting too close to the heat source. A drip pan is placed in the center of the fuel grate and an equal number of briquettes is placed on both sides. After the coals are ashen gray, the cooking grate is positioned over them and the food is placed directly over the drip pan rather than over the coals. If the cooking time is longer than forty-five to sixty minutes, it may be necessary to add additional coals.

INDOOR GRILLS

The thought of preparing food in the kitchen conjures up visions of a stew simmering in a pot or a juicy steak sizzling under the broiler.

The advent of grill-ranges has changed that image, as we now also have the capability to grill foods indoors. The principle of indoor grilling is identical to that of grilling performed outdoors: food is cooked on a specially designed grill grate directly over the heat source. Thankfully, as with an outdoor grill, there are no pots and pans!

Whether you are making a steak or a tuna filet, you will be able to delight in wonderful aromas that are as appealing as those that waft from an outdoor grill. If you yearn to bring the thrill of the grill indoors but do not own a grill-range, you needn't be discouraged. There are a host of stovetop grilling pans and broiler grill pans that can be used for this purpose with your existing range. Keep in mind, however, that these pans work best with gas or electric ranges and are not recommended for flat-induction stovetops.

JENN-AIR GRILL-RANGE

All of the recipes in this cookbook were tested on a Jenn-Air Electric Grill-Range; however, manufacturers of most other ranges offer a similar grill-range as an option. The Jenn-Air can be purchased with either an electric or a gas grill-range cooktop.

The grill-range cooktop is equipped with a removable porcelain basin pan, grill liner pan, grill element, and grill grates. Surface controls allow you to vary the intensity of the heat from the grill element or the gas burners. The gas grill-range cooktop comes with either a single grill, a grill and two surface burners, or a grill and four surface burners.

One of the important features of the Jenn-Air is the downdraft ventilation system, which draws air down through the grill top and then out through the center of the back of the range. The powerful downdraft allows some grilling aromas to persist but removes any excessive smoke or vapors that may occur while grilling, keeping your kitchen virtually smoke-free. Many other grill-ranges may have similar downdrafts, but in some, the ventilation mechanism may be located overhead.

Jenn-Air offers some very useful guidelines for using a grill-range cooktop. Most of these guidelines should be applicable to other models.

Guidelines for Using Jenn-Air Grill-Range

- Before the first use, wash new grill grates in hot soapy water, rinse thoroughly, and dry. Then "season" the surface by wiping it with a thin coating of cooking oil. Remove any excess oil with a paper towel. This procedure should be repeated each time the grates are cleaned in the dishwasher or before each grilling for which a sugar-based marinade will be used.
- Use nonmetal utensils, to avoid seriously scratching the nonstick surface of the grill grates.
- Always preheat the grill on the Hi setting for five to ten minutes. This improves the flavor of the food being cooked and will also sear in the juices.
- Excessive amounts of fat should be trimmed from meats to prevent flare-ups. A small amount of fat can remain to produce just enough smoke to give the food an outdoor flavor.
- Occasional flare-ups may occur for a second or two from grease drippings. These brief flare-ups are normal.
- Suggested cooking times are approximate, due to variations in meat. A meat thermometer will help you determine doneness.
- To get the branded look on steaks, it is important that the grill be preheated.
- Buy top-grade meats that are cut at least three quarters of an inch thick.
- Score the fat on edges to prevent meat from curling.
- Baste or apply sauces the last fifteen to twenty minutes of cooking time, unless the recipe specifies otherwise.

STOVETOP GRILL PANS

Stovetop grill pans allow you to prepare quick and flavorful grilled food indoors with a minimum of additional cost. With these nonstick pans, you can grill right on top of your gas or electric range. The nonstick raised grilling surface, or ridges, will allow you to quickly sear chicken, meats, and fish so they retain their natural juices and create grill marks on the food without adding cooking oils or fat.

These pans may be round, square, or rectangular. The round and square grill pans vary in size from nine and a half to fourteen inches in diameter, while the rectangular pans are ten by twenty inches. Some grilling pans have long handles and resemble an ordinary skillet except for the ridges, while others are designed to resemble attractive serving pieces.

BROILER GRILL PANS

Broiler grill pans consist of two basic parts: a drip pan and a cast-iron grate. Before grilling, the top rack of the oven broiler should be adjusted to allow the food on the broiler grill pan to be two to three inches from the heat source. Once the rack is positioned, pour one half inch of water into the drip pan (to reduce smoke and flare-ups) and set the cast-iron grate on top. Place the assembled grill pan on the adjusted rack of the oven broiler and preheat under broiler for ten minutes. After the pan is preheated, you can place your choice of poultry or meat on it or choose any other food you would ordinarily prepare on an outdoor grill. The pan is returned to the broiler and the food is cooked for about the same amount of time as on an outdoor grill. Exact times may vary, so follow the manufacturer's guidelines and use a meat thermometer. Turn foods once so that both sides are properly cooked.

Guidelines for Using a Stovetop
Grill Pan or a Broiler Grill Pan

- Before the first use, wash new stovetop grill pans in hot soapy water, rinse thoroughly, and dry. Then "season" the surface by wiping it with a thin coating of oil (do not use canola oil, because it bonds to the polymers of the nonstick coating on the pans). Remove any excess oil with a paper towel. This method of washing and "seasoning" the stovetop grill pan should be repeated after each use. Be aware, however, that a stovetop grill pan should never be washed in the dishwasher, since vigorous washing in harsh detergents might damage the finish. Instead, soak the pan in hot soapy water. If caked-on food remains, it can be removed by using a plastic or nylon cleaning pad with a non-abrasive cleaner.

- Broiler grill pans should be washed before the first use in the same way as stovetop grill pans. However, these pans should be "seasoned" with a thin layer of solid vegetable shortening instead of oil, making sure the entire surface is coated. Prior to the first use only, the coated pan must be placed in a preheated 300-degree oven for one hour and then allowed to return to room temperature. With repeated use, after several weeks the pan will blacken. This indicates that the pores of the iron are sealed and there will be a more durable coating to prevent sticking. As with the stovetop grill pans, the broiler grill pans should be washed (but not in the dishwasher) and then "seasoned" with vegetable shortening after each use. Pat off excessive shortening with a paper towel, and the grill is ready for its next use.

- Always preheat the stovetop grill pan on medium heat for one minute or according to the manufacturer's suggestions. If you sprinkle a drop or two of water on the pan and it sizzles, the pan is ready. It is not necessary to use high heat when cooking food, and what's more, high heat may damage the pan's non-stick coating.

- The cooking time for foods on a stovetop grill pan is very similar to that required for an outdoor grill. However, because of the great number of different grilling pans, I would suggest following the manufacturer's guidelines for the specific pan you own. In any case, a meat thermometer is always a good way to determine when the food is done.
- Cook food long enough on each side so that grill marks appear. The less you turn the food, the better the appearance and taste of the food.
- When cooking with foods that are high in fat, it may be necessary to occasionally drain the drippings.
- Use tender cuts of meat that are not more than two inches thick when using this type of grill pan.
- Baste foods with marinades the last four to five minutes of cooking time.
- Plastic or wooden utensils are recommended, to avoid damaging the nonstick cooking surface.

ELECTRIC GRILL

An electric grill, such as the Krup's Fun Grill, consists of an insulated cool-touch housing, a stainless steel drip pan, a grill rack, and a control panel with illuminated on/off switches. It is a freestanding unit that can be used on a countertop or a table. In most respects, it is similar in design to an electric grill-range, except for the absence of a ventilation system to carry away smoke. Instead, the water pan collects drippings, keeping smoke production to a minimum. This type of grill should be preheated for five minutes before using. Grilling time will vary depending on the thickness and size of the food to be cooked.

ACCESSORIES

There is no end to the number of accessories that have added new dimensions to creative grilling and at the same time have made it so easy! I have chosen to describe a few of them, most of which are mentioned in the recipes found in this cookbook. Many of these accessories are inexpensive, so becoming a fully equipped grilling chef should be relatively easy. On the other hand, you may find that with a little improvisation, some of the cooking utensils you already own can be used for the same purpose in place of some of these accessories.

WIRE BRUSH

This is an essential tool for keeping an outdoor grill clean. Each time you grill, the cooking rack should be scraped clean with a wire brush. This prevents food from sticking to the cooking rack and reduces the possibility of unpleasant flavors being added to the food. On the other hand, indoor grilling surfaces, almost all of which have a non-stick coating, must never be scraped, to avoid permanently damaging this finish.

BARBECUE TONGS

Tongs enable you to grasp foods without piercing them and allowing their natural juices to escape. They should be long enough so that your hand is safely removed from the area immediately above the hot grilling surface.

MEAT THERMOMETER

A meat thermometer is the most reliable way to determine when food is properly cooked. The thermometer reads the food's internal temperature, which is the true indicator of doneness. The tip of the thermometer should be inserted into the deepest part of the meat, but you should avoid touching the bone. There are many kinds of thermometers on the market, but the best is the instant-read variety. Once inserted into the meat, a reading will be displayed within seconds. I use the Taylor Digital Pocket Thermometer 9840. It is reasonably priced and very accurate.

INSULATED BARBECUE MITTS

Fireproof mitts are essential to the safety and enjoyment of grilling. Whether handling a chimney starter or turning metal skewers, these mitts will protect you from being burned.

GRILL WOK

The grill wok is a four-sided, porcelain-enameled steel grid with multiple small holes symmetrically placed all over the sides and bottom. It is placed directly on the cooking grate. A grill wok is invaluable for grill stir-frying, because its high sides hold the food in place while you stir. Food cannot fall through the small holes, but smoke and grilling aromas pass through them easily. This accessory is not as well suited to an indoor grill as it is to the outdoor variety.

GRILLING GRID

The grid is a flat, porcelain-enameled steel grate with multiple holes symmetrically placed all over the bottom. Like the grill wok, it is placed directly on the cooking grate. It is excellent for grilling vegetables or other foods that are too small or fragile to place over a conventional grate with widely spaced bars. I have used a grilling grid on my indoor grill-range, and although it does not fit perfectly, it still allows me to grill vegetables and other foods too fragile to be placed over the grates.

PIZZA GRID

The pizza grid is a round, porcelain-enameled grid with multiple holes symmetrically placed all over the bottom. It works equally well with an outdoor grill or an indoor grill-range. Because of the porcelain finish, pizza dough will not stick to the surface and the grid is easy to turn.

FISH AND VEGETABLE TURNER

The turner consists of two flat pieces of porcelain-enameled steel that are joined together by hinges at one edge, like a book. Used correctly, it allows you to flip food without having to use utensils. Since it grasps the entire food item at once, it is less likely to cause crumbling than a fork or tongs.

DRIP PAN

When a recipe calls for the indirect grilling method, a drip pan is placed under the food at the center of the fuel grate. Charcoal briquettes are arrayed so that they surround the pan. This arrangement allows the drippings from the food to fall into the pan rather than on the coals, which might cause flare-ups. You can make your own drip pan by folding two sheets of heavy-duty aluminum foil into the shape of a pan.

HINGED WIRE BASKET

This accessory consists of two flat, wire rectangular grids, hinged on one side. Food is placed between the wire grids and the two sides are closed, keeping the food in place. Adjustable hinged baskets are ideal for grilling hamburgers, fish, steaks, or other foods that may be too fragile to turn with a fork or a spatula.

METAL SKEWERS

Metal skewers are perfect for making kebabs. They are very long and will hold a complete individual serving of meat or fish and vegetables. They also come double-pronged, which is perfect for items such as cherry tomatoes, mushrooms, and shrimp. The second prong prevents foods like these from spinning around when the skewer is turned, making it easier to cook them evenly on both sides. Make sure to use an insulated barbecue mitt when touching a metal skewer.

If you use wooden skewers, soak them in water first for at least 30 minutes or overnight to reduce the chance of their catching fire. While on the subject of skewers, fresh rosemary skewers have become quite trendy, and for good reason. They impart a subtle aromatic flavor to meats and vegetables and are also very attractive. When using rosemary as a skewer, you should remove most of the leaves before threading meats or vegetables on it. Be sure to buy rosemary with a very thick stem; any other will not be sturdy enough to pierce the meat or vegetables, or be strong enough to support the food on the grill.

BASTING BRUSHES

Basting brushes are ideal for brushing marinades or sauces onto food. Make sure to buy one with a long handle and of good quality—there is nothing worse than finding brush hairs on your food!

SPRAY BOTTLE

Keeping a spray bottle filled with water near your outdoor grill will allow you to put out unwanted flames quickly. Just set the spray jet on the narrowest stream and aim it toward the problem area. Water should never be sprayed on a flare-up in an electric grill-range or an electric countertop grill. If a sustained flare-up occurs in an electric appliance, turn off the heat and remove the food if it can be done safely.

GUIDELINES FOR SUCCESSFUL GRILLING

Successful grilling starts with a great recipe and the proper equipment, but achieving the ultimate in grilling perfection requires attention to several details. Most of the techniques I will point out are very simple, but some are time-consuming. Nevertheless, it is worthwhile to incorporate them into your grilling routine.

- Clean your outdoor grill with a wire brush after each use. Residue left on the grill can make food taste bitter.
- To reduce flare-ups, trim all excess fat from meats.
- When grilling outdoors, grilling time will be affected by the weather. Allow for more time in cold weather.
- To brown marinated meat more evenly on an indoor or outdoor grill, blot the meat dry with a paper towel after removing it from the marinade.
- When making kebabs, leave a small amount of space between portions of meat on the skewers, to assure that each piece is cooked uniformly.
- Sprinkle fresh herbs, peppers, onions, garlic, citrus zest, or garlic zest over the hot coals of an outdoor grill. This technique will infuse foods with an additional subtle flavor while they are grilling.

- It is best to coat the grate of an outdoor grill with a nonstick vegetable spray to prevent food from sticking. This should be done before the grate is placed over the heat.
- Vegetables, whether cooked indoors or outdoors, should be coated with a cooking oil (preferably olive oil) before grilling, as an additional measure to prevent them from sticking to the cooking grate.
- Avoid running out of fuel in the middle of cooking on a gas grill. To determine the amount of gas remaining in a propane tank, pour a cup of boiling water over the tank. The part of the tank that remains cool to the touch is where there is still propane gas. Above this level, where the tank is warm, the tank is empty.

GUIDELINES FOR PREPARING
ANY KIND OF MEAT

To enhance your knowledge of the different cuts of meat available and how best to prepare them, seek the advice of the experts in the meat department of your local market. Once you have chosen the best cut for your feast, here are several pointers that will help you grill it to perfection.

- Store meat in the coldest part of the refrigerator.
- Bring meat to room temperature thirty to sixty minutes before grilling.
- Remove any visible fat to reduce flare-ups while grilling the meat and to reduce the calories.
- Using a sharp knife, make slashes along the edges of lamb and pork chops to prevent them from curling while they are grilled.
- Remove meat from the grill one to two minutes before it is done, because it will continue to cook.
- Turn steaks and roasts with tongs rather than a fork, to prevent the meat's juices from escaping.

- Once meat is removed from a marinade, the marinade should not be reused on other meats or served as a sauce, since it may contain bacteria from its contact with the uncooked meat. If you want a sauce as well as a marinade, double the recipe ingredients and divide the marinade in half. Use one half to marinate the meat, and save the other half to be heated when needed and served as a sauce over the cooked meat. The only safe way to reuse a marinade is to boil it to kill any bacteria.
- Once meat is on the grill, use clean utensils and platters that have not been in contact with the raw meat.
- After meat has been cooked, it should be kept at 140 degrees until ready to serve.

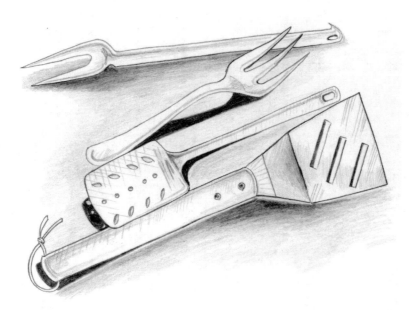

1

POULTRY

Poultry is a celebrated food enjoyed in many different cultures. While it is delicious stuffed, broiled, braised, stewed, or roasted, poultry can be elevated to a new dimension when grilled.

CHICKEN

Chicken is inherently flavorful when prepared on a grill. Not only is it infused with the smoky aroma of the grill, but it also readily picks up flavors from the spices, herbs, and sauces in a marinade. Broiler-fryers are very young birds, usually from four to six weeks old, and they vary in weight from two and a half to three and a half pounds; roasters are less than eight months old and weigh from three and a half to five pounds. Older chickens have more flavor, because of the higher amount of fat found under the skin. For this reason, roasters are more flavorful than broiler-fryers. A capon is a rooster that has been castrated while very young. Because capons are fed on a very fattening diet, they become much larger than ordinary chickens, ultimately weighing between four and ten pounds. Their meat is very tender, flavorful, and juicy.

Chicken can be purchased whole, split, quartered, or cut up, with or without the bone and skin. The most popular cuts of chicken are the thigh, breast, and drumstick. When buying chicken, look for plump birds with pale white skin.

CORNISH HEN

Cornish hens are small broiler chickens that are produced by crossing a Cornish, bantam, or small game cock with a white Plymouth Rock hen. Cornish hens are also called Cornish Rock hens, Rock Cornish hens, or Cornish game hens. At five to six weeks of age, they weigh from one to two pounds. Cornish hens can be grilled whole but are equally delicious when butterflied, that is, when cut down the backbone and then carefully opened to lie flat. Whichever way the Cornish hen is grilled, the end result is a delicate serving of all-white meat.

TURKEY

There are two kinds of turkey. The female (hen) usually weighs between eight and sixteen pounds, while the male (tom) is typically in the range of fourteen to twenty-six pounds. A tom yields more white breast meat because of its size, but both the hen and tom provide tender meat that is juicy and flavorful. When choosing your turkey, a primary consideration is the number of people you plan to serve. Allow three-quarters to one pound per serving; if you want leftovers, add at least one quarter pound per person.

Fresh turkeys taste much better than frozen turkeys. Look for Grade A turkeys with clean skin that is pearly white and unblemished. The best way to prepare a whole turkey on the grill is to use the indirect method. However, fresh turkeys that have been halved are delicious when prepared over direct heat on either an outdoor or an indoor grill. In addition to whole turkeys, turkey breasts, turkey breast tenderloins, and turkey breast steaks are readily available, as are turkey cutlets, turkey drumsticks, wings, thighs, and ground turkey.

Duck

Grilled duck is an exceptionally savory alternative to chicken and turkey. Ducks were first domesticated by the Chinese over 2,000 years ago. Thanks to an enterprising clipper ship captain in the nineteenth century, nine Peking ducks from the Imperial Palace were transported all the way to Long Island, New York. The flavorful, domestically raised Long Island ducks we enjoy today are their descendants (although more are raised in Indiana and Wisconsin than in the Empire State). Duck is delicious when grilled whole or butterflied. Because ducks are very fatty birds, I recommend removing as much visible fat as possible before grilling.

HELPFUL GUIDELINES FOR PREPARING POULTRY

- After poultry has been purchased, store it in the coldest part of the refrigerator and use it within two days.
- Always cut raw poultry on a plastic cutting board rather than a wooden one. A thorough cleaning of the board will remove any harmful bacteria that can contaminate food, whereas a wooden board may be more difficult to sanitize.
- Do not leave uncooked poultry at room temperature for more than two hours.

- To determine when poultry is done, prick the meat to see if it is white throughout and if the juices run clear. Whole chickens and turkeys should reach an internal temperature of 180 degrees and chicken breasts should reach 170 degrees. Another way to test for doneness, especially with whole chickens, turkeys, or ducks, is to grasp the end of a drumstick. If it turns easily in the socket, then it is done.

Grilled Whole Chicken with Thai Rub

SERVES 4

Chicken delightfully accepts the flavorful variety of spices in a Thai rub. This rub can also be used on Cornish hens, duck, or even beef. Serve with Jasmine Rice (page 158) and Grilled Pineapple Rings (page 330).

2 tablespoons firmly packed dark brown sugar	1 teaspoon freshly ground pepper
2 teaspoons dried lemon peel	1 teaspoon cumin
2 teaspoons coriander	1 teaspoon cayenne
2 teaspoons onion salt	1 whole chicken (3 to 3½ pounds), split down the backbone and
1 teaspoon garlic salt	wing tips removed
1 teaspoon ground ginger	

To Make Rub Combine brown sugar, lemon peel, coriander, onion salt, garlic salt, ginger, pepper, cumin, and cayenne in a small bowl and blend well. Press Thai rub on both sides of chicken and place in a nonmetal dish. Cover dish with plastic wrap and refrigerate chicken for several hours or overnight.

To Prepare Chicken on an Outdoor Grill Over moderately hot coals, place chicken on a grill coated with a nonstick vegetable spray. Cover grill and cook for 30 to 40 minutes or until a meat thermometer registers 180 degrees, turning chicken every 5 minutes. (The skin on the chicken may cause flare-ups. When you turn the chicken, make sure to extinguish any flames.)

To Prepare Chicken on an Indoor Grill Place chicken on a preheated grill and cook over moderate heat for 60 to 70 minutes or until a meat thermometer registers 180 degrees, turning chicken every 6 minutes and giving it a quarter turn occasionally.

Chicken Satay

If you ever have the good fortune to dine at an Indonesian restaurant, you will experience a variety of satays. These wonderfully tasty strips of grilled meat or fowl are served with a spicy peanut sauce for dipping.

Marinade

- 2 tablespoons soy sauce
- 1 tablespoon medium-dry sherry
- 1 tablespoon honey
- 1 tablespoon minced onion
- 1 clove garlic, minced
- ½ tablespoon oriental sesame oil (see note)
- 1 teaspoon curry powder
- ½ teaspoon fresh lemon juice
- ⅛ teaspoon cayenne
- 2 chicken breasts (12 ounces each), skinned, boned, and cut into 1-inch cubes

Peanut Sauce

- 1 cup creamy peanut butter
- ⅓ cup coconut cream (see note)
- 2 tablespoons fresh lemon juice
- 1½ tablespoons soy sauce
- 1 tablespoon garlic chili sauce (see note)
- ½ tablespoon oriental sesame oil (see note)
- ½ tablespoon curry powder
- 6 tablespoons cream

To Make Marinade Combine soy sauce, sherry, honey, onion, garlic, sesame oil, curry powder, lemon juice, and cayenne in a resealable plastic bag and blend. Add cubed chicken and turn to coat all over. Refrigerate for several hours or overnight, turning the chicken at least once.

To Make Peanut Sauce Bring ¼ cup water to a simmer in a medium saucepan over moderately high heat. Reduce heat to moderately low and add peanut butter, coconut cream, lemon juice, soy sauce, garlic chili sauce, sesame oil, curry powder, and cream and blend well. Cook for 10 minutes or until mixture is smooth and hot. Transfer sauce to the work bowl of a food processor fitted with a metal blade and process until smooth. Serve warm or at room temperature. (For a creamier sauce, add additional cream, 1 tablespoon at a time, until desired consistency.)

To Prepare Chicken on an Outdoor Grill Soak bamboo skewers in water for 30 minutes or more. Thread the cubed chicken on the skewers. Over moderately hot coals, place chicken on a grill coated with a nonstick vegetable spray. Cover grill and cook for 6 to 9 minutes, turning chicken frequently.

To Prepare Chicken on an Indoor Grill Soak bamboo skewers in water for 30 minutes or more. Thread the cubed chicken on the skewers. Place chicken on a preheated grill and cook on moderately high heat for 15 to 20 minutes, turning chicken every 8 minutes.

Note Coconut cream, garlic chili sauce, and oriental sesame oil are available in most Asian food stores.

African Chicken Breasts

This spicy chicken dish is enhanced by adding a dollop of Shelagh's Coriander and Mint Chutney (recipe below), which is a very special family recipe. Serve with couscous or Grilled Spicy Yams (page 347).

Marinade

½ cup coconut milk
1 tablespoon extra virgin olive oil
4 cloves garlic, minced
2 teaspoons paprika
½ teaspoon cayenne
½ teaspoon salt
¼ teaspoon crushed red pepper
2 chicken breasts (12 ounces each), skinned, halved, and boned

Shelagh's Coriander and Mint Chutney

2 cups loosely packed mint leaves, washed well, dried, and stems removed (see note)
1 cup loosely packed coriander leaves
1 small Vidalia onion or other sweet onion, coarsely chopped
½ to 1 hot green chile pepper (or ¼ teaspoon cayenne)
   Juice of one lemon (about ¼ cup)
½ teaspoon salt
¼ teaspoon granulated sugar

To Make Marinade Combine coconut milk, olive oil, garlic, paprika, cayenne, salt, and crushed red pepper in a resealable plastic bag and blend well. Add chicken breasts to the bag and turn to coat all over. Refrigerate for several hours or overnight, turning chicken at least once.

To Make Chutney In the work bowl of a food processor fitted with a metal blade, process mint, coriander, onion, and chile pepper until finely chopped. Add lemon juice, salt, and sugar and process until pureed. Taste for seasoning. Transfer the chutney to an airtight container and refrigerate for up to 2 to 3 days.

To Prepare Chicken on an Outdoor Grill Remove chicken breasts from marinade. Over moderately hot coals, place chicken on a grill coated with a nonstick vegetable spray. Cover grill and cook for 5 to 6 minutes on each side or until the juices run clear when chicken is pierced with a fork.

To Prepare Chicken on an Indoor Grill Remove chicken breasts from marinade. Place them on a preheated grill and cook over moderately high heat for 20 to 25 minutes or until the juices run clear when chicken is pierced with a fork, turning chicken breasts every 8 minutes.

Note To make mint chutney, omit the coriander and use 3 cups fresh mint.

Citrus-Marinated Chicken Breasts

Southwestern cuisine continues to gain in popularity among food lovers. It combines a wide variety of ingredients that provide complementary tastes but interesting contrasts in color and texture. Grapefruit, Orange, and Pineapple Salsa (page 46) adds just the right amount of zest to this flavorful dish. Serve with mugs of Gazpacho (recipe below) and Lemon Rice and Capers (page 266).

Marinade

- 3 tablespoons fresh orange juice
- 1 tablespoon fresh lime juice
- 2 tablespoons minced cilantro leaves
- 1 tablespoon pineapple juice
- 1 tablespoon extra virgin olive oil
- 2 cloves garlic, minced
- 1 teaspoon oregano
- ½ teaspoon chili powder
- ½ teaspoon coriander
- ¼ teaspoon salt
- ¼ teaspoon cayenne
- ¼ teaspoon freshly ground pepper
- 2 chicken breasts (12 ounces each), skinned, halved, and boned

Gazpacho

- 1 (1-inch-thick) slice crusty bread
- 2 large red bell peppers, seeded and quartered
- 1 large cucumber, peeled and sliced 1 inch thick
- 2 pounds plum tomatoes, quartered
- 2 cloves garlic, minced
- 2 tablespoons extra virgin olive oil
- 2 tablespoons sherry vinegar
- 1 teaspoon freshly ground pepper
- ¾ teaspoon salt
- ½ teaspoon hot pepper sauce

Gazpacho Garnish

- 1 small green bell pepper, seeded and diced
- ½ cucumber, peeled and diced
- 1 plum tomato, diced
- 2 small green onions, thinly sliced
- 1 cup croutons

To Make Marinade Combine orange juice, lime juice, cilantro, pineapple juice, olive oil, garlic, oregano, chili powder, coriander, salt, cayenne, and pepper in a resealable bag and blend. Add chicken breasts and turn to coat all over. Refrigerate for several hours or overnight, turning chicken at least once.

To Make Gazpacho Place bread in a bowl and add enough water to cover. Allow it to sit for 15 minutes, then squeeze the bread with your hands to remove as much water as possible.

In the work bowl of a food processor fitted with a metal blade, process the bread, red peppers, cucumber, tomatoes, and garlic until pureed. Add olive oil, sherry vinegar, pepper, salt, and hot pepper sauce and process until well blended. Transfer gazpacho to a large pitcher, cover, and refrigerate for several hours or overnight. When ready to serve, divide the gazpacho among six soup bowls or mugs and garnish with green pepper, cucumber, tomato, green onions, and croutons.

To Prepare Chicken on an Outdoor Grill Remove chicken breasts from marinade. Over moderately hot coals, place chicken on a grill coated with a nonstick vegetable spray. Cover grill and cook for 5 to 6 minutes on each side or until juices run clear when chicken is pierced with a fork.

To Prepare Chicken on an Indoor Grill Remove chicken breasts from marinade. Place them on a preheated grill and cook over moderately high heat for 20 to 25 minutes or until juices run clear when chicken is pierced with a fork, turning the chicken breasts every 8 minutes.

To Serve Arrange the chicken breasts on four dinner plates. Spoon a dollop of grapefruit, orange, and pineapple salsa over each and garnish with a sprig of cilantro.

Chicken Breasts with Caramelized Onions

SERVES 4

Marinating the chicken breasts and onions in lime marinade gives this dish a delightful tangy flavor. If you love caramelized onions, make extra marinade and add another onion to the mixture. Serve with Garlic Mashed Potatoes (page 78) and sourdough bread.

¼ cup fresh lime juice
2 tablespoons extra virgin olive oil
2 cloves garlic, minced
1 teaspoon thyme
½ teaspoon crushed red pepper
¼ teaspoon salt

¼ teaspoon freshly ground pepper
2 chicken breasts (12 ounces each), skinned, halved, and boned
2 large Vidalia onions or other sweet onion, thinly sliced

To Make Marinade Combine lime juice, 1 tablespoon olive oil, garlic, thyme, crushed red pepper, salt, and pepper in a large resealable plastic bag and blend. Add chicken breasts and onions and turn to coat all over. Refrigerate for several hours or overnight, turning chicken and onions at least once.

To Make Caramelized Onions Remove chicken from marinade. Set aside. Heat remaining 1 tablespoon olive oil in a large skillet over moderately low heat for 2 minutes. Add onions and marinade to skillet, partially cover, and sauté for 45 minutes, stirring occasionally. Remove cover. Raise the heat to medium and sauté onions for 15 minutes or until golden brown, stirring occasionally. Keep the caramelized onions warm over low heat.

To Prepare Chicken on an Outdoor Grill Over moderately hot coals, place chicken breasts on a grill coated with a nonstick vegetable spray. Cover grill and cook for 5 to 6 minutes on each side or until juices run clear when chicken is pierced with a fork.

To Prepare Chicken on an Indoor Grill Place chicken breasts on a preheated grill and cook over moderately high heat for 20 to 25 minutes or until juices run clear when chicken is pierced with a fork, turning the chicken breasts every 8 minutes.

To Serve Place chicken breasts on four dinner plates and distribute caramelized onions on top of each, dividing evenly. Garnish each serving with a twisted lime slice.

Chicken Breasts with Lemon and Herb Marinade

SERVES 4

This easy-to-prepare recipe features a wonderful combination of flavors from the marinade highlighted with smoky overtones from the grill. Serve with Grilled Poblano Soup (page 344) and Grilled Fruit Kebabs (page 341).

¼ cup fresh lemon juice	1 teaspoon tarragon
2 cloves garlic, minced	½ teaspoon salt
2 tablespoons Worcestershire sauce	½ teaspoon freshly ground pepper
1 tablespoon extra virgin olive oil	2 chicken breasts (12 ounces each), skinned, halved, and boned
1 teaspoon marjoram	

To Make Marinade Combine lemon juice, garlic, Worcestershire sauce, olive oil, marjoram, tarragon, salt, and pepper in a resealable plastic bag and blend. Add chicken breasts and turn to coat all over. Refrigerate for several hours or overnight, turning chicken at least once.

To Prepare Chicken on an Outdoor Grill Remove chicken breasts from marinade. Over moderately hot coals, place chicken on a grill coated with a nonstick vegetable spray. Cover grill and cook for 5 to 6 minutes on each side or until juices run clear when chicken is pierced with a fork.

To Prepare Chicken on an Indoor Grill Remove chicken breasts from marinade. Place them on a preheated grill and cook over moderately high heat for 20 to 25 minutes or until juices run clear when chicken is pierced with a fork, turning chicken breasts every 8 minutes.

Lemon-Marinated Chicken Breasts

SERVES 4

The herb-laced lemon marinade takes center stage by endowing the chicken with just enough tang to tease your taste buds. Serve with Acorn Squash with Fruited Wild Rice (page 336) and Grilled Pineapple Rings (page 330).

¼ cup fresh lemon juice
3 tablespoons minced parsley
1 tablespoon extra virgin olive oil
2 large cloves garlic, minced
2 teaspoons oregano

½ teaspoon salt
½ teaspoon freshly ground pepper
2 chicken breasts (12 ounces each), skinned, halved, and boned

To Make Marinade Combine lemon juice, parsley, olive oil, garlic, oregano, salt, and pepper in a resealable plastic bag and blend. Add chicken breasts and turn to coat all over. Refrigerate for several hours or overnight, turning chicken at least once.

To Prepare Chicken on an Outdoor Grill Remove the chicken breasts from marinade. Over moderately hot coals, place chicken on a grill coated with a nonstick vegetable spray. Cover grill and cook for 5 to 6 minutes on each side or until juices run clear when chicken is pierced with a fork.

To Prepare Chicken on an Indoor Grill Remove the chicken breasts from marinade. Place them on a preheated grill and cook over moderately high heat for 20 to 25 minutes or until juices run clear when chicken is pierced with a fork, turning the chicken breasts every 8 minutes.

Southwestern Chicken Breasts with Gazpacho Salsa

SERVES 4

These flavorful chicken breasts, adorned with Gazpacho Salsa (recipe below), are in the highest tradition of the Southwest. Serve with Garlic Mashed Potatoes (page 78).

Marinade

½ cup fresh cilantro leaves

¼ cup red wine vinegar

2 tablespoons extra virgin olive oil

4 cloves garlic, minced

1 teaspoon oregano

1 teaspoon cumin

1 teaspoon freshly ground pepper

½ teaspoon salt

2 chicken breasts (12 ounces each), skinned, halved, and boned

Gazpacho Salsa

½ cup diced red bell pepper

½ cup diced yellow bell pepper

½ cup diced red onion

½ cup diced tomato

2 tablespoons chopped cilantro leaves

2 cloves garlic, minced

2 jalapeño chiles, seeded and minced (see note)

1 tablespoon extra virgin olive oil

½ tablespoon sherry vinegar

To Make Marinade Combine cilantro, red wine vinegar, 2 tablespoons cold water, olive oil, garlic, oregano, cumin, pepper, and salt in a resealable plastic bag and blend. Add chicken breasts and turn to coat all over. Refrigerate for several hours or overnight, turning chicken at least once.

To Make Gazpacho Salsa Combine red and yellow peppers, red onion, tomato, cilantro, garlic, jalapeño chiles, olive oil, and sherry vinegar in a small dish and blend well. Refrigerate gazpacho salsa, covered, until ready to serve.

To Prepare Chicken on an Outdoor Grill Remove chicken breasts from marinade. Over moderately hot coals, place chicken on a grill coated with a nonstick vegetable spray. Cover grill and cook for 5 to 6 minutes on each side or until the juices run clear when chicken is pierced with a fork.

To Prepare Chicken on an Indoor Grill Remove chicken breasts from marinade. Place them on a preheated grill and cook over moderately high heat for 20 to 25 minutes or until the juices run clear when chicken is pierced with a fork, turning the chicken breasts every 8 minutes.

Note The seeds of jalapeño chiles are very hot. To avoid burning your skin, wear rubber or latex gloves when removing the seeds. Immediately wash the knife, cutting surface, and gloves when finished.

The Walls' Greek Grilled Chicken

SERVES 4

This flavorful recipe for chicken will transport you all the way to the beautiful islands of Greece. Imagine yourself relaxing at a seaside restaurant overlooking the Adriatic sea. The dolmathes were wonderful, the Greek salad was perfect, and now you are presented with a tempting platter of Greek grilled chicken, rice pilaf, and freshly baked pita breads. Is this good? Even on Sundays!

Greek Rub

2 tablespoons oregano (preferably Greek oregano)
1 tablespoon ground oregano (preferably ground Greek oregano)
2 teaspoons salt
2 teaspoons freshly ground pepper
1 teaspoon thyme
3 cloves garlic, minced
1 whole chicken (3 to 3½ pounds), split along the backbone and wing tips removed

Greek Salad

1 clove garlic
½ cup extra virgin olive oil
¼ cup red wine vinegar
¾ teaspoon dry mustard
¾ teaspoon Greek oregano
¼ teaspoon salt
¼ teaspoon granulated sugar
¼ teaspoon fresh lemon juice
⅛ teaspoon freshly ground pepper
1 small head escarole, torn into bite-size pieces
1 small head romaine, torn into bite-size pieces
1 large firm tomato, cut into 8 wedges
1 small Spanish onion, thinly sliced
1 green bell pepper, seeded and thinly sliced
8 pitted Greek olives (kalamatas)
8 Greek peppers (pepperoncini)
4 ounces Greek feta cheese, crumbled
4 anchovy filets, drained
2 hard-boiled eggs, each cut into 4 wedges

To Make Greek Rub Combine oregano, ground oregano, salt, pepper, thyme, and garlic in a small bowl and blend well. Press Greek rub on both sides of chicken. Place chicken in a resealable plastic bag and refrigerate for several hours or overnight.

To Make Greek Salad In the work bowl of a food processor fitted with a metal blade, process garlic until chopped. Add olive oil, red wine vinegar, dry mustard, Greek oregano, salt, sugar, lemon juice, and pepper and process until the vinaigrette is well blended. Set aside.

When ready to serve the salad, combine escarole, romaine lettuce, tomato, onion, and green pepper in a large bowl. Add just enough vinaigrette to make the salad glisten and toss well. Divide the salad among of four dinner plates and garnish each serving with 2 olives, 2 peppers, feta cheese, 1 anchovy filet, and 2 wedges hard-boiled egg.

To Prepare Chicken on an Outdoor Grill Over moderately hot coals, place chicken on a grill coated with a nonstick vegetable spray. Cover grill and cook for 30 to 40 minutes or until a meat thermometer registers 180 degrees, turning chicken every 5 minutes. (The skin on the chicken may cause flare-ups. When you turn the chicken, make sure to extinguish any flames.)

To Prepare Chicken on an Indoor Grill Place chicken on a preheated grill and cook over moderate heat for 60 to 70 minutes or until a meat thermometer registers 180 degrees, turning chicken over every 6 minutes and giving it a quarter turn occasionally.

Whole Chicken with Moroccan Rub

SERVES 4

Pressing this Moroccan rub onto whole chickens is one of the easiest yet rewarding ways to prepare chicken. The flavor is outstanding! Serve with couscous and warmed pita bread.

1	teaspoon curry powder	¼	teaspoon salt
1	teaspoon paprika	¼	teaspoon freshly ground
1	teaspoon coriander		pepper
1	teaspoon cumin	1	whole chicken (3 to 3½
½	teaspoon dried lemon peel		pounds), split along the back-
½	teaspoon cayenne		bone and wing tips removed
½	teaspoon garlic salt		

To Make Rub Combine curry, paprika, coriander, cumin, lemon peel, cayenne, garlic salt, salt, and pepper in a small bowl and blend well. Press Moroccan rub on both sides of the chicken. Place chicken in a resealable plastic bag and refrigerate for several hours or overnight.

To Prepare Chicken on an Outdoor Grill Over moderately hot coals, place chicken on a grill coated with a nonstick vegetable spray. Cover grill and cook for 30 to 40 minutes or until a meat thermometer registers 180 degrees, turning chicken every 5 minutes. (The skin on the chicken may cause flare-ups. When you turn the chicken, make sure to extinguish any flames.)

To Prepare Chicken on an Indoor Grill Place chicken on a preheated grill and cook over moderate heat for 60 to 70 minutes or until a meat thermometer registers 180 degrees, turning chicken over every 6 minutes and giving it a quarter turn occasionally.

Lime and Mustard Chicken Breasts

The lime and mustard combination endows the chicken breasts with a rich and tangy flavor. This recipe is so easy to prepare, it is certain to become one of your favorites! Serve with Lemon Rice and Capers (page 266).

¼ cup fresh lime juice
2 tablespoons Dijon mustard
2 tablespoons minced parsley
1 tablespoon extra virgin olive oil
¼ teaspoon salt
¼ teaspoon freshly ground pepper
2 chicken breasts (12 ounces each), skinned, halved, and boned

To Make Marinade Combine lime juice, Dijon mustard, parsley, olive oil, salt, and pepper in a resealable plastic bag and blend. Add chicken breasts and turn to coat all over. Refrigerate for several hours or overnight, turning chicken at least once.

To Prepare Chicken on an Outdoor Grill Remove the chicken breasts from marinade. Over moderately hot coals, place chicken on a grill coated with a nonstick vegetable spray. Cover grill and cook for 5 to 6 minutes on each side or until juices run clear when chicken is pierced with a fork.

To Prepare Chicken on an Indoor Grill Remove the chicken breasts from marinade. Place them on a preheated grill and cook over moderately high heat for 20 to 25 minutes or until juices run clear when chicken is pierced with a fork, turning the chicken breasts every 8 minutes.

Spicy Chicken Breasts

Leaving the skin on the chicken breasts while grilling allows the marinade spices to permeate the chicken. Once the chicken is done, the skin can be removed. Serve with Rice Pilaf with Toasted Almonds and Raisins (recipe below).

Marinade

- ¼ cup extra virgin olive oil
- 2 tablespoons red wine vinegar
- 4 green onions, minced
- 2 cloves garlic, minced
- 2 tablespoons minced cilantro leaves
- 2 tablespoons minced parsley
- 2 teaspoons cumin
- 2 teaspoons paprika
- ½ teaspoon salt
- ½ teaspoon freshly ground pepper
- 2 chicken breasts (12 ounces each), boned and halved

Rice Pilaf with Toasted Almonds and Raisins

- 2 tablespoons butter
- 1 small Vidalia onion or other sweet onion, minced
- 1 cup long-grain rice
- 1 can (14½ ounces) chicken broth
- ½ teaspoon salt
- ½ teaspoon freshly ground pepper
- 3 tablespoons toasted almonds (see note)
- ¼ cup raisins
- 2 tablespoons minced parsley

To Make Marinade Combine olive oil, red wine vinegar, green onions, garlic, cilantro, parsley, cumin, paprika, salt, and pepper in a resealable plastic bag and blend. Add chicken breasts and turn to coat all over. Refrigerate for several hours or overnight, turning chicken at least once.

To Make Rice Pilaf Melt butter in a medium saucepan over moderate heat. Add onion and sauté for 5 minutes, stirring frequently. Add rice and sauté for 3 minutes, stirring frequently. Add chicken broth, salt, and pepper and bring to a boil. Reduce heat to low, cover saucepan, and cook for 20 to 25 minutes or until chicken broth has been absorbed. Add almonds, raisins, and parsley and blend well. Cover and keep warm at room temperature.

To Prepare Chicken on an Outdoor Grill Remove chicken breasts from marinade. Over moderately hot coals, place chicken on a grill coated with a nonstick vegetable spray. Cover grill and cook for 5 to 6 minutes on each side or until the juices run clear when chicken is pierced with a fork.

To Prepare Chicken on an Indoor Grill Remove chicken breasts from marinade. Place them on a preheated grill and cook over moderately high heat for 20 to 25 minutes or until the juices run clear when chicken is pierced with a fork, turning the chicken breasts every 8 minutes.

Note To toast almonds: Preheat the oven to 350 degrees. Place almonds in a shallow pan and bake for 10 to 15 minutes or until golden brown.

Mary Lea's Tequila Chicken with Grapefruit, Orange, and Pineapple Salsa

SERVES 6

This recipe comes from a friend who is an extremely talented party hostess. For this special recipe, she frequently begins by offering margaritas and Grilled Red Pepper Dip (page 348). She then serves this chicken dish, topped with the salsa, and Mexican Rice on the side (page 170). Olé, and let the party begin!

Marinade
- ½ cup fresh lime juice
- ¼ cup tequila
- 3 tablespoons extra virgin olive oil
- 3 tablespoons minced cilantro leaves
- 1 tablespoon granulated sugar
- 1 teaspoon salt
- 4 cloves garlic, minced
- 1 jalapeño chile, seeded and minced (see note)
- 3 chicken breasts (12 ounces each), skinned, halved, and boned

Grapefruit, Orange, and Pineapple Salsa
- 1 navel orange, peeled and diced
- 1 ruby red grapefruit, peeled and diced
- 1 cup diced fresh pineapple
- ½ cup minced red onion
- ¼ cup minced red bell pepper
- 2 tablespoons chopped cilantro leaves
- 1 tablespoon white wine vinegar
- 1 tablespoon granulated sugar

To Make Marinade Combine lime juice, tequila, olive oil, cilantro, sugar, salt, garlic, and jalapeño chile in a resealable plastic bag and blend. Add chicken breasts and turn to coat all over. Refrigerate for several hours or overnight, turning chicken at least once.

To Make Salsa Combine orange, grapefruit, pineapple, red onion, red pepper, cilantro, white wine vinegar, and sugar in a medium bowl and blend well. Refrigerate the salsa, covered, until ready to serve.

To Prepare Chicken on an Outdoor Grill Remove chicken breasts from marinade. Over moderately hot coals, place chicken on a grill coated with a nonstick vegetable spray. Cover grill and cook for 5 to 6 minutes on each side or until juices run clear when chicken is pierced with a fork.

To Prepare Chicken on an Indoor Grill Remove chicken breasts from marinade. Place them on a preheated grill and cook over moderately high heat for 20 to 25 minutes or until juices run clear when chicken is pierced with a fork, turning the chicken breasts every 8 minutes.

Note The seeds of a jalapeño chile are very hot. To avoid burning your skin, wear rubber or latex gloves when removing the seeds. Immediately wash the knife, cutting surface, and gloves when finished.

Chicken Fajita Salad with Grilled Red Pepper Vinaigrette

SERVES 4

This is an incredibly delicious salad, composed of flavorsome grilled chicken, red onion, olives, and corn tortilla strips, all highlighted by the ultimate Grilled Red Pepper Vinaigrette (recipe below). Serve with squares of Grilled Polenta (page 322).

Marinade

¼ cup fresh lime juice

2 tablespoons tequila

½ teaspoon freshly ground pepper

¼ teaspoon salt

2 chicken breasts (10 ounces each), skinned, halved, and boned

Grilled Red Pepper Vinaigrette

1 large red bell pepper

3 cloves garlic

6 tablespoons extra virgin olive oil

2 tablespoons fresh lemon juice

2 tablespoons freshly grated Parmesan cheese

1 tablespoon red wine vinegar

2 teaspoons Dijon mustard

½ teaspoon Worcestershire sauce

½ teaspoon freshly ground pepper

¼ teaspoon salt

Grilled Chicken Fajita Salad

3 cups canola oil

3 corn tortillas, cut into ½-inch-wide strips

1 head romaine lettuce, torn into bite-size pieces (8 cups)

1 small red onion, thinly sliced

¼ cup black olives, pitted

To Make Marinade Combine lime juice, tequila, pepper, and salt in a resealable plastic bag and blend. Place chicken breasts in marinade and turn to coat all over. Refrigerate for several hours or overnight, turning chicken at least once.

To Prepare Pepper on an Outdoor Grill Over moderately hot coals, place the red pepper on a grill coated with a nonstick vegetable spray. Cover grill and cook for 20 to 24 minutes, or until the skin is charred all over, turning the pepper as skin blackens. Once grilled, place the pepper in a plastic bag and allow to steam for 15 minutes. When it is cool enough to handle, peel away the skin and remove the top and seeds (do not rinse the pepper).

To Prepare Pepper on an Indoor Grill Place the red pepper on a preheated grill over high heat and cook for 20 to 30 minutes or until the skin is charred all over, turning the pepper as skin blackens. Once grilled, place the pepper in a plastic bag and allow to steam for 15 minutes. When it is cool enough to handle, peel away the skin and remove the top and seeds (do not rinse the pepper).

To Make Grilled Red Pepper Vinaigrette In the work bowl of a food processor fitted with a metal blade, process garlic until chopped. Add red pepper and process until finely chopped. Add olive oil, lemon juice, Parmesan cheese, red wine vinegar, Dijon mustard, Worcestershire sauce, pepper, and salt and process until blended. Set aside.

To Prepare Chicken on an Outdoor Grill Remove chicken breasts from marinade. Over moderately hot coals, place chicken on a grill coated with a nonstick vegetable spray. Cover grill and cook for 5 to 6 minutes on each side or until juices run clear when chicken is pierced with a fork. Allow the chicken to cool for 10 minutes before cutting into thin slices.

To Prepare Chicken on an Indoor Grill Remove chicken breasts from marinade. Place them on a preheated grill and cook over moderately high heat for 20 to 25 minutes or until juices run clear when chicken is pierced with a fork, turning the chicken breasts every 8 minutes. Allow the chicken to cool for 10 minutes before cutting into thin slices.

To Make Tortilla Strips While grilling the chicken breasts, heat canola oil to 350 degrees in a heavy saucepan over moderately high heat. Add tortilla strips, a handful at a time, and cook for 1 to 2 minutes or until light brown. Remove strips with a slotted spoon and drain on paper towels. While the tortilla strips are warm, lightly season with salt. (The tortilla strips can be made early in the day and stored in an airtight container.)

To Serve Place the romaine lettuce, chicken, red onion, and olives in a salad bowl. Pour the grilled red pepper vinaigrette over the salad and toss well. Garnish the salad with tortilla strips.

Chicken, Fettuccine, and Creamy Red Pepper Sauce

SERVES 6

Several years ago, I was responsible, along with Ellie Densen, coauthor of one of my previous cookbooks, for orchestrating dinner for 354 people at a community function. This recipe is a variation of that memorable meal. If you plan to make it for that many people, just multiply the ingredients by 59!

Marinade
- 3 tablespoons fresh lemon juice
- 2 tablespoons extra virgin olive oil
- 2 large cloves garlic, chopped
- ½ ounce fresh basil, chopped
- 1 teaspoon crushed red pepper
- 3 chicken breasts (12 ounces each), skinned, halved, and boned

Creamy Red Pepper Sauce
- 4 red bell peppers
- ½ cup chicken broth
- ½ cup dry white wine
- 2 tablespoons butter
- 1 cup sliced fresh mushrooms
- 2 cups heavy cream
- ¼ teaspoon salt
- ⅓ cup freshly grated Parmesan cheese
- ½ ounce fresh basil, chopped

- 2 packages (9 ounces each) fresh red bell pepper, spinach, or other favorite fettuccine

To Make Marinade Combine lemon juice, olive oil, garlic, basil, and crushed red pepper in a resealable plastic bag and blend. Add chicken breasts and turn to coat all over. Refrigerate for several hours or overnight, turning chicken at least once.

To Prepare Peppers on an Outdoor Grill Over moderately hot coals, place the red peppers on a grill coated with a nonstick vegetable spray. Cover grill and cook for 20 to 24 minutes or until the skins are charred all over, turning the peppers as skins blacken. Once grilled, place the peppers in a plastic bag and allow to steam for 15 minutes. When they are cool enough to handle, peel away the skins and remove the tops and seeds (do not rinse the peppers). Slice the peppers into slivers and set aside.

To Prepare Peppers on an Indoor Grill Place the red peppers on a preheated grill over high heat and cook for 20 to 30 minutes or until the skins are charred all over, turning the peppers as skins blacken. Once grilled, place the peppers in a plastic bag and allow to steam for 15 minutes. When they are cool enough to handle, peel away the skins and remove the tops and seeds (do not rinse the peppers). Slice the peppers into slivers and set aside.

To Prepare Pepper Sauce Bring chicken broth and wine to a boil in a large saucepan over high heat and boil for 4 minutes or until mixture is reduced to 2 tablespoons.

While chicken broth and wine are boiling, melt butter in a medium skillet over moderately high heat. Add mushrooms and cook for 2 minutes, stirring occasionally. Set aside.

Add heavy cream to chicken broth and wine and boil for 4 to 5 minutes or until mixture is reduced by half. Add sliced peppers, mushrooms, and salt and blend well. Cover and set aside.

To Prepare Chicken on an Outdoor Grill Remove chicken breasts from marinade. Over moderately hot coals, place chicken on a grill coated with a nonstick vegetable spray. Cover grill and cook for 5 to 6 minutes on each side or until juices run clear when chicken is pierced with a fork.

To Prepare Chicken on an Indoor Grill Remove chicken breasts from marinade. Place them on a preheated grill and cook over moderately high heat for 20 to 25 minutes or until juices run clear when the chicken is pierced with a fork, turning the chicken breasts over every 8 minutes.

To Serve While grilling the chicken breasts, gently warm the pepper sauce on moderately low heat. Add Parmesan cheese and basil and blend well. Keep warm over low heat, stirring occasionally.

Cook the fettuccine according to package directions. Drain well. Arrange a bed of fettuccine on each of six dinner plates. Place the chicken, either sliced or whole, on the fettuccine and spoon some pepper sauce over each serving, dividing evenly. Garnish with a sprig of parsley or basil.

Mexican Chicken Salad

SERVES 4

This exceptional salad, with its colorful array of ingredients, is as visually appealing as it is flavorful. Serve with squares of corn bread.

Marinade
- 2 tablespoons fresh lime juice
- 2 cloves garlic, minced
- ½ teaspoon extra virgin olive oil
- ¼ teaspoon cumin
- ¼ teaspoon cayenne
- ¼ teaspoon chili powder
- ⅛ teaspoon freshly ground pepper
- 2 chicken breasts (10 ounces each), skinned and boned

Spicy Croutons
- 2 cups bread cubes
- 2 tablespoons pure olive oil
- ½ teaspoon cumin
- ½ teaspoon oregano
- ⅛ teaspoon cayenne
- ⅛ teaspoon freshly ground pepper

Vinaigrette
- 2 tablespoons apple cider vinegar
- 1½ teaspoons soy sauce
- 1 teaspoon granulated chicken bouillon
- 1 teaspoon tarragon
- ½ teaspoon oregano
- ⅛ teaspoon salt
- ⅛ teaspoon freshly ground pepper
- 6 tablespoons canola oil

Salad
- 2 cups spinach, washed, dried, and torn into bite-size pieces
- 2 cups romaine lettuce, torn into bite-size pieces
- 1 cup julienned jicama
- 1 avocado, cubed
- 1 cup cooked corn kernels
- 2 plum tomatoes, quartered
- ½ cup julienned red bell pepper
- ½ cup thinly sliced red onion
- ½ cup black olives, pitted
- 8 ears of baby sweet corn, optional

To Make Marinade Combine lime juice, garlic, olive oil, cumin, cayenne, chili powder, and pepper in a resealable plastic bag and blend well. Add the chicken breasts and turn to coat all over. Refrigerate for several hours or overnight, turning chicken at least once.

To Make Croutons Preheat oven to 350 degrees. Place bread cubes on a baking sheet and bake for 10 to 12 minutes or until golden brown.

Place a large skillet over moderate heat. Add olive oil and heat for 2 minutes. Add bread cubes, cumin, oregano, cayenne, and pepper and sauté for 2 minutes, shaking the pan back and forth. (The spicy croutons can be made ahead and stored in an airtight container.)

To Make Vinaigrette Combine apple cider vinegar, soy sauce, chicken bouillon, tarragon, oregano, salt, and pepper in the work bowl of a food processor fitted with a metal blade and process until blended. Add canola oil in a slow steady stream and process until well blended. Set aside.

To Prepare Chicken on an Outdoor Grill Remove chicken breasts from marinade. Over moderately hot coals, place chicken on a grill coated with a nonstick vegetable spray. Cover grill and cook for 5 to 6 minutes on each side or until juices run clear when chicken is pierced with a fork. Allow the chicken to sit for 10 minutes before cutting into thin slices.

To Prepare Chicken on an Indoor Grill Remove chicken breasts from marinade. Place them on a preheated grill and cook over moderately high heat for 20 to 25 minutes or until juices run clear when chicken is pierced with a fork, turning the chicken breasts every 8 minutes. Allow the chicken to sit for 10 minutes before cutting into thin slices.

To Serve Combine spinach, romaine lettuce, jicama, avocado, corn, tomatoes, red pepper, red onion, olives, chicken, and croutons in a large salad bowl. Add vinaigrette and toss well. Divide the salad among four dinner plates and garnish each serving with two ears of baby sweet corn, if desired.

Moroccan Chicken Breasts

SERVES 6

The nice array of spices in the marinade makes for an intense flavor throughout every bite of this savory chicken. It is fabulous topped with a spoonful of Shelagh's Coriander and Mint Chutney (page 30) and served with couscous.

6	tablespoons fresh lemon juice	1	tablespoon cumin
6	tablespoons packed minced parsley	1½	teaspoons curry powder
3	tablespoons extra virgin olive oil	¾	teaspoon salt
		¾	teaspoon freshly ground pepper
3	cloves garlic, minced	3	chicken breasts (12 ounces each), skinned, halved, and boned
1	tablespoon paprika		

To Make Marinade Combine lemon juice, parsley, olive oil, garlic, paprika, cumin, curry powder, salt, and pepper in a resealable plastic bag and blend well. Add the chicken breasts and turn to coat all over. Refrigerate for several hours or overnight, turning chicken at least once.

To Prepare Chicken on an Outdoor Grill Remove chicken breasts from marinade. Over moderately hot coals, place chicken on a grill coated with a nonstick vegetable spray. Cover grill and cook for 5 to 6 minutes on each side or until the juices run clear when chicken is pierced with a fork.

To Prepare Chicken on an Indoor Grill Remove chicken breasts from marinade. Place them on a preheated grill and cook over moderately high heat for 25 to 30 minutes or until the juices run clear when chicken is pierced with a fork, turning the chicken breasts every 8 minutes.

Mustard-Coated Whole Chicken

SERVES 4

If you like your food fiery hot, add 2 to 4 teaspoons more cayenne to this marinade! Serve with Rice Pilaf with Toasted Almonds and Raisins (page 44) and Mixed Baby Greens with Maytag Bleu Cheese (page 142).

⅓ cup Dijon mustard
2 tablespoons white wine vinegar
2 tablespoons extra virgin olive oil

2 teaspoons cayenne
1 whole chicken (3 to 3½ pounds), split down the backbone and wing tips removed

To Make Marinade Combine Dijon mustard, white wine vinegar, olive oil, and cayenne in a resealable plastic bag and blend. Add chicken and turn to coat both sides. Refrigerate for several hours or overnight, turning chicken at least once.

To Prepare Chicken on an Outdoor Grill Remove chicken from marinade. Over hot coals, place chicken on a grill coated with a nonstick vegetable spray. Cover grill and cook for 30 to 40 minutes or until a meat thermometer registers 180 degrees, turning chicken every 5 minutes. (The skin on the chicken may cause flare-ups. When you turn the chicken, make sure to extinguish any flames.)

To Prepare Chicken on an Indoor Grill Place chicken on a preheated grill and cook on moderate heat for 60 to 70 minutes or until a meat thermometer registers 180 degrees, turning chicken every 6 minutes and giving it a quarter turn occasionally.

Mustard-Coated Chicken Breasts with Red and Yellow Pepper Puree

SERVES 4

This is a versatile dish that can be served with the pepper puree spooned on whole chicken breasts, capped with grilled pepper slivers. It is also delicious when the chicken is thinly sliced and arranged on a bed of fresh red bell pepper fettuccine or other spicy fettuccine and then similarly topped with pepper puree and pepper slivers.

Marinade
- 3 tablespoons Dijon mustard
- 1½ tablespoons extra virgin olive oil
- ¾ teaspoon chili powder
- ¼ teaspoon salt
- ¼ teaspoon freshly ground pepper
- 2 chicken breasts (12 ounces each), skinned, halved, and boned

Red and Yellow Pepper Puree
- 3 large red bell peppers
- 3 large yellow bell peppers
- 3 bell peppers in assorted colors
- 1½ teaspoons extra virgin olive oil
- ¾ teaspoon freshly ground pepper
- ½ teaspoon salt
- ½ teaspoon chili powder

To Make Marinade Combine Dijon mustard, olive oil, chili powder, salt, and pepper in a resealable plastic bag and blend. Add chicken breasts and turn to coat all over. Refrigerate for several hours or overnight, turning chicken at least once.

To Prepare Peppers on an Outdoor Grill Over moderately hot coals, place the peppers on a grill coated with a nonstick vegetable spray. Cover grill and cook for 20 to 24 minutes or until the skins are charred all over, turning the peppers as skins blacken. Once grilled, place the peppers in plastic bag(s) and allow to steam for 15 minutes. When they are cool enough to handle, peel away the skins and remove the tops and seeds (do not rinse the peppers).

To Prepare Peppers on an Indoor Grill Place the peppers on a preheated grill and cook on high heat for 20 to 30 minutes or until the skins are charred all over, turning the peppers as skins blacken. Once grilled, place the peppers in plastic bag(s) and allow to steam for 15 minutes. When they are cool enough to handle, peel away the skins and remove the tops and seeds (do not rinse the peppers).

To Make the Pepper Puree In the work bowl of a food processor fitted with a metal blade, process the 3 red and 3 yellow grilled peppers until pureed. Slice the remaining peppers into slivers and set aside. Add olive oil, pepper, salt, and chili powder to red and yellow peppers and process until smooth. The pepper puree can be served at room temperature or warmed in a small saucepan over moderate heat, stirring occasionally.

To Prepare Chicken on an Outdoor Grill Remove chicken from marinade. Over moderately hot coals, place chicken breasts on a grill coated with a nonstick vegetable spray. Cover grill and cook for 5 to 6 minutes on each side or until the juices run clear when chicken is pierced with a fork.

To Prepare Chicken on an Indoor Grill Remove chicken breasts from marinade. Place them on a preheated grill and cook over moderately high heat for 20 to 25 minutes or until the juices run clear when chicken is pierced with a fork, turning the chicken breasts every 8 minutes.

To Serve Arrange a chicken breast on each of four dinner plates and spoon some pepper puree over each serving. Garnish with reserved slivered peppers.

Chicken Marinated with Rosemary and Oregano

SERVES 4

Eating grilled whole chickens with even the simplest of marinades is the ultimate taste experience. The aroma imparted from the grill intermingled with rosemary and oregano-laced lemon juice is delightful. Serve with Mashed Potatoes with Caramelized Onions (page 134).

¼	cup fresh lemon juice	2	large cloves garlic, minced
1½	tablespoons extra virgin olive oil	1	whole chicken (3 to
1	tablespoon rosemary		3½ pounds), split down
1	tablespoon oregano		the backbone and wing
¾	teaspoon freshly ground pepper		tips removed

To Make Marinade Combine lemon juice, olive oil, rosemary, oregano, pepper, and garlic in a large resealable plastic bag and blend. Add chicken and turn to coat all over. Refrigerate for several hours or overnight, turning chicken at least once.

To Prepare Chicken on an Outdoor Grill Remove chicken from marinade. Over moderately hot coals, place chicken on a grill coated with a nonstick vegetable spray. Cover grill and cook for 30 to 40 minutes or until a meat thermometer registers 180 degrees, turning chicken every 5 minutes. (The skin on the chicken may cause flare-ups. When you turn the chicken, make sure to extinguish any flames.)

To Prepare Chicken on an Indoor Grill Remove chicken from marinade. Place chicken on a preheated grill and cook over moderate heat for 60 to 70 minutes or until a meat thermometer registers 180 degrees, turning chicken every 6 minutes and giving it a quarter turn occasionally.

Rosemary-Marinated Cornish Hens

SERVES 4

This simple marinade transforms Cornish hen into a succulent and mouthwatering treat. The marinade is also sensational with whole chicken or a turkey breast. Serve with Grilled Red Pepper Flan (page 350) and Spinach and Rice (page 84).

¾ cup fresh lemon juice	¾ teaspoon salt
6 tablespoons minced parsley	¾ teaspoon freshly ground pepper
1½ tablespoons rosemary	
1½ tablespoons extra virgin olive oil	2 Cornish hens (20 ounces each), split down the backbone and wing tips removed
3 cloves garlic, minced	

To Make Marinade Combine lemon juice, parsley, rosemary, olive oil, garlic, salt, and pepper in a large nonmetal dish and blend. Add the Cornish hens and turn to coat all over. Cover the dish and refrigerate for several hours or overnight, turning hens at least once.

To Prepare Cornish Hens on an Outdoor Grill Remove Cornish hens from marinade, reserving marinade. Over moderately hot coals, place Cornish hens on a grill coated with a nonstick vegetable spray. Cover grill and cook for 20 to 25 minutes or until a meat thermometer registers 180 degrees, turning hens frequently and brushing with reserved marinade occasionally.

To Prepare Cornish Hens on an Indoor Grill Remove Cornish hens from marinade, reserving marinade. Place Cornish hens on a preheated grill and cook over moderately high heat for 40 to 45 minutes or until a meat thermometer registers 180 degrees, turning the hens frequently and giving them a quarter turn occasionally. Brush with reserved marinade the last 15 minutes.

Grilled Cornish Hens

Don't be alarmed at the Cornish hens turning a striking red. The tandoori paste in the marinade not only adds an interesting flavor but also lends a red hue. Serve with Acorn Squash with Fruited Wild Rice (page 336).

¼ cup rice wine vinegar	¼ teaspoon freshly ground pepper
2 tablespoons tandoori paste (see note)	2 tablespoons minced ginger
2 tablespoons soy sauce	2 cloves garlic, minced
2 tablespoons fresh lemon juice	2 Cornish hens (20 ounces each), split down the backbone and wing tips removed
2 teaspoons oriental sesame oil	
¼ teaspoon salt	

To Make Marinade Combine rice wine vinegar, tandoori paste, soy sauce, lemon juice, sesame oil, salt, pepper, ginger, and garlic in a large nonmetal dish and blend. Add Cornish hens and turn to coat all over. Cover dish with plastic wrap and refrigerate for several hours or overnight, turning hens at least once.

To Prepare Cornish Hens on an Outdoor Grill Remove Cornish hens from marinade, reserving marinade. Over moderately hot coals, place Cornish hens on a grill coated with a nonstick vegetable spray. Cover grill and cook for 20 to 25 minutes or until a meat thermometer registers 180 degrees, turning hens frequently and brushing with reserved marinade.

To Prepare Cornish Hens on an Indoor Grill Remove Cornish hens from marinade, reserving marinade. Place Cornish hens on a preheated grill and cook over moderately high heat for 40 to 45 minutes or until a meat thermometer registers 180 degrees, turning the hens over frequently and giving them a quarter turn occasionally. Brush with reserved marinade the last 15 minutes.

Note Tandoori paste is available in most Asian or Indian food stores.

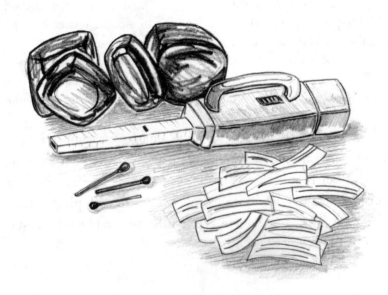

Cornish Hens with Lemongrass Marinade

A lemongrass marinade is an absolutely wonderful way to accentuate the flavor of Cornish hens, and grilling makes them sensational in both taste and appearance! Start the meal with Chilled and Spicy Grilled Red Pepper Soup (page 338) and serve the Cornish hens with Grilled Accordion Potatoes (page 328).

3   minced lemongrass stalks
2   tablespoons canola oil
2   tablespoons granulated sugar
2   tablespoons minced
    cilantro leaves
1   tablespoon soy sauce

1   large clove garlic, minced
2   teaspoons crushed red pepper
1   teaspoon salt
2   Cornish hens (20 ounces
    each), split down the back-
    bone and wing tips removed

To Make Marinade Combine lemongrass, canola oil, 2 tablespoons cold water, sugar, cilantro, soy sauce, garlic, crushed red pepper, and salt in a large nonmetal dish and blend. Add the Cornish hens and turn to coat all over. Cover the dish with plastic wrap and refrigerate for several hours or overnight, turning hens at least once.

To Prepare Cornish Hens on an Outdoor Grill Remove Cornish hens from marinade, reserving marinade. Over hot coals, place Cornish hens on a grill coated with a nonstick vegetable spray. Cover grill and cook for 20 to 25 minutes or until a meat thermometer registers 180 degrees, turning hens frequently and brushing with reserved marinade occasionally.

To Prepare Cornish Hens on an Indoor Grill Remove Cornish hens from marinade, reserving marinade. Place Cornish hens on a preheated grill and cook over moderately high heat for 40 to 45 minutes or until a meat thermometer registers 180 degrees, turning the hens frequently and giving them a quarter turn occasionally. Brush with reserved marinade the last 15 minutes.

Honey-Glazed Cornish Hens

SERVES 4

The honey glaze cloaks the Cornish hens in a pleasantly sweet flavor, and they are incredibly delicious. However, because of the honey in the marinade, the hens will have to be turned frequently to prevent them from burning. It is a little more labor-intensive, but I am certain you will agree that it is worth the effort! Serve with Basmati and Wild Rice (page 144).

6	tablespoons soy sauce		$\frac{3}{8}$	teaspoon freshly ground pepper
3	tablespoons honey		$\frac{3}{8}$	teaspoon crushed red pepper
3	tablespoons rice wine		2	Cornish hens (20 ounces each), split down the backbone and wing tips removed
3	tablespoons minced fresh ginger			
2	small cloves garlic, minced			
$1\frac{1}{2}$	tablespoons oyster sauce			
$1\frac{1}{2}$	teaspoons oriental sesame oil			

To Make Marinade Combine soy sauce, honey, rice wine, ginger, garlic, oyster sauce, sesame oil, pepper, and crushed red pepper in a nonmetal dish and blend. Add the Cornish hens and turn to coat all over. Cover the dish with plastic wrap and refrigerate for several hours or overnight, turning the hens at least once.

To Prepare Cornish Hens on an Outdoor Grill Remove Cornish hens from marinade, reserving marinade. Over moderately hot coals, place Cornish hens on a grill coated with a nonstick vegetable spray. Cover grill and cook for 20 to 25 minutes or until a meat thermometer registers 180 degrees, turning hens frequently and brushing with reserved marinade occasionally.

To Prepare Cornish Hens on an Indoor Grill Remove Cornish hens from marinade, reserving marinade. Place them on a preheated grill and cook over moderate heat for 40 to 45 minutes or until a meat thermometer registers 180 degrees, turning the hens frequently and giving them a quarter turn occasionally. Brush with reserved marinade the last 15 minutes.

Peking-Style Cornish Hens

SERVES 4

On a recent trip to Hong Kong, one of the most memorable sights was the sampans floating in Victoria Harbor. Hanging from lines stretched across many of the boats were rows of ducks destined to become one of the tastiest Chinese meals—Peking Duck. Because Cornish hens are so easy to prepare, I substituted them for duck and was delighted with the flavor and appearance. Although the hens are not hung out and dried in the traditional Chinese way, the results will surprise you. (On the other hand, if you own a sampan . . .) Serve with steamed long-grain rice.

6   tablespoons soy sauce
3   tablespoons granulated sugar
1   tablespoon canola oil
1   tablespoon minced
      fresh ginger

1   teaspoon Chinese Five Spice
      powder
2   Cornish hens (20 ounces
      each), split down the back-
      bone and wing tips removed

To Make Marinade Combine soy sauce, sugar, canola oil, ginger, and Chinese Five Spice powder in a large nonmetal dish and blend. Add Cornish hens and turn to coat all over. Cover the dish with plastic wrap and refrigerate for several hours or overnight, turning hens at least once.

To Prepare Cornish Hens on an Outdoor Grill Remove Cornish hens from marinade, reserving marinade. Over moderately hot coals, place Cornish hens on a grill coated with a nonstick vegetable spray. Cover grill and cook for 20 to 25 minutes or until a meat thermometer registers 180 degrees, turning hens frequently and brushing with reserved marinade.

To Prepare Cornish Hens on an Indoor Grill Remove Cornish hens from marinade, reserving marinade. Place Cornish hens on a preheated grill and cook over moderate heat for 40 to 45 minutes or until a meat thermometer registers 180 degrees, turning the hens frequently and giving them a quarter turn occasionally. Brush with reserved marinade the last 15 minutes.

Orange-Glazed Cornish Hens

SERVES 4

The orange glaze is fabulous! Try it on duck, chicken, or even a turkey breast for a true epicurean experience. Serve these delectable Cornish hens with Garlic Mashed Potatoes (page 78) and Lemon-Glazed Carrots (page 218).

1	can (12 ounces) frozen orange juice, thawed	¼	teaspoon crushed red pepper
⅓	cup dry red wine	1	clove garlic, minced
¼	cup Dijon mustard	2	Cornish hens (20 ounces each), split down the backbone and wing tips removed
1	tablespoon soy sauce		
1½	teaspoons rosemary		

To Make Marinade Combine orange juice, red wine, Dijon mustard, soy sauce, rosemary, crushed red pepper, and garlic in a large nonmetal dish and blend. Add Cornish hens and turn to coat all over. Cover the dish with plastic wrap and refrigerate for several hours or overnight, turning hens at least once.

To Prepare Cornish Hens on an Outdoor Grill Remove Cornish hens from marinade, reserving marinade. Over moderately hot coals, place Cornish hens on a grill coated with a nonstick vegetable spray. Cover grill and cook for 20 to 25 minutes or until a meat thermometer registers 180 degrees, turning hens frequently and brushing with reserved marinade the last 15 minutes.

To Prepare Cornish Hens on an Indoor Grill Remove Cornish hens from marinade, reserving marinade. Place Cornish hens on a preheated grill and cook over moderately high heat for 40 to 45 minutes or until a meat thermometer registers 180 degrees, turning the hens frequently and giving them a quarter turn occasionally. Brush with reserved marinade the last 15 minutes.

Turkey Tenderloins Marinated with Tequila and Orange Marmalade

SERVES 4

You thought tequila was only for margaritas. Try this marinade on turkey tenderloins and you'll gain a new perspective on the bottle with a worm. The marinade would also enhance turkey breasts, Cornish hens, or chicken. Serve with Grilled Spicy Yams (page 347).

¼ cup tequila	½ teaspoon salt
¼ cup orange marmalade	½ teaspoon freshly ground pepper
¼ cup fresh lime juice	
1 tablespoon extra virgin olive oil	4 turkey tenderloins (6 ounces each)
4 large cloves garlic, minced	

To Make Marinade Combine tequila, marmalade, lime juice, olive oil, garlic, salt, and pepper in a resealable plastic bag and blend.

Place turkey tenderloins between two pieces of waxed paper. Using a meat tenderizer, flatten each turkey tenderloin into a ¼-inch-thick filet. Place turkey in marinade and turn to coat both sides. Refrigerate for several hours or overnight, turning turkey at least once.

To Prepare Turkey on an Outdoor Grill Remove turkey tenderloins from marinade. Over moderately hot coals, place turkey on a grill coated with a nonstick vegetable spray. Cover grill and cook for 5 to 6 minutes on each side.

To Prepare Turkey on an Indoor Grill Remove turkey tenderloins from marinade. Place them on a preheated grill and cook over moderately high heat for 8 to 10 minutes on each side, turning the turkey tenderloins every 8 minutes.

Tandoori Cornish Hens

SERVES 4

A tandoor is a pitlike Indian oven that is made of red clay and capable of reaching intensely hot temperatures. Using a tandoor is the optimal way to prepare this wonderful Indian dish, although it is still delicious even when cooked on an indoor grill, because of the unique combination of spices and the tenderizing effect of acidic yogurt on the Cornish hens. Serve with Basmati Rice.

Marinade

1   cup plain yogurt
4   cloves garlic, minced
4   teaspoons minced
    fresh ginger
2   tablespoons tandoori paste
2   tablespoons fresh lime juice
1   teaspoon salt
1   teaspoon chili powder

¼   teaspoon turmeric
¼   teaspoon cumin
2   Cornish hens (20 ounces
    each), split along the back-
    bone and wing tips removed

Basmati Rice

1   cup basmati rice

To Make Marinade Combine yogurt, garlic, ginger, tandoori paste, lime juice, salt, chili powder, turmeric, and cumin in a large nonmetal dish and blend. Add the Cornish hens and turn to coat all over. Cover the dish with plastic wrap and refrigerate for several hours or overnight, turning hens at least once.

To Prepare Cornish Hens on an Outdoor Grill Remove Cornish hens from marinade, reserving marinade. Over moderately hot coals, place Cornish hens on a grill coated with a nonstick vegetable spray. Cover grill and cook for 20 to 25 minutes or until a meat thermometer registers 180 degrees, turning hens frequently and brushing with reserved marinade occasionally.

To Prepare Cornish Hens on an Indoor Grill Remove Cornish hens from marinade, reserving marinade. Place Cornish hens on a preheated grill and cook over moderately high heat for 40 to 45 minutes or until a meat thermometer registers 180 degrees, turning the hens frequently and giving them a quarter turn occasionally. Brush with reserved marinade the last 15 minutes.

To Make Basmati Rice While grilling the tandoori Cornish hens, bring 2 cups water to a boil in a medium saucepan over high heat. Add rice and reduce heat to low. Cover the saucepan and cook for 20 minutes or until water is absorbed.

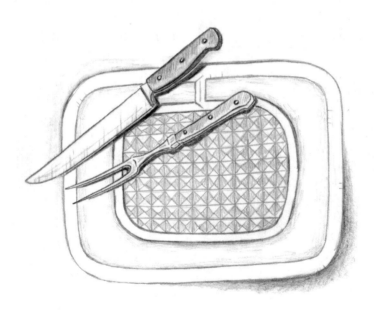

Grilled Turkey

SERVES 6

Turkey halves cooked on an outdoor grill not only remain moist and succulent, but also incorporate a smoky aroma from the grill. Succulent turkey can also be prepared on an indoor grill, but the smoke flavor will not be as intense. Serve with Cranberry Chutney (recipe below).

Cranberry Chutney

- 1 cup granulated sugar
- ½ cup chopped onions
- 4 whole cloves
- 1 teaspoon cinnamon
- ½ teaspoon salt
- ¼ cup white distilled vinegar
- 2 cups fresh or frozen cranberries
- ½ cup raisins
- ½ cup chopped dates
- ¼ cup chopped preserved ginger
- ¼ cup firmly packed dark brown sugar

Turkey Seasoning

- 2 teaspoons salt
- ¾ teaspoon seasoning salt
- ⅜ teaspoon dry mustard
- ⅜ teaspoon paprika
- ⅜ teaspoon poultry seasoning
- ¼ teaspoon nutmeg
- 1 fresh turkey half (3 to 3½ pounds), wing tips removed
  Canola oil

To Make Chutney Combine sugar, 1 cup cold water, onions, cloves, cinnamon, salt, and vinegar in a large saucepan over moderate heat. Bring to a boil, then reduce heat to moderately low and simmer for 5 minutes. Add cranberries, raisins, dates, preserved ginger, and brown sugar and blend well. Simmer for 12 minutes. Remove saucepan from heat and allow chutney to come to room temperature. Refrigerate cranberry chutney in a covered container.

To Make Turkey Seasoning Combine salt, seasoning salt, dry mustard, paprika, poultry seasoning, and nutmeg in a small jar and blend well.

Press turkey seasoning all over the inside and outside of the turkey. Brush the turkey with canola oil.

To Prepare Turkey on an Outdoor Grill Prepare a grill with a drip pan in the center of the lower grate and place an equal number of briquettes on both sides. When coals are moderately hot, place turkey centered over drip pan on a grill coated with a nonstick vegetable spray. Cover grill and cook for 1 hour or until a meat thermometer registers 180 degrees.

To Prepare Turkey on an Indoor Grill Place turkey on a preheated grill over moderate heat. Cover turkey with a piece of aluminum foil, leaving an opening on the vent side of the grill. Cook for 1 hour and 30 to 45 minutes or until a meat thermometer registers 180 degrees, turning turkey over and giving it a quarter turn occasionally. Brush with canola oil, if necessary.

New Delhi Turkey

Inspiration for this recipe came from a recent trip to India. Just walking down the streets, one could not help but be impressed by the wonderful aromas emanating from homes and restaurants. Serve with an Indian vegetable curry and naan, a tender Indian flatbread.

⅓ cup fresh lemon juice	½ teaspoon garam masala
2 tablespoons extra virgin olive oil	¼ teaspoon cayenne
1 tablespoon chopped fresh ginger	¼ teaspoon turmeric
2 cloves garlic, minced	¼ teaspoon cumin
1 teaspoon coriander	¼ teaspoon freshly ground pepper
½ teaspoon salt	1 fresh turkey half (3 pounds), wing tips removed

To Make Marinade Combine lemon juice, olive oil, ginger, garlic, coriander, salt, garam masala, cayenne, turmeric, cumin, and pepper in a resealable plastic bag and blend. Add turkey and turn to coat all over. Refrigerate for several hours or overnight.

To Prepare Turkey on an Outdoor Grill Prepare a grill with a drip pan in the center of the lower grate and place an equal number of briquettes on both sides. When coals are moderately hot, remove turkey from marinade, reserving marinade. Place turkey centered over drip pan on a grill coated with a nonstick vegetable spray. Cover grill and cook for 1 hour or until a meat thermometer registers 180 degrees, brushing occasionally with marinade.

To Prepare Turkey on an Indoor Grill Remove turkey from marinade, reserving marinade. Place turkey on a preheated grill over moderate heat. Cover turkey with a piece of aluminum foil, leaving an opening on the vent side of the grill. Cook for 1 hour and 30 to 45 minutes or until a meat thermometer registers 180 degrees, giving turkey a quarter turn occasionally and turning over to other side every 30 minutes. Brush occasionally with marinade.

Cilantro-Marinated Turkey Tenderloins with Garlic Mashed Potatoes

Cilantro combined with a pleasing array of spices adds a new dimension to the flavor of turkey. This dish is exceptional when served on a bed of Garlic Mashed Potatoes (recipe below) and topped with Gazpacho Salsa (page 38).

Marinade

1 cup chopped cilantro leaves
6 cloves garlic, minced
¾ cup fresh lime juice
1 tablespoon extra virgin
  olive oil
1¼ teaspoons cumin
1¼ teaspoons oregano
1¼ teaspoons thyme
1¼ teaspoons freshly ground
  pepper
⅛ teaspoon salt
6 turkey tenderloins
  (6 ounces each)

Garlic Mashed Potatoes

3 cups milk
2 pounds potatoes, peeled and
  cubed
8 cloves garlic, chopped
4 tablespoons butter, at room
  temperature
½ teaspoon salt
¼ teaspoon freshly ground
  pepper

To Make Marinade Combine cilantro, garlic, lime juice, olive oil, cumin, oregano, thyme, pepper, and salt in a resealable plastic bag and blend.

Place turkey tenderloins between two pieces of waxed paper. Using a meat tenderizer, flatten each turkey tenderloin into a ¼-inch-thick filet. Place turkey in marinade and turn to coat both sides. Refrigerate for several hours or overnight, turning turkey at least once.

To Make Potatoes Combine milk, potatoes, and garlic in a large saucepan over moderate heat and bring to a boil. Reduce heat to moderately low and simmer, covered, for 25 minutes or until potatoes are fork-tender. Place a sieve over a bowl. Transfer potatoes to sieve, reserving the milk and garlic in the bowl. Place potatoes in a large mixing bowl and mash with a potato masher. Add butter, salt, and pepper and blend well. Add reserved milk and garlic, blending in a small amount at a time, until potatoes are desired consistency. Taste for seasoning. Transfer mashed potatoes to a double boiler, cover, and keep warm over moderate heat.

To Prepare Turkey on an Outdoor Grill Remove turkey from marinade. Over moderately hot coals, place turkey tenderloins on a grill coated with a nonstick vegetable spray. Cover grill and cook for 5 to 6 minutes on each side.

To Prepare Turkey on an Indoor Grill Remove turkey tenderloins from marinade. Place them on a preheated grill over moderately high heat and cook for 8 to 10 minutes on each side, turning turkey tenderloins every 8 minutes.

To Serve Divide the garlic mashed potatoes among four dinner plates and top each serving with a turkey tenderloin. Garnish with a sprig of cilantro.

Cobb Salad with Grilled Turkey

Cobb salad is traditionally made with chicken; however, grilled turkey adds an interesting dimension to this cornucopia of spinach, avocado, bacon, tomatoes, and bleu cheese. Serve with French baguettes.

Champagne Vinaigrette

- 1 clove garlic
- ½ cup canola oil
- ¼ cup Champagne vinegar (see note)
- 1 tablespoon Dijon mustard
- ½ teaspoon salt
- ½ teaspoon granulated sugar
- ½ teaspoon dry mustard
- ½ teaspoon Worcestershire sauce
- ½ teaspoon paprika
- ½ teaspoon freshly ground pepper

Cobb Salad

- 2 turkey tenderloins (8 ounces each)
- ½ cup bottled Italian dressing
- 6 cups packed fresh baby spinach
- 6 slices bacon, cooked, drained, and crumbled
- 3 plum tomatoes, sliced
- 2 avocados, peeled and cubed
- 2 hard-boiled eggs, cut into quarters
- 3 ounces Maytag Bleu cheese, crumbled

To Make Vinaigrette In the work bowl of a food processor fitted with a metal blade, process garlic until finely chopped. Add canola oil, Champagne vinegar, Dijon mustard, salt, sugar, dry mustard, Worcestershire sauce, paprika, and pepper and process until well blended. Transfer vinaigrette to a bowl, cover with plastic wrap, and set aside.

To Marinate Place turkey tenderloins between two pieces of waxed paper. Using a meat tenderizer, flatten each turkey tenderloin into a ¼-inch-thick filet. Place Italian dressing in a resealable bag and add turkey tenderloins. Turn to coat all over. Refrigerate for 2 to 3 hours, turning turkey at least once.

To Prepare Turkey on an Outdoor Grill Remove turkey from marinade. Over moderately hot coals, place turkey tenderloins on a grill coated with a nonstick vegetable spray. Cover grill and cook for 5 to 6 minutes on each side. Allow turkey to cool for 10 minutes before cutting into thin slices.

To Prepare Turkey on an Indoor Grill Remove turkey tenderloins from marinade. Place them on a preheated grill over moderately high heat and cook for 8 to 10 minutes on each side, turning turkey tenderloins every 8 minutes. Allow turkey to cool for 10 minutes before cutting into thin slices.

To Make Cobb Salad Layer spinach, turkey, bacon, tomatoes, avocados, eggs, and cheese in a large salad bowl. Add vinaigrette and toss well.

Note If Champagne vinegar is unavailable, substitute white wine vinegar.

Southwestern Turkey Burgers

SERVES 4

Cumin, coriander, and cilantro give these turkey burgers a rich, Southwestern flavor. They are delicious topped with Corn Salsa (page 254) and accompanied with Sweet Potato Hash (recipe below).

Turkey Burgers

- 1 tablespoon extra virgin olive oil
- 1 small red bell pepper, diced
- 1 small onion, diced
- 2 cloves garlic, minced
- 1½ pounds freshly ground turkey
- 1 tablespoon cilantro leaves
- 2 teaspoons coriander
- 1 teaspoon cumin
- ¼ teaspoon salt
- ¼ teaspoon freshly ground pepper

Sweet Potato Hash

- 2 tablespoons extra virgin olive oil
- 3 large green onions, thinly sliced
- 2 large cloves garlic, minced
- 1 small red bell pepper, diced
- 3 sweet potatoes (or yams), 8 ounces each, baked and cut into ½-inch cubes (see note)
- 2 jalapeño chiles, seeded and minced (see note)
- 1 tablespoon chopped cilantro leaves
- ½ teaspoon freshly ground pepper
- ¼ teaspoon salt

- 4 hamburger buns

To Make Burgers Coat a medium skillet with a nonstick vegetable spray and add olive oil. Place over moderate heat and heat for 2 minutes. Add red pepper, onion, and garlic and sauté for 5 minutes, stirring occasionally. Set aside to cool.

Combine turkey, red pepper mixture, cilantro, coriander, cumin, salt, and pepper in a medium bowl and blend well. Form the turkey mixture into 4 patties.

To Prepare Burgers on an Outdoor Grill Over moderately hot coals, place turkey burgers on a grill coated with a nonstick vegetable spray. Cover grill and cook for 4 to 5 minutes on each side.

To Prepare Burgers on an Indoor Grill Place turkey burgers on a preheated grill and cook on moderately high heat for 12 to 13 minutes on each side.

To Make Hash While grilling the turkey burgers, place a large skillet over moderate heat and add olive oil. Heat for 2 minutes. Add green onions and garlic and sauté for 4 minutes, stirring occasionally. Add red pepper and sweet potatoes and sauté for 2 minutes, stirring frequently. Add jalapeño chiles, cilantro, pepper, and salt and sauté for 1 to 2 minutes or until heated through, stirring frequently.

To Serve Place a turkey burger on bottom half of each of four hamburger buns. Cover with remaining buns. Serve with sweet potato hash and garnish with a sprig of cilantro.

Note To bake the sweet potatoes, preheat the oven to 400 degrees. Prick sweet potatoes all over with a fork. Bake for 45 minutes or until tender when lightly squeezed. Cool before cutting.

Note The seeds of jalapeño chiles are very hot. To avoid burning your skin, wear rubber or latex gloves when removing the seeds. Immediately wash the knife, cutting surface, and gloves when finished.

Lemon-Marinated Turkey with Lemon and Caper Sauce

SERVES 4

The piquant lemon sauce is an excellent way to elevate the flavor of the lemon-marinated turkey. This sauce would also be wonderful on chicken or pork. Serve with Spinach and Rice (recipe below).

Marinade
- ½ cup fresh lemon juice
- 1 tablespoon extra virgin olive oil
- 2 cloves garlic, minced
- ½ teaspoon rosemary
- ½ teaspoon thyme
- ½ teaspoon oregano
- ½ teaspoon freshly ground pepper
- ½ teaspoon salt
- 4 turkey tenderloins (6 ounces each)

Spinach and Rice
- 2 tablespoons extra virgin olive oil
- 1 medium Vidalia onion or other sweet onion, coarsely chopped
- 1 cup long-grain rice

- 1 Anaheim chile, seeded and chopped
- ¼ cup chopped celery leaves
- 2 large cloves garlic, minced
- 1 can (14½ ounces) chicken broth
- ½ teaspoon salt
- ¼ teaspoon freshly ground pepper
- ½ cup thinly sliced prewashed, fresh spinach
- 2 tablespoons minced parsley
- 1 tablespoon butter, at room temperature

Lemon and Caper Sauce
- 4 tablespoons butter
- 3 tablespoons minced parsley
- ¼ cup fresh lemon juice
- 2 tablespoons capers

To Make Marinade Combine lemon juice, olive oil, garlic, rosemary, thyme, oregano, pepper, and salt in a resealable plastic bag and blend.

Place turkey tenderloins between two pieces of waxed paper. Using a meat tenderizer, flatten each turkey tenderloin into a ¼-inch-thick filet. Place turkey in marinade and turn to coat both sides. Refrigerate for several hours or overnight, turning turkey at least once.

To Make Spinach and Rice Heat olive oil in a medium saucepan over moderate heat. Add onion and sauté for 5 minutes, stirring occasionally. Reduce heat to moderately low, add rice, and sauté for 3 minutes, stirring occasionally. Add Anaheim chile, celery, garlic, chicken broth, salt, and pepper and bring to a boil over moderately high heat. Boil for 3 minutes. Reduce heat to low, cover, and cook for 15 minutes. Add spinach and blend. Cover saucepan and cook for 5 minutes. Add parsley and butter and blend. Cover and keep warm at room temperature.

To Prepare Turkey on an Outdoor Grill Remove turkey tenderloins from marinade. Over moderately hot coals, place turkey on a grill coated with a nonstick vegetable spray. Cover grill and cook for 5 to 6 minutes on each side.

To Prepare Turkey on an Indoor Grill Remove turkey tenderloins from marinade. Place them on a preheated grill over moderately high heat and cook for 8 to 10 minutes on each side, turning turkey tenderloins every 8 minutes.

To Make Lemon and Caper Sauce While grilling the turkey tenderloins, melt butter in a small saucepan over moderate heat. Remove saucepan from the heat and add parsley, lemon juice, and capers and blend.

To Serve Place a turkey tenderloin on each of four dinner plates and spoon some lemon and caper sauce over each. Spoon a serving of spinach and rice beside the turkey.

Southwestern Turkey Tenderloins with Blue Corn Tortillas

SERVES 4

Native Americans in the Southwest have been cultivating blue corn for thousands of years. The color reflects the plants' natural pigmentation. These colorful tortillas are especially eye-appealing and delicious when served on a plate beside slices of grilled turkey, with individual bowls of sour cream, Jo Gail's Guacamole (recipe below), and salsa.

Marinade

- 6 tablespoons fresh lime juice
- 1 tablespoon extra virgin olive oil
- 2 tablespoons packed minced cilantro leaves
- 1 teaspoon cumin
- ⅛ teaspoon cayenne
- ⅛ teaspoon oregano
- ⅛ teaspoon thyme
- ⅛ teaspoon salt
- ⅛ teaspoon freshly ground pepper
- 1 jalapeño chile, minced (see note)
- 1 clove garlic, minced

- 2 turkey tenderloins (10 ounces each)

Jo Gail's Guacamole

- 2 ripe avocados, peeled
- 2 tablespoons salsa
- 2 tablespoons fresh lemon juice
- 2 teaspoons mayonnaise
- ⅛ teaspoon garlic powder
- ⅛ teaspoon salt
- ⅛ teaspoon cayenne

- 8 blue corn tortillas, warmed (see note)
- ½ cup sour cream
- 1 cup salsa

To Make Marinade Combine lime juice, olive oil, cilantro, cumin, cayenne, oregano, thyme, salt, pepper, jalapeño chile, and garlic in a resealable plastic bag and blend.

Place turkey tenderloins between two pieces of waxed paper. Using a meat tenderizer, flatten each turkey tenderloin into a ¼-inch-thick filet. Place turkey in marinade and turn to coat both sides. Refrigerate for several hours or overnight, turning turkey at least once.

To Make Guacamole Place the avocado pulp (reserve one pit) in a small bowl and mash with a fork until smooth. Add salsa, lemon juice, mayonnaise, garlic powder, salt, and cayenne and blend well. If not serving the guacamole immediately, place the reserved pit in the center to prevent it from turning brown. Cover the bowl with plastic wrap and refrigerate.

To Prepare Turkey on an Outdoor Grill Remove turkey from marinade. Over moderately hot coals, place turkey tenderloins on a grill coated with a nonstick vegetable spray. Cover grill and cook for 5 to 6 minutes on each side. Cut the turkey tenderloins into thin slices.

To Prepare Turkey on an Indoor Grill Remove turkey tenderloins from marinade. Place them on a preheated grill and cook over moderately high heat for 8 to 10 minutes on each side, turning the turkey tenderloins every 8 minutes. Cut the turkey tenderloins into thin slices.

To Serve On each of four dinner plates, place two blue corn tortillas off to one side with turkey slices slightly overlapping the tortillas. Place individual bowls of guacamole, sour cream, and salsa beside the turkey slices.

Note The seeds of a jalapeño chile are very hot. To avoid burning your skin, wear rubber or latex gloves when removing the seeds. Immediately wash the knife, cutting surface, and gloves when finished.

Note Blue corn tortillas are available in most specialty or natural food stores.

Turkey Glazed with Honey and Mustard

SERVES 6

I like the flavor of Jack Daniel's Dijon mustard; however, any Dijon would work equally as well with this recipe. Adding honey to the mustard in the marinade is a nice balance of flavors. Serve with Cranberry Chutney (page 74)—Green Pepper Jelly (page 160) would also nicely complement this dish—and Acorn Squash with Fruited Wild Rice (page 336).

¼ cup Jack Daniel's Dijon mustard or other Dijon mustard
¼ cup dry white wine
2 tablespoons honey
1 tablespoon extra virgin olive oil
1 shallot, chopped

1 clove garlic, chopped
½ teaspoon cinnamon
½ teaspoon freshly ground pepper
⅛ teaspoon salt
1 fresh turkey half (3 to 3½ pounds), wing tips removed

To Make Marinade Combine Dijon mustard, white wine, honey, olive oil, shallot, garlic, cinnamon, pepper, and salt in a large resealable plastic bag and blend. Add turkey and turn to coat all over. Refrigerate for several hours or overnight, turning turkey at least once.

To Prepare Turkey on an Outdoor Grill Prepare a grill with a drip pan in the center of the lower grate and place an equal number of briquettes on both sides. When coals are moderately hot, remove turkey from marinade, reserving marinade. Place turkey centered over drip pan on a grill coated with a nonstick vegetable spray. Cover grill and cook for 1 hour or until a meat thermometer registers 180 degrees, brushing occasionally with marinade.

To Prepare Turkey on an Indoor Grill Remove turkey from marinade, reserving marinade. Place turkey on a preheated grill over moderate heat. Cover turkey with a piece of aluminum foil, leaving an opening on the vent side of the grill. Cook for 1 hour and 30 to 45 minutes or until a meat thermometer registers 180 degrees, giving turkey a quarter turn occasionally and turning over to the other side every 30 minutes. Brush occasionally with reserved marinade.

Grilled Turkey in Rosemary Marinade

Speckles of rosemary make a stunning presentation. These speckles not only are for show, but also add a wonderful, rustic flavor. Serve with Cranberry Chutney (page 74) and Grilled Spicy Yams (page 347).

¼ cup fresh lemon juice
2 tablespoons extra virgin olive oil
2 tablespoons minced garlic
1 tablespoon rosemary
1 tablespoon oregano
½ teaspoon crushed red pepper
½ teaspoon salt
½ teaspoon freshly ground pepper
1 fresh turkey half (3 to 3½ pounds), wing tips removed

To Make Marinade Combine lemon juice, olive oil, garlic, rosemary, oregano, crushed red pepper, salt, and pepper in a large resealable plastic bag and blend. Add turkey and turn to coat all over. Refrigerate for several hours or overnight, turning turkey at least once.

To Prepare Turkey on an Outdoor Grill Prepare a grill with a drip pan in the center of the lower grate and place an equal number of briquettes on both sides. When coals are moderately hot, remove turkey from marinade, reserving marinade. Place turkey centered over drip pan on a grill coated with a nonstick vegetable spray. Cover grill and cook for 1 hour or until a meat thermometer registers 180 degrees, brushing occasionally with reserved marinade.

To Prepare Turkey on an Indoor Grill Remove turkey from marinade, reserving marinade. Place turkey on a preheated grill over moderate heat. Cover turkey with a piece of aluminum foil, leaving an opening on the vent side of the grill. Cook for 1 hour and 30 to 45 minutes or until a meat thermometer registers 180 degrees, giving turkey a quarter turn occasionally and turning over to other side every 30 minutes. Brush occasionally with reserved marinade.

Greek Turkey Burgers

Because Mediterranean cuisine is a favorite of mine, grilling these Greek Turkey Burgers is a true labor of love. Serve with Tabbouleh (recipe below).

Tabbouleh

1½	cups boiling water
1	cup bulgur
¼	cup fresh lemon juice
¼	cup extra virgin olive oil
1	cup packed minced parsley
½	cup minced green onions
6	tablespoons minced fresh mint
2	tomatoes, chopped
1	teaspoon minced garlic
¾	teaspoon salt
¼	teaspoon freshly ground pepper

Turkey Burgers

1	pound freshly ground turkey
1	small egg
4	pimiento-stuffed olives, chopped
2	tablespoons minced parsley
1	teaspoon minced garlic
¼	teaspoon cinnamon
⅛	teaspoon nutmeg
	Salt and freshly ground pepper, to taste
¼	cup fat-free sour cream
4	pita breads, warmed
1	small cucumber, diced
¼	cup feta cheese, crumbled

To Make Tabbouleh Combine boiling water and bulgur in a medium bowl and cover with a piece of plastic wrap. Allow it to sit for 20 minutes. Pour bulgur into a colander lined with cheesecloth. Twist the cheesecloth around the bulgur and squeeze out the water. Transfer bulgur to a large bowl.

Combine lemon juice and olive oil in a small jar and blend well. Add mixture to bulgur and blend well. Add parsley, green onions, mint, tomatoes, garlic, salt, and pepper and blend well. Refrigerate tabbouleh, covered, for several hours or overnight. Stir before serving.

To Make Burgers Combine turkey, egg, olives, parsley, garlic, cinnamon, nutmeg, salt, and pepper in a medium bowl and blend well. (If the mixture is not firm, add bread crumbs, a tablespoon at a time, until the right consistency is reached.) Form mixture into 4 patties.

To Prepare Burgers on an Outdoor Grill Over moderately hot coals, place turkey burgers on a grill coated with a nonstick vegetable spray. Cover grill and cook for 4 to 5 minutes on each side.

To Prepare Burgers on an Indoor Grill Place turkey burgers on a preheated grill and cook over moderately high heat for 12 to 13 minutes on each side.

To Serve Spread 1 tablespoon sour cream on each warmed pita bread. Place a turkey burger on bottom half of pita and top each with cucumber and 1 tablespoon feta cheese. Fold over top half of pita bread.

Spicy Turkey Meatballs, Pita, and Tahini Sauce

SERVES 4

These spicy meatballs are so delicious, you may want to make extra just to have them as snacks or for lunch the next day. They are stuffed into pita bread, along with tomatoes and lettuce, and topped with a wonderful Tahini Sauce (recipe below). If you are watching calories, top the sandwiches with Raita (page 174) instead of the tahini sauce. Serve with Tabbouleh (page 92).

Tahini Sauce

- ½ cup coarsely chopped parsley
- 2 cloves garlic
- 6 tablespoons plain yogurt
- ¼ cup fresh lemon juice
- 3 tablespoons tahini paste
- 1½ tablespoons cumin
- ⅛ teaspoon salt
- ⅛ teaspoon freshly ground pepper

Meatballs

- ¼ cup coarsely chopped onion
- 2 tablespoons coarsely chopped parsley
- 1½ teaspoons fresh oregano leaves
- 1 clove garlic
- 1¼ pounds freshly ground turkey
- 6 tablespoons bread crumbs
- 1 teaspoon fresh lemon juice
- ¾ teaspoon freshly ground pepper
- ¼ teaspoon salt

- 4 pita breads, warmed
- 1 tomato, thinly sliced
- 1 cup shredded lettuce leaves

To Make Tahini Sauce In the work bowl of a food processor fitted with a metal blade, process parsley and garlic until finely chopped. Add yogurt, lemon juice, tahini paste, cumin, salt, and pepper and process until blended. Refrigerate tahini sauce for up to 1 hour before serving.

To Make Meatballs Soak bamboo skewers in water for 30 minutes or more. In a clean work bowl of a food processor fitted with a metal blade, process onion, parsley, oregano, and garlic until finely chopped.

Transfer mixture to a medium bowl and add turkey, bread crumbs, lemon juice, pepper, and salt and blend well. Form turkey mixture into 8 large meatballs and slightly flatten them so they will cook evenly. Thread the turkey meatballs on the skewers.

To Prepare Meatballs on an Outdoor Grill Over moderately hot coals, place meatball skewers on a grill coated with a nonstick vegetable spray. Cover grill and cook for 20 to 24 minutes, turning skewers every 6 minutes.

To Prepare Meatballs on an Indoor Grill Place meatball skewers on a preheated grill and cook over moderate heat for 45 to 50 minutes, turning skewers every 6 minutes.

To Serve Make a horizontal cut across each pita, about 1 inch down from the top, to make a pocket. Place 2 turkey meatballs in each pocket, along with tomato slices and lettuce. Spoon some tahini sauce on top of each.

Thanksgiving Turkey Burgers

SERVES 8

Flavoring ground turkey with sage turns these burgers into a treat even on nonholidays. For an added festive touch, top each burger with Cranberry Chutney (page 74) and serve with Sugar's Yams in Orange Cups (recipe below).

Sugar's Yams in Orange Cups

1   can (29 ounces) yams, mashed
½   cup orange marmalade
2   eggs
3   tablespoons butter, at room temperature, plus 2½ table-spoons, cut into small pieces
2   tablespoons firmly packed dark brown sugar
½   teaspoon salt
8   firm oranges
⅔   cup chopped pecans

Turkey Burgers

3   pounds freshly ground turkey
3   tablespoons sage
1½   teaspoons freshly ground pepper
1½   teaspoons tarragon
½   teaspoon salt

To Make Yams Preheat oven to 400 degrees. Combine yams, marmalade, eggs, 3 tablespoons butter, brown sugar, and salt in a large bowl and blend until smooth.

Slice off top portion of oranges. Using a sharp knife, carefully remove the pulp. Fill the oranges with the yam filling. Top the yam filling with chopped pecans and dot with remaining 2½ tablespoons butter. Bake for 20 to 25 minutes.

To Make Burgers Combine turkey, sage, pepper, tarragon, and salt in a medium bowl and blend well. Form mixture into 8 patties.

To Prepare Burgers on an Outdoor Grill Over moderately hot coals, place turkey burgers on a grill coated with a nonstick vegetable spray. Cover grill and cook for 4 to 5 minutes on each side.

To Prepare Burgers on an Indoor Grill Place turkey burgers on a preheated grill and cook over moderately high heat for 12 to 13 minutes on each side.

Note After the tops of the oranges and pulp are removed, the oranges can be scalloped by using a sharp paring knife and cutting out small wedges all around the top edge.

Duck with Three-Fruit Marinade

SERVES 4

Because duck is exceptionally fatty, I like to split it down the backbone and remove as much visible fat as possible. This method also makes it easier to prepare on either an indoor or an outdoor grill. Rose's Select Orange Marmalade, with its additional ingredients (grapefruit and lime), is a change from the traditional orange marmalade and nicely emboldens the flavor of the marinade. Serve with Acorn Squash with Fruited Wild Rice (page 336).

1   cup fresh orange juice
¼   cup rice wine
⅓   cup Rose's Select Orange Marmalade or other orange marmalade
1   tablespoon soy sauce
1   tablespoon canola oil

1   tablespoon minced fresh ginger
1   teaspoon thyme
¼   teaspoon salt
1   duck (4 to 5 pounds), split down the backbone, wing tips and all visible fat removed

To Make Marinade Combine orange juice, rice wine, marmalade, soy sauce, canola oil, ginger, thyme, and salt in a large resealable plastic bag and blend well. Add the duck and turn to coat all over. Refrigerate for several hours or overnight, turning duck at least once.

To Prepare Duck on an Outdoor Grill Remove duck from marinade, reserving marinade. Over moderately hot coals, place duck on a grill coated with a nonstick vegetable spray. Cover grill and cook for 30 to 40 minutes or until a meat thermometer registers 180 degrees, or when the end of a drumstick turns easily in the socket. Turn the duck every 5 minutes and brush occasionally with reserved marinade. (The skin and fat on the duck may cause flare-ups. When you turn the duck, make sure to extinguish any flames.)

To Prepare Duck on an Indoor Grill Remove duck from marinade, reserving marinade. Place duck on a preheated grill and cook over moderate heat for 1 hour and 20 to 25 minutes or until a meat thermometer registers 180 degrees, or when the end of a drumstick turns easily in the socket. Turn the duck every 5 minutes and give it a quarter turn occasionally. Brush with reserved marinade the last 15 minutes.

Honey-Glazed Duck

SERVES 4

In this glaze, there is an ample touch of garlic chili sauce, which gives it a rich flavor. Leftover duck (if there is any) can be made into a delicious salad, composed of mixed baby greens, goat cheese, and hearts of palm, laced with a Raspberry Vinaigrette (page 140).

Glaze

- 3 tablespoons honey
- 1 tablespoon garlic chili sauce
- 1 tablespoon Dijon mustard
- 1 tablespoon fresh lime juice

Rub

- 2 tablespoons extra virgin olive oil
- 1½ teaspoons garlic salt
- 1½ teaspoons salt
- 1½ teaspoons freshly ground pepper
- 1 duck (4 to 5 pounds), split down the backbone, wing tips and all visible fat removed

To Make Glaze Combine honey, garlic chili sauce, Dijon mustard, and lime juice in a small bowl and blend well. Set aside.

To Make Rub Combine olive oil, garlic salt, salt, and pepper in a small dish and blend well. Rub inside and outside of duck with olive oil rub.

To Prepare Duck on an Outdoor Grill Over moderately hot coals, place duck on a grill coated with a nonstick vegetable spray. Cover grill and cook for 30 to 40 minutes or until a meat thermometer registers 180 degrees, or when the end of a drumstick turns easily in the socket. Turn the duck every 5 minutes. Brush the duck with honey glaze the last 15 minutes of cooking time. (The skin and fat on the duck may cause flare-ups. When you turn the duck, make sure to extinguish any flames.)

To Prepare Duck on an Indoor Grill Place duck on a pre-heated grill and cook over moderate heat for 1 hour and 20 to 25 minutes or until a meat thermometer registers 180 degrees, or when the end of a drumstick turns easily in the socket. Turn the duck over every 5 minutes and give it a quarter turn occasionally. Brush the duck with honey glaze the last 15 minutes of cooking time.

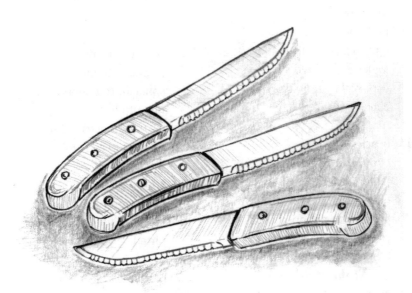

Pasta with Grilled Turkey and Pesto Sauce

SERVES 4

This fabulous pasta dish is delicious with grilled turkey. However, it could easily become a vegetarian dish by eliminating the turkey and adding equal amounts of your favorite grilled vegetables. Serve with an Italian salad and sourdough bread.

Pesto Sauce
2½ cups packed fresh basil
¼ cup pine nuts
1 tablespoon chopped garlic
¼ teaspoon salt
6 tablespoons extra virgin olive oil, plus olive oil as needed
¼ cup freshly grated pecorino cheese

Marinade
¼ cup fresh lemon juice
1 tablespoon extra virgin olive oil
1 tablespoon chopped basil
2 cloves garlic, chopped

¼ teaspoon salt
¼ teaspoon freshly ground pepper
4 turkey tenderloins (5 ounces each)

2 red bell peppers
1 package (9 ounces) fresh spinach, red pepper, or favorite fettuccine
1 jar (6½ ounces) quartered marinated artichoke hearts, drained
¼ cup sun-dried tomatoes, quartered
16 Greek olives (kalamatas), pitted

To Make Pesto In the work bowl of a food processor fitted with a metal blade, process basil, pine nuts, garlic, and salt until finely chopped. Add 6 tablespoons olive oil and puree. Add pecorino cheese and blend well. Transfer pesto to a container and pour enough olive oil on top to completely cover. Refrigerate pesto, covered, until ready to use.

To Make Marinade Combine lemon juice, olive oil, basil, garlic, salt, and pepper in a resealable plastic bag and blend.

Place turkey tenderloins between two pieces of waxed paper. Using a meat tenderizer, flatten each turkey tenderloin into a ¼-inch-thick filet. Place turkey in marinade and turn to coat both sides. Refrigerate for several hours or overnight, turning turkey at least once.

To Prepare Peppers on an Outdoor Grill Over moderately hot coals, place the red peppers on a grill coated with nonstick vegetable spray. Cover grill and cook for 20 to 24 minutes or until skins are charred all over, turning the peppers as skins blacken. Once grilled, place the peppers in a plastic bag and allow to steam for 15 minutes. When they are cool enough to handle, peel away the skins and remove the tops and seeds (do not rinse the peppers). Thinly slice the red peppers and set aside.

To Prepare Peppers on an Indoor Grill Place the red peppers on a preheated grill over high heat and cook for 20 to 30 minutes or until skins are charred all over, turning the peppers as skins blacken. Once grilled, place the peppers in a plastic bag and allow to steam for 15 minutes. When they are cool enough to handle, peel away the skins and remove the tops and seeds (do not rinse the peppers). Thinly slice the red peppers and set aside.

To Prepare Turkey on an Outdoor Grill Remove turkey tenderloins from marinade. Over moderately hot coals, place turkey on a grill coated with a nonstick vegetable spray. Cover grill and cook for 5 to 6 minutes on each side. Cut the turkey into thin slices and cover with plastic wrap until ready to serve.

To Prepare Turkey on an Indoor Grill Remove turkey tenderloins from marinade. Place them on a preheated grill over moderately high heat and cook for 8 to 10 minutes on each side, turning turkey tenderloins every 8 minutes. Cut the turkey into thin slices and cover with plastic wrap until ready to serve.

CONTINUED

To Serve While grilling the turkey tenderloins, combine 2 tablespoons water and ½ cup pesto and blend well. Set aside.

Cook fettuccine according to package directions. Drain well.

Place fettuccine, artichoke hearts, tomatoes, olives, and pesto (reserve some pesto to spoon over turkey and red peppers) in a large serving bowl and blend well. Divide fettuccine among four dinner plates and decoratively arrange turkey and red pepper slices on top. Spoon reserved pesto over each serving. Garnish with fresh basil leaves or toasted pine nuts, if desired. Alternatively, the fettuccine, turkey, red peppers, tomatoes, olives, and pesto can be combined together in a large serving bowl.

2

BEEF

Beef has been a dietary staple in our society for centuries. It is no wonder that for most of us the mere sight or smell of a juicy steak sizzling on a grill evokes a Pavlovian response. Although there is some concern about the health risks of consuming too much red meat, beef consumption has been on the rise in the 1990s. Beef has become increasingly popular, because it is being bred leaner than it was years ago, and as we become more nutritionally aware and able to make wise choices about healthier cuts and reasonable serving sizes, it becomes easier to include beef in a health-conscious diet.

The United States Department of Agriculture (USDA) recognizes eight grades of meat. The top four are prime, choice, select, and standard. The best grades for grilling are prime and choice.

Prime is the top grade, has the most marbling (streaks or flecks of fat in meat, which make it juicy and tender), and is the most flavorful. Only 2 percent of all beef is prime, and the majority of it is purchased by restaurants or upscale meat shops.

Choice has less marbling than prime but is still an excellent selection for grilling.

The most tender cuts come from the muscles of the animal that are used the least. These sections include the sirloin, rib, short loin, and flank steak.

SIRLOIN

Sirloin steaks are somewhat chewier than rib steaks but are just as delicious when grilled.

RIB

Ribeye steak and rib steak are both derived from the rib. These steaks are more tender than sirloins. Because rib steaks still have their bone, they tend to be more juicy than the ribeye.

SHORT LOIN

Filet (including filet mignon, chateaubriand, and tournedo), porterhouse steak, T-bone steak, strip steak, and club steak all originate from the short loin. They are the most expensive of all the cuts of beef, and for good reason: they are exceptionally tender and intensely flavored.

FLANK STEAK

Flank steak comes from the lower hindquarters, or flank. It is very suitable for grilling, but because it is so lean, marinating it is a necessity. It should be quickly grilled and served rare, otherwise it loses its tenderness.

GROUND BEEF

Ground beef, also known as hamburger, is a universal favorite for grilling. Ground beef is made from select cuts of meat, such as sirloin, round, and chuck; the label should specify the origin. "Regular" ground beef on the label identifies it as 80 percent lean, i.e., that 80 percent of the beef is a combination of different cuts of meat ground together while the remaining 20 percent is fat. The leanest ground beef, 95 percent lean, is usually made from meat that comes from the short loin, while ground sirloin is 85 percent lean. When making hamburger patties, handle them as little as possible so the burgers will remain moist and juicy. Also, if using beef with a higher fat content, the patties should be made larger to allow for the shrinkage that will occur when the burgers are cooked.

Remember, to eliminate all traces of potentially dangerous bacteria in the meat, ground beef patties must be cooked so that the center registers 160 degrees on a meat thermometer.

HELPFUL GUIDELINES FOR SELECTING AND GRILLING BEEF

- Leaner cuts of meat tend to be less tender and less tasty. However, marinating them for several hours or overnight in a liquid or paste mixture will tenderize them as well as add flavor. A useful rule of thumb to follow when looking for leaner cuts of beef is to look for the words "loin" or "round" in the name. The leanest cuts are beef eye round, top round, round tip, top sirloin, top loin, and tenderloin.
- When buying beef, look for brightly colored, red to deep red cuts with a moderate amount of marbling.
- To seal in the juices when grilling beef, sear it first by cooking the meat for 1 minute on each side. Test for doneness by

inserting a meat thermometer to measure the temperature of the thickest part of the meat or by observing the color of the beef through a slit made near its center. If the thermometer registers 120 to 135 degrees, or if the center is bluish-maroon and the outer portion is pale brown, then it is rare. If the thermometer registers 135 to 140 degrees, or if the center is deep red and the outer portion is light to medium brown, then it is medium rare. A temperature of 140 to 150 degrees or a light pink center and medium to dark brown outer portion indicates that it is medium. A reading of 155 to 165 degrees, or beef that appears uniformly brown throughout, suggests that the meat is well-done. For steaks, another way to determine how long to cook the meat is to follow guidelines that relate to thickness. The Weber's Owner's Guide provides a useful chart for outdoor charcoal grilling:

COOKING TIME (IN MINUTES)

Steak Thickness	Rare 1st Side	Rare 2nd Side	Medium 1st Side	Medium 2nd Side	Well-Done 1st Side	Well-Done 2nd Side
1 inch thick	2	3	4	4	5	6
1½ inches thick	5	6	7	8	9	10
2 inches thick	7	8	9	9	10	11

- Grilling indoors may require slightly longer times for similar results. Even with time guidelines, meat temperature and color are always effective measures of doneness.
- It bears repeating that for safety from dangerous bacteria, ground beef must *always* be cooked so that its internal temperature reaches at least 160 degrees.

Chicago Hot Dogs

SERVES 4

Because I grew up in Chicago, one of my favorite food memories is the Vienna all-beef hot dog sold at hot dog stands. They have been a tradition in Chicago for over a hundred years. Pushcart vendors used to call them Vienna Red Hots, and they were an all-time favorite treat at baseball games. The hot dogs were steamed, then placed in a special Vienna poppy seed hot dog bun; celery salt was sprinkled on the hot dog, and it was smothered with chopped onions, tomatoes, relish, and yellow mustard (you could also add hot peppers). This glorious delight was served in a red plastic basket with lots of French fries. With this recipe, you can enjoy your own taste of Chicago but add a new twist by grilling the hot dogs.

4	kosher all-beef hot dogs		Yellow mustard
4	poppy seed hot dog buns, warmed	1	onion, chopped
	Celery salt, to taste	1	large tomato, chopped
			Relish

To Prepare Hot Dogs on an Outdoor Grill Over moderately hot coals, place hot dogs on a grill coated with a nonstick vegetable spray. Cover grill and cook for 8 to 12 minutes or until brown all over, turning hot dogs occasionally.

To Prepare Hot Dogs on an Indoor Grill Place hot dogs on a preheated grill over high heat and cook for 8 to 12 minutes or until brown all over, turning hot dogs occasionally.

To Serve Place hot dogs in buns and season with celery salt. Garnish with mustard, onion, tomato, and relish. Enjoy!

Beef Filets with Mushroom Sauce

Serving beef filets is such an elegant yet easy way to entertain friends. Although the beef is delicious by itself, spooning a mushroom sauce over it adds a contrast in flavor, color, and texture. Serve with Potato and Turnip Au Gratin (page 124) and Mixed Baby Greens with Goat Cheese (page 140).

1   filet of beef (1½ pounds), cut
    into 4 steaks
    Salt and freshly ground
    pepper, to taste

Mushroom Sauce

2   tablespoons butter
¾   pound fresh mushrooms,
    thinly sliced
1   cup sour cream
2   tablespoons brandy
2   tablespoons chopped parsley
    Dash of salt

To Prepare Beef on an Outdoor Grill Season the filets with salt and pepper. Over moderately hot coals, place filets on a grill coated with a nonstick vegetable spray. Sear the filets for 1 minute on each side. Cover grill and cook for 4 to 5 minutes on each side or until a meat thermometer registers 145 degrees.

To Prepare Beef on an Indoor Grill Season the filets with salt and pepper. Place them on a preheated grill over high heat and cook for 18 to 20 minutes or until a meat thermometer registers 145 degrees, turning the filets every 7 minutes.

To Make Mushroom Sauce While grilling the beef filets, melt butter in a medium saucepan over moderate heat. Add mushrooms and sauté for 5 to 7 minutes or until mushrooms are soft. Add sour cream, brandy, parsley, and salt and blend well. Keep the mushroom sauce warm until ready to serve.

To Serve Arrange the beef filets on four dinner plates and spoon some mushroom sauce over each serving. Garnish with a sprig of parsley.

Greek Marinated Filet of Beef with Caramelized Onions

This savory marinade highlights the flavor of the beef filets. However, if time is of the essence, omit the marinade, season the filets with salt and pepper before grilling, and savor the fabulous addition of caramelized onions that seem to melt in your mouth. Serve with Garlic Mashed Potatoes (page 78).

Marinade

¼ cup dry white wine

¼ cup fresh lemon juice

1 tablespoon extra virgin olive oil

3 large cloves garlic, minced

2 tablespoons dried dill weed

2 tablespoons chopped green onions

2 tablespoons parsley

1 teaspoon oregano

1 filet of beef (1½ pounds), cut into 4 steaks

Caramelized Onions

2 tablespoons extra virgin olive oil

2 large onions, thinly sliced

½ teaspoon salt

½ teaspoon freshly ground pepper

To Make Marinade Combine wine, lemon juice, olive oil, garlic, dill weed, green onions, parsley, and oregano in a resealable plastic bag and blend. Add filets and turn to coat all over. Refrigerate for several hours or overnight, turning filets at least once.

To Make Onions Heat olive oil in a large skillet over moderate heat for 3 minutes. Add onions and season with salt and pepper. Sauté onions for 15 minutes, stirring occasionally. Keep the caramelized onions warm.

To Prepare Beef on an Outdoor Grill Remove the filets from marinade. Over moderately hot coals, place filets on a grill coated with a nonstick vegetable spray. Sear the filets for 1 minute on each side. Cover grill and cook for 4 to 5 minutes on each side or until a meat thermometer registers 145 degrees.

To Prepare Beef on an Indoor Grill Remove the filets from marinade. Place them on a preheated grill over high heat and cook for 18 to 20 minutes or until a meat thermometer registers 145 degrees, turning the filets every 7 minutes.

To Serve Arrange a filet of beef on each of four dinner plates. Spoon caramelized onions over beef and garnish with a sprig of dill or parsley.

Beef

Filet of Beef with Wild Mushrooms

SERVES 4

This is a great dish to serve at a dinner party. The filets are quickly grilled, and a variety of wild mushrooms cloaked in a velvety rich cream sauce adds a touch of elegance. Serve with Asparagus with Lemon Crumbs (page 228) and Sautéed New Potatoes (page 186).

4 tablespoons butter
1 pound fresh wild mushrooms (shiitake, morels, cepes, porcini, or chanterelles), thinly sliced
¼ teaspoon salt, plus salt to taste

¼ teaspoon freshly ground pepper, plus pepper to taste
½ cup heavy cream
1 filet of beef (1½ pounds), cut into 4 steaks

To Make Mushrooms Melt butter in a medium saucepan over moderate heat. Add mushrooms and sauté for 2 to 3 minutes. Add ¼ teaspoon salt and ¼ teaspoon pepper and blend. Reduce heat to moderately low, cover saucepan, and cook for 10 to 15 minutes or until mushrooms are soft, adding more butter, one tablespoon at a time, if necessary. Raise heat to moderate and add heavy cream. Cook for 10 minutes or until sauce thickens, stirring frequently. Keep the wild mushroom sauce warm until ready to serve.

To Prepare Beef on an Outdoor Grill Season the filets with salt and pepper. Over moderately hot coals, place filets on a grill coated with a nonstick vegetable spray. Sear the filets for 1 minute on each side. Cover grill and cook for 4 to 5 minutes on each side or until a meat thermometer registers 145 degrees.

To Prepare Beef on an Indoor Grill Season the filets with salt and pepper. Place them on a preheated grill over high heat and cook for 18 to 20 minutes or until a meat thermometer registers 145 degrees, turning the filets every 7 minutes.

To Serve Place a beef filet on each of four dinner plates. Spoon some wild mushrooms over each serving and garnish with a sprig of parsley.

Gingered Beef Kebabs

This recipe definitely lends itself to being prepared in large quantities, and it does wonderful things to beef. So have a party! These tender cubes of marinated beef intermingling with pineapple chunks, orange bell peppers, shiitake mushrooms, and green onions seem to beckon friends to join you in a fabulous feast. Serve with Savory Wild Rice (page 120).

¼ cup minced fresh ginger

3 large cloves garlic, minced

2 tablespoons shoyu sauce

2 tablespoons rice wine vinegar

2 tablespoons dry sherry

2 tablespoons canola oil

½ tablespoon oriental sesame oil

1 sirloin steak (1½ pounds), cut into 1¼-inch cubes

1 orange bell pepper, seeded and cut into 8 squares

8 fresh pineapple chunks

8 shiitake mushrooms, stems removed

4 green onions, cut into 2-inch pieces

To Make Marinade Combine ginger, garlic, shoyu sauce, rice wine vinegar, sherry, canola oil, and sesame oil in a resealable plastic bag and blend. Add cubed sirloin and turn to coat all over. Refrigerate for several hours, turning beef cubes at least once.

To Prepare Kebabs on an Outdoor Grill Soak bamboo skewers in water for 30 minutes or more. Remove cubed steak from marinade. Alternate the beef, orange pepper, pineapple, mushrooms, and green onions on skewers. Over moderately hot coals, place the kebabs on a grill coated with a nonstick vegetable spray. Cover grill and cook for 5 to 6 minutes on each side or until a meat thermometer registers 145 degrees.

To Prepare Kebabs on an Indoor Grill Soak bamboo skewers in water for 30 minutes or more. Remove cubed steak from marinade. Alternate the beef, orange pepper, pineapple, mushrooms, and green onions on skewers. Place the kebabs on a preheated grill over high heat and cook for 20 minutes or until a meat thermometer registers 145 degrees, turning kebabs every 7 minutes.

Thara's Marinated Flank Steak

The recipe for this marinade comes from a Japanese friend. It transforms beef tenderloins and flank or skirt steak into an epicurean delight. Serve with Jasmine Rice (page 158) and Japanese Cucumber Salad (recipe below).

Marinade

¼ sweet apple, peeled and cored
¼ onion
1 small clove garlic
¼ cup sake
¼ cup rice wine
¼ cup shoyu sauce
1½ teaspoons white miso, optional
1 teaspoon oriental sesame oil
½ teaspoon crushed red pepper
1 flank steak (2¼ pounds)

Japanese Cucumber Salad

2 medium-size cucumbers
1 large carrot, peeled
¼ cup white wine vinegar
1 tablespoon granulated sugar
½ teaspoon salt
½ teaspoon freshly ground pepper

To Make Marinade In the work bowl of a food processor fitted with a metal blade, process apple, onion, and garlic until finely chopped. Transfer mixture to a resealable plastic bag and add sake, rice wine, shoyu sauce, miso, sesame oil, and crushed red pepper and blend well.

Score the flank steak by making diagonal cuts across the grain, 1 inch apart, to form a diamond pattern. Place the steak in the marinade and turn to coat both sides. Refrigerate for several hours or overnight, turning steak at least once.

To Make Cucumber Salad Using a fork, start at one end of each cucumber and move the fork down to the other end of the cucumber, slightly piercing the skin. Repeat this process around the entire cucumber. Remove ends and thinly slice each cucumber.

Cut 4 equally spaced V-shaped grooves down length of carrot, making sure that the points of each V do not touch each other. Thinly slice the carrot.

Combine white wine vinegar, sugar, salt, and pepper in a medium bowl and blend. Add cucumber and carrot slices and turn to coat all over. Refrigerate the Japanese cucumber salad, covered, for several hours or overnight.

To Prepare Steak on an Outdoor Grill Remove the flank steak from marinade. Over moderately hot coals, place the steak on a grill coated with a nonstick vegetable spray. Sear the steak for 1 minute on each side. Cover grill and cook for 5 to 6 minutes on each side or until a meat thermometer registers 145 degrees. Carve the flank steak across the grain into very thin slices.

To Prepare Steak on an Indoor Grill Remove the flank steak from marinade. Place it on a preheated grill over high heat and cook for 18 to 20 minutes or until a meat thermometer registers 145 degrees, turning the steak every 7 minutes. Carve the flank steak across the grain into very thin slices.

Judy's Filet of Beef

This recipe comes from a friend who is one of the best cooks I know. It is one of my favorites. Serve with Savory Wild Rice (recipe below).

Marinade

½ cup beef or chicken broth
¼ cup honey
¼ cup soy sauce
½ teaspoon ground ginger
¼ teaspoon dry mustard
½ clove garlic, crushed
1 to 2 jiggers bourbon or gin
1 filet of beef (1½ pounds), cut
   into 4 steaks

Savory Wild Rice

2 tablespoons butter
1 medium Vidalia onion or
   other sweet onion, chopped
1 cup wild rice, rinsed in
   cold water
2 cans (14½ ounces each)
   chicken broth
3 tablespoons toasted almonds
   (see note)
3 tablespoons raisins
2 tablespoons minced
   fresh parsley
½ teaspoon salt
½ teaspoon freshly
   ground pepper

To Make Marinade Combine broth, honey, soy sauce, ginger, mustard, and garlic in a small saucepan over moderate heat. Bring to a boil and simmer for 5 minutes. Add bourbon or gin and blend. Set aside to cool for 10 minutes.

Place the filets in a nonmetal dish and pour the marinade on top. Cover the dish and refrigerate for several hours or overnight, turning filets at least once.

To Make Wild Rice Melt butter in a medium saucepan over moderate heat. Add onion and sauté for 5 minutes, stirring occasionally. Transfer onions to a dish and set aside. In the same saucepan, bring rice and chicken broth to a boil over high heat. Reduce heat to moderately high and cook, uncovered, for 25 to 30 minutes or just until rice begins to open. Drain well.

Add onions, almonds, raisins, parsley, salt, and pepper to wild rice and blend well. Cover and keep warm at room temperature.

To Prepare Beef on an Outdoor Grill Remove filets from marinade. Over moderately hot coals, place filets on a grill coated with a nonstick vegetable spray. Sear the filets for 1 minute on each side. Cover grill and cook for 4 to 5 minutes on each side or until a meat thermometer registers 145 degrees.

To Prepare Beef on an Indoor Grill Remove filets from marinade. Place them on a preheated grill over high heat and cook for 18 to 20 minutes or until a meat thermometer registers 145 degrees, turning steaks every 7 minutes.

Note To toast almonds: Preheat the oven to 350 degrees. Place almonds in a shallow pan and bake for 10 to 15 minutes or until golden brown.

Sirloin Steaks with Mike's Special Marinade

SERVES 4

This special marinade does wonderful things to steaks. It can also be used to baste steaks, if you don't have time to marinate them. Any leftover marinade that has not been in contact with the raw steak can be refrigerated and simply refreshed by adding crushed garlic. Serve the steaks with Garlic-Basted Grilled Corn on the Cob (page 317) and Joanne's Spinach Salad (page 178).

½ cup soy sauce or tamari sauce
2 cloves garlic, crushed
¼ cup firmly packed dark
    brown sugar
2 tablespoons canola oil or
    extra virgin olive oil

½ teaspoon ground ginger
½ teaspoon freshly ground
    pepper
4 sirloin steaks (6 ounces each)

To Make Marinade Combine soy sauce, garlic, brown sugar, oil, ground ginger, and pepper in a jar with a tight-fitting lid and shake well.

Place marinade in a resealable plastic bag and add steaks. Turn to coat all over. Refrigerate for several hours or overnight, turning steaks at least once.

To Prepare Steaks on an Outdoor Grill Remove the sirloin steaks from marinade. Over moderately hot coals, place the steaks on a grill coated with a nonstick vegetable spray and cook for 3 minutes. Using tongs, turn the steaks about 45 degrees to make a cross-hatch mark and cook an additional 3 minutes. Turn steaks over, cover grill, and cook for 6 to 7 minutes or until a meat thermometer registers 145 degrees.

To Prepare Steaks on an Indoor Grill Remove the sirloin steaks from marinade. Place them on a preheated grill over high heat and cook for 12 to 19 minutes on each side or until a meat thermometer registers 145 degrees.

Pepper-Coated Filet of Beef

Coating beef tenderloin steaks with a mix of freshly ground pepper-corns—green, pink, black, and white—gives them a real bite. The steaks can be served alone or topped with Grilled Red Pepper Hollandaise Sauce (page 354). Serve with Potato and Turnip Au Gratin (recipe below).

Potato and Turnip Au Gratin

1   clove garlic, peeled and halved
1   tablespoon butter, at room temperature
1   cup milk
½   cup heavy cream
1½   pounds baking potatoes, peeled and thinly sliced
½   pound turnip, peeled and thinly sliced
3   tablespoons butter, divided into tablespoons and each cut into small pieces
     Salt and freshly ground pepper, to taste

Filet of Beef

2   tablespoons extra virgin olive oil
¼   cup freshly ground four peppercorn mix (green, pink, black, and white)
1   filet of beef (1½ pounds), cut into 4 steaks

To Make Gratin Preheat oven to 400 degrees. Rub the garlic first and then the butter all over the inside of a 13 × 8½ × 1¾-inch gratin dish. Set aside.

Bring milk and heavy cream to a simmer in a heavy, medium saucepan over moderate heat. Distribute one third of the potatoes and turnip in gratin dish, top with one third of milk and heavy cream mixture, dot with 1 tablespoon butter, and season with salt and pepper. Repeat this process two more times. Bake for 50 minutes or until potatoes and turnip are brown.

To Coat Beef Place ½ tablespoon olive oil on one plate and 1 tablespoon ground peppercorns on another plate. Coat both sides of one steak in olive oil first and then in peppercorn mix. Replenish each plate with new olive oil and peppercorn mix for each remaining steak, and repeat the process.

To Prepare Beef on an Outdoor Grill Over moderately hot coals, place steaks on a grill coated with a nonstick vegetable spray. Sear steaks for 1 minute on each side. Cover grill and cook for 4 to 5 minutes on each side or until a meat thermometer registers 145 degrees.

To Prepare Beef on an Indoor Grill Place steaks on a pre-heated grill over high heat and cook for 18 to 20 minutes or until a meat thermometer registers 145 degrees, turning steaks every 7 minutes.

Filet of Beef with Vidalia Onion, Mustard, and Honey Sauce

SERVES 4

When company is arriving on short notice and I want to prepare a meal that is quick, yet special, this is one of my favorite entrees. The sauce can be prepared beforehand and the steaks can be grilled while sharing a glass of wine and some appetizers with your guests. Serve with Alsatian Garlic Potatoes (recipe below) and a mixed green salad.

Sauce

- 2 tablespoons canola oil
- 2 Vidalia onions or other sweet onion, coarsely chopped
- 6 large cloves garlic, minced
- 2 stalks celery, coarsely chopped
- 2 carrots, coarsely chopped
- ¼ teaspoon salt
- ¼ teaspoon freshly ground pepper
- ¾ cup dry red wine
- 2 cans (14½ ounces each) chicken broth
- ½ cup Dijon mustard
- ½ cup grainy mustard
- 6 tablespoons honey
- 8 tablespoons (1 stick) butter, cut into 8 pieces

Alsatian Garlic Potatoes

- 2 pounds potatoes, peeled and cubed
- 2 tablespoons butter, at room temperature
- 2 eggs, beaten
- 2 tablespoons flour
- 3 cloves garlic, minced
- 2 tablespoons minced parsley
- ½ teaspoon freshly ground pepper
- ⅜ teaspoon salt
  Dash of nutmeg
- 2 tablespoons butter, melted

- 1 filet of beef (1½ pounds), cut into 4 steaks
  Salt and pepper, to taste

To Make Sauce Heat canola oil in a medium saucepan over moderate heat for 2 minutes. Add onions, garlic, celery, carrots, salt, and pepper and sauté for 5 minutes, stirring occasionally. Increase heat to high, add wine, and boil quickly for 5 minutes. Add chicken broth, Dijon and grainy mustards, and honey and cook over moderately high heat, stirring occasionally, for 30 to 40 minutes or until sauce is thick and reduced to a scant 2 cups. Place a sieve over the top of a double boiler and pour the sauce into the sieve, pressing down on the vegetables with the back of a spoon. Discard vegetables. Place the sauce over moderate heat and add butter, one piece at a time, stirring constantly. The sauce can be kept warm in the double boiler until ready to serve (see note).

To Make Potatoes Preheat oven to 350 degrees and lightly grease a baking dish. Place potatoes in a large saucepan filled with boiling water and simmer over moderately high heat for 30 minutes or until fork-tender. Drain.

Place potatoes in a large bowl and mash with a potato masher. Add butter and eggs and blend well. Add flour, garlic, parsley, pepper, salt, and nutmeg and blend. Transfer potatoes to the prepared baking dish and bake for 20 to 25 minutes or until top is lightly browned. Pour melted butter on top before serving.

To Prepare Beef on an Outdoor Grill Season the filets with salt and pepper. Over moderately hot coals, place filets on a grill coated with a nonstick vegetable spray. Sear filets for 1 minute on each side. Cover grill and cook for 4 to 5 minutes on each side or until a meat thermometer registers 145 degrees.

To Prepare Beef on an Indoor Grill Season the filets with salt and pepper. Place them on a preheated grill over high heat and cook for 18 to 20 minutes or until a meat thermometer registers 145 degrees, turning filets every 7 minutes.

To Serve Spoon some Vidalia onion, mustard, and honey sauce on one side of each of four dinner plates. Center the filet of beef on the sauce and garnish with a sprig of watercress or parsley. Place a serving of Alsatian garlic potatoes beside each steak.

   Note The sauce can be made into a wild mushroom sauce by adding 1 to 1½ pounds wild mushrooms, thinly sliced, to the sauce while warming it in the double boiler. In one to two hours, the mushrooms are tender and the sauce is delicious!

Flank Steak in Oriental Marinade

SERVES 4

Sriracha hot chili sauce is a smooth, Asian red sauce made from serrano chiles. When a spicy dish is in order, Sriracha hot chili sauce will add just the right amount of zing. It can be found in most Asian food stores. Serve the flank steak with a Chinese noodle salad.

1 tablespoon canola oil
1 tablespoon Sriracha hot chili sauce
1 tablespoon granulated sugar
1 tablespoon soy sauce
2 teaspoons chopped green onion

1 teaspoon oriental sesame oil
1 clove garlic, minced
1 flank steak (1½ pounds), pierced all over with a fork

To Make Marinade Combine canola oil, Sriracha hot chili sauce, sugar, soy sauce, green onion, sesame oil, and garlic in a resealable plastic bag and blend. Add flank steak and turn to coat all over. Refrigerate for several hours or overnight, turning steak at least once.

To Prepare Steak on an Outdoor Grill Remove the flank steak from marinade. Over moderately hot coals, place the steak on a grill coated with a nonstick vegetable spray. Sear the steak for 1 minute on each side. Cover grill and cook for 5 to 6 minutes on each side or until a meat thermometer registers 145 degrees. Carve the flank steak across the grain into very thin slices.

To Prepare Steak on an Indoor Grill Remove the flank steak from marinade. Place the steak on a preheated grill over high heat and cook for 20 to 24 minutes or until a meat thermometer registers 145 degrees, turning the steak every 5 minutes. Carve the flank steak across the grain into very thin slices.

Grilled Hamburgers with Crispy Onions

The Tartars used to place their raw meat under their saddles as they engaged in warfare. They later shredded this now tenderized meat, or tartar steak, and ate it raw. They introduced it to Germany before the fourteenth century, and it soon became a common meal among the poor. And it was in Hamburg, Germany, that it got its name: hamburger steak. Today, the universal popularity of the hamburger among rich and poor cannot be disputed, and happily the grill has replaced the saddle as a preparation technique. Hamburgers can be served with slices of tomatoes, green pepper, lettuce, and onions; however, my family likes them topped with crispy onions. Serve with Dill and Basil Potato Salad (recipe below).

Dill and Basil Potato Salad

- 2½ pounds new potatoes
- 5 eggs
- ¾ cup mayonnaise
- 2 tablespoons apple cider vinegar
- 1½ tablespoons Dijon mustard
- 1 tablespoon chopped fresh dill
- 1 tablespoon chopped fresh basil
- 1 tablespoon honey
- 2½ teaspoons freshly ground pepper
- 1¼ teaspoons salt
- 1 red bell pepper, seeded and diced

Crispy Onions

- 3 large red onions, cut into ½-inch slices

Hamburgers

- 2¼ pounds lean ground beef
- 6 tablespoons minced parsley
- 3 cloves garlic, minced
- 1½ tablespoons Dijon mustard
- ½ teaspoon Worcestershire sauce
- ¾ teaspoon salt
- ¾ teaspoon freshly ground pepper
- 6 whole-wheat hamburger buns

To Make Potato Salad Place potatoes and eggs in a large pot and fill with enough water to cover. Bring to a boil over moderately high heat. Turn off heat, cover pot, and allow the potatoes and eggs to come to room temperature. When cool, remove egg shells from eggs. Cube the potatoes and coarsely chop the eggs.

Combine the mayonnaise, apple cider vinegar, Dijon mustard, dill, basil, honey, pepper, and salt in a large bowl and blend well. Add the potatoes, eggs, and red pepper and gently blend. Cover the bowl and refrigerate the dill and basil potato salad for several hours.

To Make Crispy Onions Place a large nonstick skillet over moderate heat for 2 minutes. Spread onions in a single layer in pan and cook for 20 minutes. Turn onions over and cook an additional 20 minutes or until crisp, stirring occasionally. Set aside.

To Make Hamburgers Combine ground beef, parsley, garlic, Dijon mustard, Worcestershire sauce, salt, and pepper in a medium bowl and blend well. Form the mixture into 6 hamburger patties and slightly flatten them.

To Prepare Hamburgers on an Outdoor Grill Over moderately hot coals, place hamburgers on a grill coated with a nonstick vegetable spray. Cover grill and cook for 4 minutes on each side or until a meat thermometer registers 160 degrees.

To Prepare Hamburgers on an Indoor Grill Place hamburgers on a preheated grill and cook over high heat for 8 to 10 minutes on each side or until a meat thermometer registers 160 degrees.

To Serve Place a hamburger and some crispy onions in each hamburger bun. Serve with dill and basil potato salad on the side.

Peppered Filet of Beef with Three-Mustard Sauce

SERVES 4

The blend of three mustards in this savory sauce is a delicious complement to beef tenderloin. I like to use good-quality mustards to bring out the individual flavors and to make a richly flavored sauce. The sauce also goes well with grilled poultry or pork. Serve with Grilled Accordion Potatoes (page 328).

Pepper Sauce Baste
- ¼ cup Spicy Peppa mustard (or other hot mustard)
- 1 tablespoon freshly ground pepper
- 1 tablespoon minced parsley
- ¼ teaspoon cayenne

Three-Mustard Sauce
- ¼ cup dry white wine
- 1 cup heavy cream
- 2 tablespoons Dijon mustard
- 2 tablespoons yellow mustard
- 2 tablespoons grainy mustard

- 1 filet of beef (1½ pounds), cut into 4 steaks
  Parsley

To Make Pepper Sauce Baste Combine Spicy Peppa mustard, pepper, parsley, and cayenne in a small dish and blend well.

To Make Three-Mustard Sauce Bring wine to a boil in a large skillet over moderately high heat and boil for 2 minutes. Reduce heat to moderate and add heavy cream and Dijon, yellow, and grainy mustards and cook for 2 to 3 minutes or until sauce thickens, stirring occasionally. Keep warm over low heat, stirring occasionally.

To Prepare Beef on an Outdoor Grill Over moderately hot coals, place steaks on a grill coated with a nonstick vegetable spray. Sear steaks for 1 minute on each side. Brush the tops of steaks with pepper sauce baste and turn them over. Cover grill, and cook for 4 to 5 minutes. Brush tops of steaks with pepper sauce baste and turn over. Cover grill and cook for 4 to 5 minutes or until a meat thermometer registers 145 degrees.

To Prepare Beef on an Indoor Grill Brush pepper sauce baste on one side of each steak. Place steaks, basted side down, on a preheated grill over high heat and cook for 7 minutes. Brush pepper sauce baste on tops of steaks, turn over, and cook for 7 minutes. Turn steaks again and cook for an additional 4 to 6 minutes or until a meat thermometer registers 145 degrees.

To Serve Spoon some three-mustard sauce on each of four dinner plates. Center a filet on the sauce and garnish with a sprig of parsley.

Kathy's Marinated Flank Steak

Kathy gives some of the best dinner parties in Iowa City. She was kind enough to share with me some of her favorite recipes that always receive rave reviews. She considers her marinated flank steak and Mashed Potatoes with Caramelized Onions (recipe below) a winning combination. I think you will agree!

Marinade

¼ cup red wine vinegar
2 tablespoons canola oil
2 tablespoons soy sauce
2 tablespoons ketchup
¼ teaspoon garlic powder
¼ teaspoon freshly ground pepper
¼ teaspoon onion salt
1 flank steak (2¼ pounds), pierced all over with a fork

Mashed Potatoes with Caramelized Onions

2 tablespoons butter
1 large Vidalia onion or other sweet onion, coarsely chopped
3 large potatoes, peeled and cubed
3 carrots, peeled and cubed
1 package (8 ounces) cream cheese, at room temperature
½ teaspoon salt
½ teaspoon freshly ground pepper

To Make Marinade Combine red wine vinegar, canola oil, soy sauce, ketchup, garlic powder, pepper, and onion salt in a resealable plastic bag and blend. Add flank steak and turn to coat all over. Refrigerate for several hours or overnight, turning steak at least once.

To Make Potatoes Melt butter in a heavy, medium saucepan over moderately high heat. Add onion and sauté for 10 minutes, stirring occasionally.

While the onion is cooking, place potatoes and carrots in a large saucepan filled with boiling water over moderately high heat. Cook for 15 to 20 minutes or until vegetables are fork-tender. Drain well. Transfer potatoes and carrots to a large bowl and mash with a potato masher. Add cream cheese, salt, and pepper and mash together until mixture is well blended. Add the caramelized onion and blend well. Transfer the mashed potatoes to a double boiler, cover, and keep warm over moderate heat.

To Prepare Steak on an Outdoor Grill Remove the flank steak from marinade. Over moderately hot coals, place the steak on a grill coated with a nonstick vegetable spray. Sear the steak for 1 minute on each side. Cover grill and cook for 5 to 6 minutes on each side or until a meat thermometer registers 145 degrees. Carve the flank steak across the grain into very thin slices.

To Prepare Steak on an Indoor Grill Remove the flank steak from marinade. Place it on a preheated grill over high heat and cook for 20 to 24 minutes or until a meat thermometer registers 145 degrees, turning the steak every 5 minutes. Carve the flank steak across the grain into very thin slices.

Ribeye Steaks with Curry Butter

SERVES 4

Anything made with curry has to taste good! This sensational curry butter is just delicious when placed on a sizzling steak hot off the grill. Serve with Grilled Artichokes (page 332) and Grilled Spicy Yams (page 347).

Curry Butter

4 tablespoons butter, at room temperature
1 tablespoon Dijon mustard
1 teaspoon curry powder
½ teaspoon Worcestershire sauce

¼ teaspoon salt
¼ teaspoon freshly ground pepper

½ cup Madeira
2 ribeye steaks (12 ounces each)
Parsley

To Make Curry Butter Combine butter, Dijon mustard, curry powder, Worcestershire sauce, salt, and pepper in a small dish and blend well. Transfer curry butter to a piece of plastic wrap and twist both ends to completely enclose butter. Refrigerate curry butter for several hours or overnight. Bring to room temperature before serving.

To Marinate Steaks Combine the Madeira and ribeye steaks in a resealable plastic bag. Turn to coat all over. Refrigerate for several hours or overnight, turning steaks at least once.

To Prepare Steaks on an Outdoor Grill Remove the ribeye steaks from marinade. Over moderately hot coals, place the steaks on a grill coated with a nonstick vegetable spray and cook for 3 minutes. Using tongs, turn the steak about 45 degrees to make a crosshatch mark and cook an additional 3 minutes. Turn steaks over, cover grill, and cook for 6 to 7 minutes or until a meat thermometer registers 145 degrees. Cut each steak into 2 pieces.

To Prepare Steaks on an Indoor Grill Remove the ribeye steaks from marinade. Place them on a preheated grill over high heat and cook for 12 to 19 minutes on each side or until a meat thermometer registers 145 degrees. Cut each steak into 2 pieces.

To Serve Place a ribeye steak on each of four dinner plates and immediately top with a dollop of curry butter. Garnish with a sprig of parsley.

Soy-Glazed Steaks with Spicy Pineapple Fried Rice

SERVES 4

This savory steak recipe came from a group that knows their beef: the Iowa Beef Industry Council. The suggested accompaniment for this extraordinary steak is Spicy Pineapple Fried Rice (recipe below).

Glaze

¼ cup pineapple syrup, drained from 1 can (8 ounces) crushed pineapple (reserve crushed pineapple)

¼ cup soy sauce

2 tablespoons packed brown sugar

1 teaspoon cornstarch

4 top sirloin or ribeye steaks (6 ounces each)

Spicy Pineapple Fried Rice

2 tablespoons canola oil

1 clove garlic, crushed

1 teaspoon finely chopped fresh ginger

⅛ to ¼ teaspoon crushed red pepper

3 cups cold, cooked long-grain rice

¼ cup soy sauce

Reserved crushed pineapple from glaze

¼ cup thinly sliced green onions

To Make Glaze To make the glaze in the microwave, combine pineapple syrup, soy sauce, brown sugar, and cornstarch in a 1-cup glass measure and blend well. Microwave on high for 2½ to 3 minutes or until thickened. Set aside. To make the glaze on the stove, combine pineapple syrup and cornstarch in a small saucepan. Add soy sauce and brown sugar and blend well. Place saucepan over moderate heat and cook for 6 to 7 minutes or until soy glaze comes to a boil, stirring occasionally. Boil for 1 minute. Remove saucepan from heat and set aside.

To Prepare Steaks on an Outdoor Grill Over medium ash-covered coals, place the steaks on a grill coated with a nonstick vegetable spray. Sear the steaks for 1 minute on each side. Cook sirloin steaks for 17 to 21 minutes (ribeye steaks for 11 to 14 minutes) or until a meat thermometer registers 135 degrees for medium-rare and 140 degrees for medium. Turn occasionally and brush both sides with some glaze the last 5 minutes of grilling. Carve steak crosswise into slices and drizzle with remaining glaze.

To Prepare Steaks on an Indoor Grill Place steaks on a preheated grill over high heat and cook for 12 to 19 minutes on each side or until a meat thermometer registers 145 degrees, brushing with some glaze the last 5 minutes of cooking time. Carve steak crosswise into slices and drizzle with remaining glaze.

To Make Fried Rice Heat canola oil in a large nonstick skillet over moderately low heat for 2 minutes. Add garlic, ginger, and crushed red pepper and sauté for 2 minutes. Increase heat to moderately high and add rice and soy sauce. Cook for 2 minutes, stirring frequently. Add pineapple and blend. Sprinkle with green onions before serving.

Oriental Glazed Flank Steak

The mélange of spices and ingredients that make up this oriental marinade add exotic and delicious flavors to beef. Scoring the flank steak before placing it in the marinade further enhances the distinctive flavor found in every bite. Serve with sautéed zucchini and carrots sticks and Mixed Baby Greens with Goat Cheese (recipe below).

Marinade
¼ cup soy sauce
2 tablespoons canola oil
3 tablespoons honey
2 tablespoons rice wine vinegar
1½ teaspoons garlic powder
1½ teaspoons ground ginger
1 flank steak (1½ pounds)

Raspberry Vinaigrette
1 shallot
½ cup canola oil
2 tablespoons raspberry vinegar
1 tablespoon Dijon mustard
⅛ teaspoon salt
⅛ teaspoon freshly ground pepper

Mixed Baby Greens with Goat Cheese
6 cups mixed baby greens
4 (½-inch-thick) slices goat cheese, preferably Montrachet

To Make Marinade Combine soy sauce, canola oil, honey, rice wine vinegar, garlic powder, and ground ginger in a resealable plastic bag and blend.

Score the flank steak by making diagonal cuts across the grain, 1 inch apart, to form a diamond pattern. Place steak in marinade and turn to coat both sides. Refrigerate for several hours or overnight, turning steak at least once.

To Make Vinaigrette In the work bowl of a food processor fitted with a metal blade, process the shallot until chopped. Add canola oil, raspberry vinegar, Dijon mustard, salt, and pepper and process until blended.

To Serve Place mixed baby greens in a salad bowl and add just enough raspberry vinaigrette to make greens glisten. Divide salad among four salad plates and garnish each with a slice of cheese.

To Prepare Steak on an Outdoor Grill Remove the flank steak from marinade. Over moderately hot coals, place the steak on a grill coated with a nonstick vegetable spray. Sear the steak for 1 minute on each side. Cover grill and cook for 5 to 6 minutes on each side or until a meat thermometer registers 145 degrees. Carve the flank steak across the grain into very thin slices.

To Prepare Steak on an Indoor Grill Remove the flank steak from marinade. Place it on a preheated grill over high heat and cook for 18 to 20 minutes or until a meat thermometer registers 145 degrees, turning the steak every 7 minutes. Carve the flank steak across the grain into very thin slices.

Savory Ribeye Steaks

A savory marinade cloaks the ribeye steaks with a fabulous aromatic flavor. Serve with Garlic Mashed Potatoes (page 78) and Mixed Baby Greens with Maytag Bleu Cheese (recipe below).

Marinade

- 3 tablespoons extra virgin olive oil
- 3 tablespoons chicken broth
- 3 tablespoons cumin
- 1½ tablespoons paprika
- 3 teaspoons ground ginger
- 3 teaspoons coriander
- 1½ teaspoons freshly ground pepper
- ⅜ teaspoon salt
- ⅜ teaspoon cayenne
- 3 ribeye steaks (12 ounces each)

Mixed Baby Greens with Maytag Bleu Cheese

- 1 red bell pepper
- 6 tablespoons extra virgin olive oil
- 2 tablespoons balsamic vinegar
- ¼ teaspoon salt
- ¼ teaspoon freshly ground pepper
- 6 cups mixed baby greens
- 4 green onions, thinly sliced
- 3 ounces Maytag Bleu cheese, crumbled
- ⅓ cup Praline Pecans (page 273)

To Make Marinade Combine olive oil, chicken broth, cumin, paprika, ground ginger, coriander, pepper, salt, and cayenne in a resealable plastic bag and blend. Add the ribeye steaks and turn to coat all over. Refrigerate for several hours or overnight, turning steaks at least once.

To Prepare Pepper on an Outdoor Grill Over moderately hot coals, place the red pepper on a grill coated with nonstick vegetable spray. Cover and cook for 20 to 24 minutes or until the skin is charred all over, turning the pepper as skin blackens. Once grilled, place the pepper in a plastic bag and allow to steam for 15 minutes. When it is cool enough to handle, peel away the skin and remove the top and seeds (do not rinse the pepper). Slice the pepper into slivers and set aside.

To Prepare Pepper on an Indoor Grill Place the red pepper on a preheated grill over high heat and cook for 20 to 30 minutes or until the skin is charred all over, turning the pepper as skin blackens. Once grilled, place the pepper in a plastic bag and allow to steam for 15 minutes. When it is cool enough to handle, peel away the skin and remove the top and seeds (do not rinse the pepper). Slice the pepper into slivers and set aside.

To Make Greens Combine olive oil, balsamic vinegar, salt, and pepper in a jar and blend well. Set aside vinaigrette at room temperature for up to 2 hours.

When ready to serve salad, combine baby greens, green onions, and cheese in a large salad bowl. Add just enough vinaigrette to make lettuce glisten. Arrange salad on six salad plates and garnish with red pepper slivers.

To Prepare Steaks on an Outdoor Grill Remove the ribeye steaks from marinade. Over moderately hot coals, place the steaks on a grill coated with a nonstick vegetable spray and cook for 3 minutes. Using tongs, turn the steak about 45 degrees to make a crosshatch mark and cook an additional 3 minutes. Turn steaks over, cover grill, and cook for 6 to 7 minutes or until a meat thermometer registers 145 degrees. Cut each steak into 2 pieces.

To Prepare Steaks on an Indoor Grill Remove the ribeye steaks from marinade. Place them on a preheated grill over high heat and cook for 12 to 19 minutes on each side or until a meat thermometer registers 145 degrees. Cut each steak into 2 pieces.

Yamada's Everyday Japanese Marinated Flank Steak

SERVES 6

This recipe comes from a very good friend. The very versatile marinade imparts a Japanese flavor to any meat. Pierce the steak with a fork several times throughout the marinating process. Serve this delectable entree with Basmati and Wild Rice (recipe below).

Marinade
- 2 tablespoons sake
- 2 tablespoons shoyu sauce
- 2 tablespoons granulated sugar
- 1 tablespoon chopped fresh ginger
- 1 clove garlic, minced
- 1 flank steak (2¼ pounds), pierced all over with a fork

Basmati and Wild Rice
- ½ cup wild rice, rinsed with cold water
- 2 cans (14½ ounces each) chicken broth
- 2 cups basmati rice
- ¼ teaspoon salt
- ¼ teaspoon freshly ground pepper
- ¼ cup raisins
- ¼ cup toasted almonds (see note)

To Make Marinade Combine sake, shoyu sauce, sugar, ¼ cup water, ginger, and garlic in a resealable plastic bag and blend. Add flank steak and turn to coat all over. Refrigerate for several hours, piercing steak with a fork occasionally.

To Make Rice Combine wild rice, chicken broth, and 1 cup water in a large saucepan over moderately high heat and bring to a boil. Cook for 10 minutes. Reduce heat to low, add basmati rice, salt, and pepper and cook, covered, for 25 minutes or until all liquid is absorbed. Add raisins and almonds and blend well. Cover and keep warm at room temperature.

To Prepare Steak on an Outdoor Grill Remove the flank steak from marinade. Over moderately hot coals, place the steak on a grill coated with a nonstick vegetable spray. Sear the steak for 1 minute on each side. Cover grill and cook for 5 to 6 minutes on each side or until a meat thermometer registers 145 degrees. Carve the flank steak across the grain into very thin slices.

To Prepare Steak on an Indoor Grill Remove the flank steak from marinade. Place it on a preheated grill over high heat and cook for 18 to 20 minutes or until a meat thermometer registers 145 degrees, turning the steak every 7 minutes. Carve the flank steak across the grain into very thin slices.

Note To toast almonds: Preheat the oven to 350 degrees. Place almonds in a shallow pan and bake for 10 to 15 minutes or until golden brown.

Sirloin Steaks with Oregano and Red Pepper Sauce

SERVES 4

Oregano and Red Pepper Sauce (recipe below) is definitely for oregano lovers! When first given this recipe by a friend, I was somewhat skeptical about how it might taste, but now I am a believer. It is the perfect complementary sauce to serve with grilled meats. Accompany the steaks with Zucchini and Yellow Squash Soufflé (page 302) and Grilled Potatoes (page 346).

2	red bell peppers	1	cup chicken broth
1	pasilla chile (see note)	2	tablespoons fresh oregano
3	tablespoons butter		leaves, chopped
1	cup coarsely chopped Vidalia onion or other sweet onion	1	tablespoon fresh thyme leaves, chopped
2	cloves garlic, minced	4	sirloin steaks (6 ounces each)
¼	cup red wine vinegar		Salt and freshly ground
¼	cup dry red wine		pepper, to taste

To Prepare Peppers on an Outdoor Grill Over moderately hot coals, place the red peppers and pasilla chile on a grill coated with nonstick vegetable spray. Cover and cook for 20 to 24 minutes or until skins are charred all over, turning the peppers as skins blacken. Once grilled, place the peppers in a plastic bag and allow to steam for 15 minutes. When they are cool enough to handle, peel away the skins and remove the tops and seeds (do not rinse the peppers). Slice the peppers into slivers and set aside.

To Prepare Peppers on an Indoor Grill Place the red peppers and pasilla chile on a preheated grill over high heat and cook for 20 to 30 minutes or until skins are charred all over, turning the peppers as skins blacken. Once grilled, place the peppers in a plastic bag and allow to steam for 15 minutes. When they are cool enough to handle, peel away the skins and remove the tops and seeds (do not rinse the peppers). Slice the peppers into slivers and set aside.

To Make Sauce Melt 2 tablespoons butter in a medium saucepan over moderate heat. Add onion and garlic and sauté for 5 minutes, stirring occasionally. Add red wine vinegar and red wine and bring to a boil. Boil for 5 minutes or until mixture is reduced by half. Add grilled red and pasilla peppers and chicken broth and bring to a boil. Boil for 10 to 15 minutes or until mixture is thick. Transfer sauce to the work bowl of a food processor fitted with a metal blade and process until coarsely chopped. Add oregano and thyme and lightly blend. Return sauce to saucepan and set aside.

To Prepare Steaks on an Outdoor Grill Season the sirloin steaks with salt and pepper. Over moderately hot coals, place the steaks on a grill coated with a nonstick vegetable spray. Sear steaks for 1 minute on each side. Cover grill and cook for 6 minutes on each side or until a meat thermometer registers 145 degrees.

To Prepare Steaks on an Indoor Grill Season the sirloin steaks with salt and pepper. Place them on a preheated grill over high heat and cook for 12 to 19 minutes on each side or until a meat thermometer registers 145 degrees.

To Serve Slowly reheat oregano and red pepper sauce over moderately low heat. Add remaining 1 tablespoon butter and blend. Place a sirloin steak on each of four dinner plates and spoon some sauce over each. Garnish with a sprig of oregano.

Note The pasilla chile pepper is a long, wrinkled chile. It is found in the produce section of most supermarkets.

Oriental Glazed Beef Kebabs

You will enjoy the taste of these beef kebabs. They are exceptionally delicious, spicy, and a beautiful contrast in colors. Serve with Basmati Rice (page 72).

2   tablespoons rice wine vinegar
2   tablespoons soy sauce
1   tablespoon canola oil
1   tablespoon granulated sugar
2   teaspoons Sriracha hot chili sauce (see note)
3   cloves garlic, minced

⅛   teaspoon salt
1   sirloin steak (1½ pounds), cut into 1¼-inch cubes
8   shiitake mushrooms
1   red bell pepper, seeded and cut into 8 pieces
1   to 2 star fruit, cut into 8 stars

To Make Marinade Combine rice wine vinegar, soy sauce, canola oil, sugar, Sriracha hot chili sauce, garlic, and salt in a resealable plastic bag and blend. Add cubed sirloin and turn to coat all over. Refrigerate for several hours, turning beef cubes at least once.

To Prepare Kebabs on an Outdoor Grill Soak bamboo skewers in water for 30 minutes or more. Remove cubed steak from marinade. Alternate beef, shiitake mushrooms, red pepper, and star fruit on skewers. Over moderately hot coals, place the kebabs on a grill coated with a nonstick vegetable spray. Cover grill and cook for 8 to 10 minutes or until a meat thermometer registers 145 degrees, turning kebabs frequently.

To Prepare Kebabs on an Indoor Grill Soak bamboo skewers in water for 30 minutes or more. Remove cubed steak from marinade. Alternate beef, shiitake mushrooms, red pepper, and star fruit on skewers. Place them on a preheated grill over high heat and cook for 20 to 24 minutes or until a meat thermometer registers 145 degrees, turning kebabs frequently.

Note Sriracha hot chili sauce is an Asian sauce made from serrano chiles. It is available in most Asian food stores.

Southwestern Flank Steak with Corn and Black Bean Salsa

SERVES 4

This colorful salsa is a sensational combination of Southwestern flavors and textures and is a great complementary accent to steak. Serve with Sweet Potato Hash (page 82).

Marinade
- ¼ cup fresh lime juice
- ½ tablespoon extra virgin olive oil
- 3 cloves garlic, minced
- 1 tablespoon minced cilantro leaves
- 1 teaspoon cumin
- 1 teaspoon chili powder
- ½ teaspoon cayenne
- ½ teaspoon freshly ground pepper
- 1 flank steak (1½ pounds), pierced all over with a fork

Corn and Black Bean Salsa
- 1 cup cooked black beans, rinsed
- 1 cup cooked corn kernels
- 1 red bell pepper, seeded and diced
- 2 plum tomatoes, seeded and diced
- ¼ cup finely chopped cilantro leaves
- 2 tablespoons fresh lime juice
- 1½ teaspoons gold Aztec tequila
- ¼ teaspoon salt
- ¼ teaspoon freshly ground pepper

To Make Marinade Combine lime juice, olive oil, garlic, cilantro, cumin, chili powder, cayenne, and pepper in a resealable plastic bag and blend. Add flank steak and turn to coat both sides. Refrigerate for several hours or overnight, turning steak at least once.

To Make Salsa Combine black beans, corn, red pepper, tomatoes, cilantro, lime juice, tequila, salt, and pepper in a medium bowl and blend well. Refrigerate the corn and black bean salsa, covered, until ready to serve.

To Prepare Steak on an Outdoor Grill Remove the flank steak from marinade. Over moderately hot coals, place the steak on a grill coated with a nonstick vegetable spray. Sear the steak for 1 minute on each side. Cover grill and cook for 5 to 6 minutes on each side or until a meat thermometer registers 145 degrees. Carve the flank steak across the grain into very thin slices.

To Prepare Steak on an Indoor Grill Remove the flank steak from marinade. Place it on a preheated grill over high heat and cook for 18 to 20 minutes or until a meat thermometer registers 145 degrees, turning the steak every 7 minutes. Carve the flank steak across the grain into very thin slices.

To Serve Arrange steak slices on each of four dinner plates and spoon corn and black bean salsa over or beside each serving.

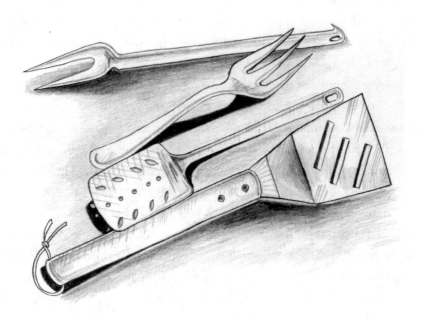

Malaysian Flank Steak

This spicy flank steak has a real kick. It is marinated in a spicy marinade that captures the essence of Asian cooking. Serve with Pat's Vegetable Byriani (page 194).

2 tablespoons extra virgin olive oil	1 teaspoon turmeric
3 large cloves garlic, minced	½ teaspoon coriander
1 stalk lemongrass, minced	½ teaspoon cumin
1 tablespoon soy sauce	½ teaspoon salt
2 teaspoons granulated sugar	½ teaspoon freshly ground pepper
1 teaspoon fresh lemon juice	1 flank steak (1½ pounds), pierced all over with a fork
1 teaspoon curry powder	

To Make Marinade Combine olive oil, 2 tablespoons cold water, garlic, lemongrass, soy sauce, sugar, lemon juice, curry powder, turmeric, coriander, cumin, salt, and pepper in a resealable plastic bag and blend. Add flank steak and turn to coat all over. Refrigerate for several hours or overnight, turning steak at least once.

To Prepare Steak on an Outdoor Grill Remove the flank steak from marinade. Over moderately hot coals, place the steak on a grill coated with a nonstick vegetable spray. Sear the steak for 1 minute on each side. Cover grill and cook for 5 to 6 minutes on each side or until a meat thermometer registers 145 degrees. Carve the flank steak across the grain into very thin slices.

To Prepare Steak on an Indoor Grill Remove the flank steak from marinade. Place it on a preheated grill over high heat and cook for 18 to 20 minutes or until a meat thermometer registers 145 degrees, turning the steak every 7 minutes. Carve the flank steak across the grain into very thin slices.

3

LAMB

Lamb is one of the most distinctively flavored meats. Lamb comes from sheep that are less than two years old. A milk-fed lamb (sometimes called baby lamb) is between six and eight weeks old and was never weaned to eat grass or grain. This lamb will have an exceptionally sweet flavor and will be very tender. A spring lamb is slightly older, between three and nine months. Spring lamb has a mild flavor and tender meat. A yearling is between twelve and twenty-four months old, and its meat is tougher and gamier. Mutton is derived from sheep that are over two years old and cannot be called a lamb anymore.

LAMB CHOPS

The most tender cuts of lamb come from the loin and rib section and include the all-time favorite, the lamb chop. There are two types of lamb chops. Rib lamb chops are the meatiest but can be very expensive. They make the most elegant presentation. Loin and shoulder lamb chops are less meaty and have more fat, but have an equally appealing taste when grilled.

LEG OF LAMB

The plumpest legs of lamb have a higher ratio of meat to bone and contain more fat, making for a more tasty and tender cut of meat. The parchment-like covering, or "fell," on a leg of lamb helps retain its juices during grilling. To butterfly a leg of lamb, ask the butcher to remove the bone in the leg and to spread the meat so it will lie flat while grilled. Test for doneness by inserting a meat thermometer to measure the temperature of the thickest part of the meat. If the thermometer registers 145 to 150 degrees, it is medium-rare; if it registers 160 degrees, it is medium.

Spicy Lamb Patties

I like to serve these spicy lamb patties topped with Raita (page 174) to balance the flavors. The patties can also be stuffed in warmed pita breads topped with raita or Tahini Sauce (page 94) and filled with thinly sliced tomatoes and red onions. Serve with Tabbouleh (page 92).

1½	pounds freshly ground lamb	½	teaspoon cinnamon
6	tablespoons minced Vidalia onion or other sweet onion	½	teaspoon ground ginger
6	tablespoons minced cilantro leaves	½	teaspoon coriander
4	cloves garlic, minced	½	teaspoon cumin
2	tablespoons mango chutney	¼	teaspoon cayenne
		¼	teaspoon paprika

To Make Lamb Patties Combine lamb, onion, cilantro, garlic, chutney, cinnamon, ground ginger, coriander, cumin, cayenne, and paprika in a medium bowl and blend well. Form mixture into 4 patties.

To Prepare Patties on an Outdoor Grill Over moderately hot coals, place lamb patties on a grill coated with a nonstick vegetable spray. Cover grill and cook for 10 to 12 minutes, turning lamb frequently.

To Prepare Patties on an Indoor Grill Place lamb patties on a preheated grill over moderately high heat and cook for 25 minutes, turning frequently.

Butterflied Leg of Lamb in Ginger Marinade

Serves 4

In this recipe, the rich combination of ginger and lemongrass, along with the other ingredients in the marinade, creates a fabulous lamb feast. Serve with Indian vegetables and naan, a tender Indian flatbread.

¼ cup fresh lemon juice
2 tablespoons extra virgin olive oil
2 tablespoons chopped fresh ginger
1 tablespoon minced lemongrass
3 cloves garlic, minced
2 teaspoons coriander
½ teaspoon salt
½ teaspoon cumin
½ teaspoon garam masala
½ teaspoon turmeric
½ teaspoon crushed red pepper
½ teaspoon freshly ground pepper
1 butterflied leg of lamb (1½ pounds)

To Make Marinade Combine lemon juice, olive oil, ginger, lemongrass, garlic, coriander, salt, cumin, garam masala, turmeric, crushed red pepper, and pepper in a resealable plastic bag and blend. Add lamb and turn to coat all over. Refrigerate for several hours or overnight, turning lamb at least once.

To Prepare Lamb on an Outdoor Grill Remove lamb from marinade. Over moderately hot coals, place lamb on a grill coated with a nonstick vegetable spray. Sear lamb for 1 minute on each side. Cover grill and cook for 25 to 30 minutes or until a meat thermometer registers 150 degrees for medium-rare or 160 degrees for medium, turning lamb every 10 minutes. Allow lamb to sit for 5 minutes before carving into thin slices.

To Prepare Lamb on an Indoor Grill Remove lamb from marinade. Place lamb on a preheated grill over moderately high heat and cook for 40 to 50 minutes or until a meat thermometer registers 150 degrees for medium-rare or 160 degrees for medium, turning lamb over every 10 minutes and giving it a quarter turn occasionally. Allow lamb to sit for 5 minutes before carving into thin slices.

Oriental Lamb Kebabs

These lamb kebabs are exceptionally appealing because of their fragrance and spicy flavor. They are delicious when served with Jasmine Rice (recipe below).

Marinade

¼ cup fresh orange juice

2 tablespoons mushroom soy sauce or soy sauce

2 tablespoons oyster sauce

2 teaspoons oriental sesame oil

1 teaspoon Chinese Five Spice powder

2 large cloves garlic, minced

1 boneless leg of lamb (1½ pounds), cut into 1¼-inch cubes

Kebabs

8 shiitake mushrooms, stems trimmed

1 orange or red bell pepper, cut into 8 squares

4 large green onions, cut into 8 (2-inch) pieces

Jasmine Rice

2 cups jasmine rice

To Make Marinade Combine orange juice, mushroom soy sauce, oyster sauce, sesame oil, Chinese Five Spice powder, and garlic in a resealable plastic bag and blend. Add lamb and turn to coat all over. Refrigerate for several hours or overnight, turning lamb at least once.

To Prepare Kebabs on an Outdoor Grill Soak bamboo skewers in water for 30 minutes or more. Remove cubed lamb from marinade. Alternate lamb, shiitake mushrooms, bell pepper, and green onions on skewers. Over moderately hot coals, place lamb kebabs on a grill coated with a nonstick vegetable spray. Cover grill and cook for 12 to 16 minutes or until a meat thermometer registers 150 degrees for medium-rare or 160 degrees for medium, turning lamb every 6 minutes.

To Prepare Kebabs on an Indoor Grill Soak bamboo skewers in water for 30 minutes or more. Remove cubed lamb from marinade. Alternate lamb, shiitake mushrooms, bell pepper, and green onions on skewers. Place them on a preheated grill over moderately high heat and cook for 25 to 30 minutes or until a meat thermometer registers 150 degrees for medium-rare or 160 degrees for medium, turning lamb every 8 minutes.

To Make Jasmine Rice While grilling the lamb kebabs, place jasmine rice in a fine-sieved strainer and rinse with cold water until the water runs clear. Combine rice and 2½ cups water in a medium saucepan and bring to a boil over moderate heat. Reduce heat to low, cover, and cook for 5 minutes.

Butterflied Leg of Lamb with Green Pepper Jelly

Lamb is one of the tastiest meats when grilled, whether indoors or outdoors. It blends well with most marinades, and as this recipe proves, it is especially well complemented by Green Pepper Jelly (recipe below). Green Pepper Jelly is very versatile; it can be used as a glaze when grilling lamb chops, and it also makes a wonderful appetizer when served with cream cheese and crackers. For a main course, serve with Grilled Bermuda Onions (page 331) and Savory Wild Rice (page 120).

Green Pepper Jelly

- 3 green bell peppers, coarsely chopped
- 6 jalapeño chiles, seeded and stems removed (see note)
- 1 cup white distilled vinegar
- 5 cups granulated sugar
- 1 package (6 ounces) liquid pectin
- 12 to 16 drops green food coloring

Marinade

- 2 tablespoons Spicy Peppa mustard (or other hot mustard)
- 2 tablespoons soy sauce
- 2 tablespoons extra virgin olive oil
- 2 cloves garlic, chopped
- 1 tablespoon red wine vinegar
- 1 tablespoon rosemary
- ¼ teaspoon crushed red pepper
- ¼ teaspoon salt
- 1 butterflied leg of lamb (1½ pounds)

To Make Green Pepper Jelly In the large work bowl of a food processor fitted with a metal blade, process the green peppers and jalapeño chiles for 1 minute or until finely chopped. Add white vinegar and blend well. Transfer mixture to a large pot over moderate heat and add sugar. Bring to a boil, stirring occasionally. Reduce heat to low and continue to boil for 4 minutes, stirring constantly.

Remove pot from heat and skim off the foam. Add liquid pectin and green food coloring and blend well. Immediately pour the green pepper jelly into 6 sterilized pint-size jars and seal. Once the green pepper jelly has set, store in a cool, dark place. Refrigerate after opening.

To Make Marinade Combine Spicy Peppa mustard, soy sauce, olive oil, garlic, red wine vinegar, rosemary, crushed red pepper, and salt in a resealable plastic bag and blend. Add lamb and turn to coat all over. Refrigerate for several hours or overnight, turning lamb at least once.

To Prepare Lamb on an Outdoor Grill Remove lamb from marinade. Over moderately hot coals, place lamb on a grill coated with a nonstick vegetable spray. Sear lamb for 1 minute on each side. Cover grill and cook for 25 to 30 minutes or until a meat thermometer registers 150 degrees for medium-rare or 160 degrees for medium, turning lamb every 10 minutes. Allow lamb to sit for 5 minutes before carving into thin slices.

To Prepare Lamb on an Indoor Grill Remove lamb from marinade. Place lamb on a preheated grill over moderately high heat and cook for 40 to 50 minutes or until a meat thermometer registers 150 degrees for medium-rare or 160 degrees for medium, turning lamb every 10 minutes. Allow lamb to sit for 5 minutes before carving into thin slices.

To Serve Arrange slices of lamb on each of four dinner plates and spoon a dollop of green pepper jelly on the side. Pass additional jelly in a pretty serving dish.

Note The seeds of jalapeño chiles are very hot. To avoid burning your skin, wear rubber or latex gloves when removing the seeds. Immediately wash the knife, cutting surface, and gloves when finished.

Delhi Leg of Lamb

SERVES 4

Garam masala is an Indian spice made of a combination of cardamom, cinnamon, cloves, cayenne, cumin, mace, and nutmeg. Combining it with other spices in a marinade adds a distinctive and unmistakably Indian flavor to lamb. Serve with chutney, Indian vegetables, and naan, a tender Indian flatbread.

2	tablespoons canola oil	1½	teaspoons garam masala
1	tablespoon honey	1	teaspoon curry powder
1	tablespoon packed brown sugar	¼	teaspoon crushed red pepper
1	tablespoon soy sauce	2	cloves garlic, chopped
1	tablespoon turmeric	1	butterflied leg of lamb (1½ pounds)

To Make Marinade Combine 3 tablespoons cold water, canola oil, honey, brown sugar, soy sauce, turmeric, garam masala, curry powder, crushed red pepper, and garlic in a resealable plastic bag and blend. Add lamb and turn to coat all over. Refrigerate for several hours or overnight, turning lamb at least once.

To Prepare Lamb on an Outdoor Grill Remove lamb from marinade. Over moderately hot coals, place lamb on a grill coated with a nonstick vegetable spray. Sear lamb for 1 minute on each side. Cover grill and cook for 25 to 30 minutes or until a meat thermometer registers 150 degrees for medium-rare or 160 degrees for medium, turning lamb every 10 minutes. Allow lamb to sit for 5 minutes before carving into thin slices.

To Prepare Lamb on an Indoor Grill Remove lamb from marinade. Place lamb on a preheated grill over moderately high heat and cook for 40 to 50 minutes or until a meat thermometer registers 150 degrees for medium-rare or 160 degrees for medium, turning lamb every 5 minutes and giving it a quarter turn occasionally. Allow lamb to sit for 10 minutes before carving into thin slices.

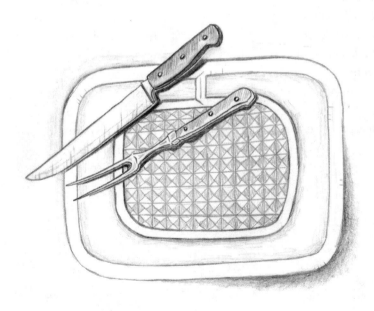

Greek Lamb Burgers

One of the things my children enjoy is a casual dinner out on the patio. One of their favorite meals is this one. I simply prepare a Greek Salad (page 40) and Rice Pilaf with Toasted Almonds and Raisins (page 44), and I have plenty of warmed pita breads on a tray, along with sliced red onions and tomatoes, lettuce, and a bowl of Cucumber and Mint Yogurt Sauce (recipe below) to spoon on top of the lamb burgers.

Cucumber and Mint Yogurt Sauce

- ½ cup plain yogurt
- ½ cup peeled diced cucumber
- 2 tablespoons minced red onion
- 2 tablespoons chopped cilantro leaves
- 1 tablespoon minced fresh mint
- 1 clove garlic, minced
- ⅛ teaspoon salt
- ⅛ teaspoon freshly ground pepper

Lamb Burgers

- 1½ pounds freshly ground lamb
- 2 ounces feta cheese, crumbled
- 1 clove garlic, minced
- 1 teaspoon coriander
- 1 teaspoon cumin
- ½ teaspoon salt
- ⅛ teaspoon cloves
- ⅛ teaspoon nutmeg
- ⅛ teaspoon cayenne
- ⅛ teaspoon freshly ground pepper
- 4 pita breads, warmed
- 4 red onion slices
- 4 tomato slices
  Lettuce

To Make Yogurt Sauce Combine yogurt, cucumber, red onion, cilantro, mint, garlic, salt, and pepper in a medium bowl and blend well. Cover the cucumber and mint yogurt sauce and refrigerate for several hours.

To Make Burgers Combine lamb, cheese, garlic, coriander, cumin, salt, cloves, nutmeg, cayenne, and pepper in a medium bowl and blend well. Form the mixture into 4 patties.

To Prepare Burgers on an Outdoor Grill Over hot coals, place lamb patties on a grill coated with a nonstick vegetable spray. Cover grill and cook for 10 to 12 minutes, turning lamb frequently.

To Prepare Burgers on an Indoor Grill Place lamb patties on a preheated grill over moderately high heat and cook for 25 minutes, turning frequently.

To Serve Make a pocket in the pita bread by cutting across the top, about 1 inch down. Place a Greek lamb burger in each pita bread and fill with red onion, tomato, and lettuce. Spoon some cucumber and mint yogurt sauce over each lamb burger.

Grilled Butterflied Leg of Lamb with Lemongrass Marinade

SERVES 4

Lemongrass, also known as fevergrass, is a tropical grass that can reach heights of up to six feet or more. Its subtle lemon flavor, found only in the lower stem of the plant, is especially complementary to lamb. Serve with Grilled Vegetable Kebabs (page 356) and Pat's Vegetable Byriani (page 194).

2 tablespoons rice wine	1 teaspoon nutmeg
2 tablespoons canola oil	½ tablespoon turmeric
2 tablespoons soy sauce	¼ teaspoon salt
1 tablespoon minced lemongrass	¼ teaspoon freshly ground pepper
2 cloves garlic, minced	1 butterflied leg of lamb (1½ pounds)
1 tablespoon minced fresh ginger	

To Make Marinade Combine rice wine, canola oil, soy sauce, lemongrass, garlic, ginger, nutmeg, turmeric, salt, and pepper in a resealable plastic bag and blend. Add lamb and turn to coat all over. Refrigerate for several hours or overnight, turning lamb at least once.

To Prepare Lamb on an Outdoor Grill Remove lamb from marinade. Over moderately hot coals, place lamb on a grill coated with a nonstick vegetable spray. Sear lamb for 1 minute on each side. Cover grill and cook for 25 to 30 minutes or until a meat thermometer registers 150 degrees for medium-rare or 160 degrees for medium, turning lamb every 10 minutes. Allow lamb to sit for 5 minutes before carving into thin slices.

To Prepare Lamb on an Indoor Grill Remove lamb from marinade. Place it on a preheated grill over moderately high heat and cook for 40 to 50 minutes or until a meat thermometer registers 150 degrees for medium-rare or 160 degrees for medium, turning lamb over every 10 minutes and giving it a quarter turn occasionally. Allow lamb to sit for 5 minutes before carving into thin slices.

Grilled Lamb Chops

My family enjoys nothing more than grilled lamb chops. For a special touch, I top each lamb chop with a dollop of Green Pepper Jelly (page 160). Serve with Grilled Spicy Yams (page 347) and Artichoke Rice Salad (recipe below).

Artichoke Rice Salad

3 jars (6½ ounces each)
    artichoke hearts
½ cup mayonnaise
1 tablespoon curry powder
2 boxes (6.9 ounces each)
    Rice-A-Roni

2 packages (3 ounces each)
    slivered almonds, toasted
    (see note)
4 green onions, thinly sliced

6 loin lamb chops
    (6 ounces each)
    Salt and freshly ground
    pepper, to taste

To Make Salad Drain the artichokes and reserve the liquid and the artichokes in separate containers. Combine mayonnaise, curry powder, and reserved artichoke liquid in a small bowl and blend well. Refrigerate.

Cook Rice-A-Roni according to package directions, cutting water by ¾ cup per package. Allow rice to come to room temperature.

Combine Rice-A-Roni, reserved artichokes, almonds, and green onions in a large bowl and blend. Add mayonnaise mixture and blend well. Refrigerate the artichoke and rice salad, covered, for several hours or overnight. Stir before serving.

To Prepare Lamb on an Outdoor Grill Season lamb chops with salt and pepper. Over moderately hot coals, place lamb chops on a grill coated with a nonstick vegetable spray. Cover grill and cook for 4 to 5 minutes on each side or until a meat thermometer registers 150 degrees for medium-rare or 160 degrees for medium.

To Prepare Lamb on an Indoor Grill Season lamb chops with salt and pepper. Place them on a preheated grill over moderately high heat and cook for 25 minutes or until a meat thermometer registers 150 degrees for medium-rare or 160 degrees for medium, turning lamb every 8 minutes.

Note To toast almonds: Preheat oven to 350 degrees. Place almonds in a shallow pan and bake for 10 to 15 minutes or until golden brown.

Southwestern Butterflied Leg of Lamb

The flavors of the Southwest ride again! This is perfect fare when having friends over for a casual dinner. Serve margaritas and mugs of Gazpacho (page 32) as starters, followed by this lamb dish with Gazpacho Salsa (page 38), Mexican Rice (recipe below), and Garlic-Basted Grilled Corn on the Cob (page 317).

Marinade

- 6 tablespoons fresh lime juice
- ¼ cup minced cilantro leaves
- 2 tablespoons extra virgin olive oil
- 1½ teaspoons cumin
- 1 teaspoon salt
- 1 teaspoon freshly ground pepper
- ½ teaspoon coriander
- ½ teaspoon chili powder
- 4 cloves garlic, minced
- ⅛ teaspoon cayenne
- 1 butterflied leg of lamb (2¼ pounds)

Mexican Rice

- 1 tablespoon extra virgin olive oil
- 1 red bell pepper, diced
- 1 medium onion, diced
- ¾ cup chopped cilantro leaves
- 3 plum tomatoes, seeded and diced
- 2 cloves garlic, minced
- 1½ cups long-grain rice
- 1 can (14½ ounces) chicken broth
- ½ teaspoon cumin
- ½ teaspoon salt
- ½ teaspoon freshly ground pepper

To Make Marinade Combine lime juice, cilantro, olive oil, cumin, salt, pepper, coriander, chili powder, garlic, and cayenne in a resealable plastic bag and blend. Add lamb and turn to coat all over. Refrigerate for several hours or overnight, turning lamb at least once.

To Prepare Lamb on an Outdoor Grill Remove lamb from marinade. Over moderately hot coals, place lamb on a grill coated with a nonstick vegetable spray. Sear lamb for 1 minute on each side. Cover grill and cook for 25 to 30 minutes or until a meat thermometer registers 150 degrees for medium-rare or 160 degrees for medium, turning lamb every 10 minutes. Allow lamb to sit for 5 minutes before carving into thin slices.

To Prepare Lamb on an Indoor Grill Remove lamb from marinade. Place lamb on a preheated grill over moderately high heat and cook for 40 to 50 minutes or until a meat thermometer registers 150 degrees for medium-rare or 160 degrees for medium, turning lamb every 10 minutes. Allow lamb to sit for 5 minutes before carving into thin slices.

To Make Mexican Rice While grilling the lamb, coat a large saucepan with nonstick olive oil spray. Add olive oil and place over moderate heat for 2 minutes. Add red pepper, onion, cilantro, tomatoes, and garlic and sauté for 10 minutes, stirring occasionally. Add rice and sauté for 3 minutes, stirring occasionally. Add chicken broth, cumin, salt, and pepper and bring to a boil. Reduce heat to low, cover, and cook for 25 minutes or until all liquid is absorbed. Stir before serving and taste for seasoning.

Grilled Lamb Chops in Red Wine Vinegar Marinade

The red wine vinegar marinade would also nicely complement flank steak or a pork roast. Start the meal with Chilled and Spicy Grilled Red Pepper Soup (page 338) and serve Connie's Three-Onion Casserole (recipe below) with the lamb chops.

Marinade

- 3 tablespoons red wine vinegar
- 3 tablespoons extra virgin olive oil
- 3 cloves garlic, minced
- 1½ teaspoons dry mustard
- ¾ teaspoon salt
- ¾ teaspoon freshly ground pepper
- 6 loin lamb chops (6 ounces each)

Connie's Three-Onion Casserole

- 3 tablespoons butter
- 2 large yellow onions, thinly sliced
- 1½ cups freshly grated havarti cheese
- 2 large red onions, thinly sliced
- 2 cartons (5.2 ounces each) Boursin cheese, crumbled
- 4 medium leeks, washed, green tops removed, and white part thinly sliced
- 1½ cups freshly grated Gruyere cheese
- Salt and freshly ground pepper, to taste
- ½ cup dry white wine

To Make Marinade Combine red wine vinegar, olive oil, garlic, dry mustard, salt, and pepper in a resealable plastic bag and blend. Add lamb chops and turn to coat all over. Refrigerate for several hours or overnight, turning lamb at least once.

To Make Casserole Preheat oven to 350 degrees. Coat an 8-cup baking dish with butter. Place yellow onions in a layer in the dish and sprinkle havarti cheese on top. Make another layer with the red onions and top with Boursin cheese. Make a final layer of the leeks and top with Gruyere cheese. Season with salt and pepper and pour the white wine over all. Bake for 1 hour.

To Prepare Lamb on an Outdoor Grill Remove lamb chops from marinade. Over moderately hot coals, place lamb chops on a grill coated with a nonstick vegetable spray. Cover grill and cook for 4 to 5 minutes on each side or until a meat thermometer registers 150 degrees for medium-rare or 160 degrees for medium.

To Prepare Lamb on an Indoor Grill Remove lamb chops from marinade. Place them on a preheated grill over moderately high heat and cook for 25 minutes or until a meat thermometer registers 150 degrees for medium-rare or 160 degrees for medium, turning lamb every 8 minutes.

Lamb

Indian Lamb Kebabs

The cuisine of India is one of my favorites. Yogurt, exotic spices, and special cooking techniques create some of the most delectable dishes that can be experienced. These Indian Lamb Kebabs are one example of the endless ways to transform a simple lamb into a gourmet experience. Serve with Shelagh's Coriander and Mint Chutney (page 30), Raita (recipe below), and Pat's Vegetable Byriani (page 194).

Marinade
1   cup plain yogurt
1   tablespoon canola oil
1   teaspoon ground ginger
1   teaspoon cumin
1   teaspoon coriander
1   teaspoon turmeric
½   teaspoon cinnamon
¼   teaspoon salt
⅛   teaspoon allspice
⅛   teaspoon nutmeg
1   boneless leg of lamb
    (1½ pounds), cut into
    1½-inch cubes

Raita
2   cups plain yogurt
2   cucumbers, peeled
    and grated
1   medium onion,
    finely chopped
½   teaspoon cumin
¼   teaspoon salt

Kebabs
1   red bell pepper, cut into
    1-inch cubes
8   fresh button mushrooms
1   red onion, cut into 8 wedges
8   cherry tomatoes

To Make Marinade Combine yogurt, canola oil, ground ginger, cumin, coriander, turmeric, cinnamon, salt, allspice, and nutmeg in a resealable plastic bag and blend. Add cubed lamb and turn to coat all over. Refrigerate for several hours or overnight, turning lamb at least once.

To Make Raita Place a fine-sieved strainer over a bowl and spoon yogurt into strainer. Place cucumbers in another fine-sieved strainer placed over another bowl. Allow the yogurt and cucumbers to sit at room temperature for 1 hour.

Discard liquid from yogurt and cucumbers. Combine yogurt, cucumbers, onion, cumin, and salt in a medium bowl and blend. Refrigerate the raita, covered, for several hours.

To Prepare Kebabs on an Outdoor Grill Soak bamboo skewers in water for 30 minutes or more. Remove cubed lamb from marinade. Alternate lamb, red pepper, mushrooms, onion, and tomatoes on skewers. Over moderately hot coals, place the kebabs on a grill coated with a nonstick vegetable spray. Cover grill and cook for 10 to 12 minutes or until a meat thermometer registers 150 degrees for medium-rare or 160 degrees for medium, turning kebabs every 6 minutes.

To Prepare Kebabs on an Indoor Grill Soak bamboo skewers in water for 30 minutes or more. Remove cubed lamb from marinade. Alternate lamb, red pepper, mushrooms, onion, and tomatoes on skewers. Place the kebabs on a preheated grill over moderately high heat and cook for 25 to 30 minutes or until a meat thermometer registers 150 degrees for medium-rare or 160 degrees for medium, turning lamb every 8 minutes.

Indonesian Lamb Chops

Kecap manis (sweet soy sauce) is a delightful Indonesian condiment. It is thicker than regular soy sauce and adds a marvelous flavor to marinades and other sauces. If kecap manis is not available, soy sauce can be substituted. Serve these lamb chops with Acorn Squash with Fruited Wild Rice (page 336).

3 tablespoons kecap manis or soy sauce	1 teaspoon oriental sesame oil
1 tablespoon Dijon mustard	1 teaspoon ground ginger
2 teaspoons Sriracha hot chili sauce	2 cloves garlic, minced
	4 loin lamb chops (6 ounces each)

To Make Marinade Combine kecap manis, Dijon mustard, Sriracha hot chili sauce, sesame oil, ground ginger, and garlic in a resealable plastic bag and blend. Add lamb chops and turn to coat all over. Refrigerate for 2 to 3 hours, turning lamb chops at least once.

To Prepare Lamb on an Outdoor Grill Remove lamb chops from marinade. Over moderately hot coals, place lamb chops on a grill coated with a nonstick vegetable spray. Cover grill and cook for 4 to 5 minutes on each side or until a meat thermometer registers 150 degrees for medium-rare or 160 degrees for medium.

To Prepare Lamb on an Indoor Grill Remove lamb chops from marinade. Place them on a preheated grill over moderately high heat and cook for 25 minutes or until a meat thermometer registers 150 degrees for medium-rare or 160 degrees for medium, turning lamb every 8 minutes.

Marinated Lamb Chops

Lamb is delicious when grilled without any seasonings, but for variety, different sauces or marinades can add a new dimension to this perennial favorite. Serve with Grilled Artichokes (page 332) and Grilled Polenta (page 322).

1 tablespoon Dijon mustard	1 teaspoon soy sauce
1 tablespoon white wine vinegar	1 teaspoon Worcestershire sauce
1 tablespoon firmly packed dark brown sugar	¼ teaspoon salt
1 tablespoon extra virgin olive oil	¼ teaspoon freshly ground pepper
1 tablespoon minced parsley	4 loin lamb chops (6 ounces each)
1 clove garlic, minced	

To Make Marinade Combine Dijon mustard, white wine vinegar, brown sugar, olive oil, parsley, garlic, soy sauce, Worcestershire sauce, salt, and pepper in a resealable plastic bag and blend. Add lamb chops and turn to coat all over. Refrigerate for several hours or overnight, turning lamb chops at least once.

To Prepare Lamb on an Outdoor Grill Remove lamb chops from marinade. Over moderately hot coals, place lamb chops on a grill coated with a nonstick vegetable spray. Cover grill and cook for 4 to 5 minutes on each side or until a meat thermometer registers 150 degrees for medium-rare or 160 degrees for medium.

To Prepare Lamb on an Indoor Grill Remove lamb chops from marinade. Place them on a preheated grill over moderately high heat and cook for 25 minutes or until a meat thermometer registers 150 degrees for medium-rare or 160 degrees for medium, turning lamb every 8 minutes.

Lamb Burgers with Goat Cheese

These lamb burgers are more exotic than the classic all-American hamburger. They are made with a filling of goat cheese blended with sun-dried tomatoes and can be eaten with or without a bun. Serve with Joanne's Spinach Salad (recipe below) and Grilled Accordion Potatoes (page 328).

Lamb Burgers

- 6 ounces goat cheese
- 5 tablespoons minced marinated sun-dried tomatoes in olive oil, drained
- 2¼ pounds freshly ground lamb
- 6 tablespoons minced parsley
- 4 large cloves garlic, minced
- 1¼ teaspoons freshly ground pepper
- ¾ teaspoon salt

Joanne's Spinach Salad

- ⅔ cup canola oil
- ¼ cup garlic wine vinegar
- 2 tablespoons dry white wine
- 2 teaspoons soy sauce
- 1 teaspoon dry mustard
- ½ teaspoon curry powder
- ½ teaspoon salt
- ½ teaspoon freshly ground pepper
- 1 package (10 ounces) prewashed baby spinach
- 5 slices bacon, cooked, drained, and crumbled
- 2 hard-boiled eggs, finely chopped

To Make Burgers Combine goat cheese and sun-dried tomatoes in a small bowl and blend well. Divide the mixture into 6 portions and form into balls.

Combine lamb, parsley, garlic, pepper, and salt in a medium bowl and blend well. Divide the lamb mixture into 6 portions and form into flat patties. Place a cheese ball on each patty and press the lamb around cheese to completely enclose it. Gently flatten the lamb burgers.

To Make Salad Combine canola oil, garlic wine vinegar, wine, soy sauce, dry mustard, curry powder, salt, and pepper in the work bowl of a food processor fitted with a metal blade and process until well blended. (The vinaigrette can be made ahead and kept in a covered container until ready to use.)

When ready to serve the salad, place the spinach in a salad bowl and toss with enough vinaigrette to make spinach glisten. Arrange spinach on each of six salad plates, and garnish each serving with bacon and eggs.

To Prepare Burgers on an Outdoor Grill Over moderately hot coals, place lamb burgers on a grill coated with a nonstick vegetable spray. Cover grill and cook for 5 to 6 minutes on each side.

To Prepare Burgers on an Indoor Grill Place lamb burgers on a preheated grill over moderately high heat and cook for 35 minutes, turning frequently.

Lamb Chops with Grilled Red Pepper Chutney

SERVES 4

A traditional way to serve lamb chops is with a side dollop of mint jelly. However, once you are introduced to Grilled Red Pepper Chutney (recipe below), I feel confident you will become a convert. Serve this simple but delicious fare with Grilled Vegetable Kebabs (page 356).

Grilled Red Pepper Chutney

1   large red bell pepper
1   tablespoon extra virgin olive oil
3   large green onions, thinly sliced
2   large cloves garlic, minced
4   plum tomatoes, minced
1   tablespoon rice wine vinegar
1   tablespoon granulated sugar
⅛   teaspoon cayenne

⅛   teaspoon cumin
⅛   teaspoon coriander
⅛   teaspoon turmeric
⅛   teaspoon nutmeg
    Dash of salt
1   tablespoon tomato paste

8   to 12 lamb rib chops (3 to 4 ounces each)
    Salt and freshly ground pepper, to taste

To Prepare Pepper on an Outdoor Grill Over hot coals, place the red pepper on a grill coated with a nonstick vegetable spray. Cover grill and cook for 20 to 24 minutes or until skin is charred all over, turning the pepper as skin blackens. Once grilled, place the pepper in a plastic bag and allow to steam for 15 minutes. When the pepper is cool enough to handle, peel away the skin and remove the top and seeds (do not rinse the pepper). Dice the red pepper.

To Prepare Pepper on an Indoor Grill Place the red pepper on a preheated grill over high heat and cook for 20 to 30 minutes or until skin is charred all over, turning the pepper as skin blackens. Once grilled, place the pepper in a plastic bag and allow to steam for 15 minutes. When it is cool enough to handle, peel away the skin and remove the top and seeds (do not rinse the pepper). Dice the red pepper.

To Make Chutney Heat olive oil in a heavy, medium saucepan over moderate heat for 2 minutes. Add diced red pepper, green onions, and garlic and sauté for 2 minutes, stirring occasionally. Add the tomatoes and sauté for 2 minutes, stirring occasionally. Add the rice wine vinegar, sugar, cayenne, cumin, coriander, turmeric, nutmeg, and salt and blend well. Cook an additional 2 minutes, stirring occasionally. Add the tomato paste and blend. Cook over low heat for 20 minutes, stirring occasionally. Allow the chutney to come to room temperature. Transfer the grilled red pepper chutney to a covered container and refrigerate for several hours or overnight. Serve at room temperature.

To Prepare Lamb on an Outdoor Grill Season lamb chops with salt and pepper. Over moderately hot coals, place lamb chops on a grill coated with a nonstick vegetable spray. Cover grill and cook for 4 to 5 minutes on each side or until a meat thermometer registers 150 degrees for medium-rare or 160 degrees for medium.

To Prepare Lamb on an Indoor Grill Season lamb chops with salt and pepper. Place them on a preheated grill over moderately high heat and cook for 25 minutes or until a meat thermometer registers 150 degrees for medium-rare or 160 degrees for medium, turning lamb every 8 minutes.

To Serve Place two to three lamb chops on each of four dinner plates. Top each with a dollop of grilled red pepper chutney.

Butterflied Leg of Lamb in Red Wine Marinade

Red wine marinade is an elegant way to bring out the true flavor of lamb and to transform it into a dinner fit for your most discerning guests. Serve with Grilled Red Pepper Flan (page 350), Savory Wild Rice (page 120), and Joanne's Spinach Salad (page 178).

½ cup dry red wine
2 tablespoons extra virgin olive oil
1 tablespoon chopped parsley
2 cloves garlic, chopped
1 tablespoon rosemary
½ teaspoon salt
½ teaspoon freshly ground pepper

½ teaspoon marjoram
½ teaspoon oregano
½ teaspoon thyme
½ teaspoon crushed red pepper
½ teaspoon Worcestershire sauce
1 butterflied leg of lamb (1½ pounds)

To Make Marinade Combine red wine, olive oil, parsley, garlic, rosemary, salt, pepper, marjoram, oregano, thyme, crushed red pepper, and Worcestershire sauce in a resealable plastic bag and blend. Add lamb and turn to coat all over. Refrigerate for several hours or overnight, turning lamb at least once.

To Prepare Lamb on an Outdoor Grill Remove lamb from marinade. Over moderately hot coals, place lamb on a grill coated with a nonstick vegetable spray. Sear lamb for 1 minute on each side. Cover grill and cook for 25 to 30 minutes or until a meat thermometer registers 150 degrees for medium-rare or 160 degrees for medium, turning lamb every 10 minutes. Allow lamb to sit for 5 minutes before carving into thin slices.

To Prepare Lamb on an Indoor Grill Remove lamb from marinade. Place lamb on a preheated grill over moderately high heat and cook for 40 to 50 minutes or until a meat thermometer registers 150 degrees for medium-rare or 160 degrees for medium, turning lamb over every 10 minutes and giving it a quarter turn occasionally. Allow lamb to sit for 5 minutes before carving into thin slices.

Butterflied Leg of Lamb with Green Peppercorn Sauce

SERVES 4

As the berries of the pepper plant ripen, they are first green and less pungent in taste. As they get darker in color, their pungency increases. The green berries (peppercorns) have been pickled and used whole or mashed in a variety of ways for cooking. Adding them to a creamy sauce complements grilled lamb or beef specialties. Serve with Lemon-Glazed Carrots (page 218) and Sautéed New Potatoes (page 186).

1 butterflied leg of lamb (1½ pounds)	**Green Peppercorn Sauce**
Salt and freshly ground pepper, to taste	¾ cup dry white wine
	1 cup heavy cream
	¼ cup green peppercorns, rinsed and drained
	¼ teaspoon salt

To Prepare Lamb on an Outdoor Grill Season lamb with salt and pepper. Over moderately hot coals, place lamb on a grill coated with a nonstick vegetable spray. Sear lamb for 1 minute on each side. Cover grill and cook for 25 to 30 minutes or until a meat thermometer registers 150 degrees for medium-rare or 160 degrees for medium, turning lamb every 10 minutes. Allow lamb to sit for 5 minutes before carving into thin slices.

To Prepare Lamb on an Indoor Grill Season lamb with salt and pepper. Place lamb on a preheated grill over moderately high heat and cook for 40 to 50 minutes or until a meat thermometer registers 150 degrees for medium-rare or 160 degrees for medium, turning lamb over every 10 minutes and giving it a quarter turn occasionally. Allow lamb to sit for 5 minutes before carving into thin slices.

To Make Sauce While grilling the lamb, bring wine to a boil in a small saucepan over high heat. Boil for 6 to 7 minutes or until wine is reduced to 5 tablespoons. Reduce heat to moderately high and add heavy cream, peppercorns, and salt and boil for 8 to 10 minutes or until sauce is thick, stirring occasionally. If sauce begins to boil over, reduce heat for a few seconds.

To Serve Arrange slices of lamb on each of four dinner plates and spoon green peppercorn sauce over each serving. Garnish with a sprig of parsley.

Lamb Chops with Oriental Rub

The naturally strong flavor of lamb can be further accentuated when chops are coated with an Oriental rub before grilling. Serve with Grilled Red Pepper Flan (page 350) and Sautéed New Potatoes (recipe below).

Rub

- 2 tablespoons packed brown sugar
- 2 tablespoons dried lemon peel
- 1 tablespoon coriander
- 2 teaspoons garlic powder
- 2 teaspoons ground ginger
- 1½ teaspoons crushed red pepper
- 1 teaspoon cumin
- 1 teaspoon freshly ground pepper
- 4 loin lamb chops (6 ounces each)

Sautéed New Potatoes

- 2 tablespoons butter
- 2 tablespoons extra virgin olive oil
- 2 pounds new potatoes, quartered
- ½ teaspoon salt
- ½ teaspoon freshly ground pepper

To Make Rub Combine brown sugar, lemon peel, coriander, garlic powder, ground ginger, crushed red pepper, cumin, and pepper in a jar and blend well. Press rub on both sides of lamb chops. Place lamb chops in a nonmetal dish, cover, and refrigerate for up to 2 hours.

To Make Potatoes Place butter and olive oil in a large nonstick skillet over moderate heat. When butter has melted, add potatoes. Sauté the potatoes for 15 minutes, then season with salt and pepper. Continue cooking for 40 to 45 minutes or until potatoes are fork-tender and brown, stirring occasionally. Garnish with chopped parsley.

To Prepare Lamb on an Outdoor Grill Over moderately hot coals, place lamb chops on a grill coated with a nonstick vegetable spray. Cover grill and cook for 4 to 5 minutes on each side or until a meat thermometer registers 150 degrees for medium-rare or 160 degrees for medium.

To Prepare Lamb on an Indoor Grill Place lamb chops on a preheated grill over moderately high heat and cook for 25 minutes or until a meat thermometer registers 150 degrees for medium-rare or 160 degrees for medium, turning lamb every 8 minutes.

Lamb Shish Kebabs

SERVES 8

Shish kebabs are perfect party fare when having friends over for a casual dinner. Serve mugs of Gazpacho (page 32) for starters, followed by the lamb shish kebabs and Savory Wild Rice (page 120). Alternatively, the lamb shish kebabs can be served Nepalese style: mound a serving of rice in the center of each dinner plate, then section by section around the rice, spoon a serving of lamb (skewers removed), curried lentils, sautéed spinach and mushrooms, and chicken curry. On a recent trip to Nepal, we found wild boar also arrayed around the rice (this may be hard to come by at the local supermarket). For the ultimate Nepalese experience, place seat cushions around a coffee table, sit on the floor, contemplate a trek in the Himalayas, and enjoy this bountiful meal.

1 small onion, sliced
¼ cup fresh lemon juice
2 tablespoons extra virgin olive oil
2 teaspoons dry mustard
2 cloves garlic, minced
¼ teaspoon salt
¼ teaspoon freshly ground pepper
1 boneless leg of lamb (2½ pounds), cut into 1¼-inch cubes

8 firm cherry tomatoes
8 fresh mushrooms
1 green bell pepper, cut into 8 pieces
1 red bell pepper, cut into 8 pieces
1 Bermuda onion, cut into 8 wedges

To Make Marinade Combine onion, lemon juice, olive oil, dry mustard, garlic, salt, and pepper in resealable plastic bag. Add lamb and turn to coat all over. Refrigerate for several hours or overnight, turning lamb at least once.

To Prepare Kebabs on an Outdoor Grill Soak bamboo skewers in water for 30 minutes or more. Remove lamb from the marinade. Alternate lamb, tomatoes, mushrooms, green and red peppers, and onion on skewers. Over moderately hot coals, place skewers on a grill coated with a nonstick vegetable spray. Cover grill and cook for 12 to 16 minutes or until a meat thermometer registers 150 degrees for medium-rare or 160 degrees for medium, turning kebabs every 4 minutes.

To Prepare Kebabs on an Indoor Grill Soak bamboo skewers in water for 30 minutes or more. Remove lamb from the marinade. Alternate lamb, tomatoes, mushrooms, green and red peppers, and onion on skewers. Place them on a preheated grill over moderately high heat and cook for 25 to 30 minutes or until a meat thermometer registers 150 degrees for medium-rare or 160 degrees for medium, turning lamb every 8 minutes.

Butterflied Leg of Lamb with Assorted Roasted Peppers

SERVES 6

Rosemary is the ultimate herb that highlights the true characteristics of lamb. It is an evergreen shrub of the mint family and is native to the Mediterranean. Serve this fragrant dish topped with slivers of grilled peppers and Zucchini and Yellow Squash Soufflé (page 302) on the side.

⅓ cup fresh lemon juice
3 tablespoons red wine vinegar
2 tablespoons extra virgin olive oil
2 tablespoons Dijon mustard
4 cloves garlic, minced
1 tablespoon rosemary
1 tablespoon oregano
1 tablespoon freshly ground pepper

¾ teaspoon salt
½ teaspoon crushed red pepper
1 butterflied leg of lamb (2¼ pounds)
1 red bell pepper
1 yellow bell pepper
1 orange bell pepper

To Make Marinade Combine lemon juice, red wine vinegar, 3 tablespoons cold water, olive oil, Dijon mustard, garlic, rosemary, oregano, pepper, salt, and crushed red pepper in a resealable plastic bag and blend. Add lamb and turn to coat all over. Refrigerate for several hours or overnight, turning lamb at least once.

To Prepare Peppers on an Outdoor Grill Over moderately hot coals, place the peppers on a grill coated with nonstick vegetable spray. Cover and cook for 20 to 24 minutes or until skins are charred all over, turning the peppers as skins blacken. Once grilled, place the peppers in a plastic bag and allow to steam for 15 minutes. When they are cool enough to handle, peel away the skins and remove the tops and seeds (do not rinse the peppers). Slice the peppers into slivers and set aside.

To Prepare Peppers on an Indoor Grill Place the peppers on a preheated grill over high heat and cook for 20 to 30 minutes or until skins are charred all over, turning the peppers as skins blacken. Once grilled, place the peppers in a plastic bag and allow to steam for 15 minutes. When they are cool enough to handle, peel away the skins and remove the tops and seeds (do not rinse the peppers). Slice the peppers into slivers and set aside.

To Prepare Lamb on an Outdoor Grill Remove lamb from marinade. Over moderately hot coals, place lamb on a grill coated with a nonstick vegetable spray. Sear lamb for 1 minute on each side. Cover grill and cook for 25 to 30 minutes or until a meat thermometer registers 150 degrees for medium-rare or 160 degrees for medium, turning lamb every 10 minutes. Allow lamb to sit for 5 minutes before carving into thin slices.

To Prepare Lamb on an Indoor Grill Remove lamb from marinade. Place lamb on a preheated grill over moderately high heat and cook for 40 to 50 minutes or until a meat thermometer registers 150 degrees for medium-rare or 160 degrees for medium, turning lamb every 8 minutes. Allow lamb to sit for 5 minutes before carving into thin slices.

Mediterranean Ground Lamb Kebabs with Yogurt Sauce

These kebabs taste so good, you might want to double the recipe so you can have leftovers to enjoy the next day. They are served in warmed pita breads and can be topped with Tahini Sauce (page 94) or Raita (page 174).

1¼	pounds freshly ground lamb	½	teaspoon cayenne
½	cup minced onion	½	teaspoon paprika
½	cup minced cilantro leaves	½	teaspoon freshly ground pepper
4	cloves garlic, minced		
1	teaspoon cumin	⅛	teaspoon ground ginger
1	teaspoon coriander	⅛	teaspoon allspice
½	teaspoon salt	⅛	teaspoon cinnamon

To Make Lamb Kebabs Soak bamboo skewers in water for 30 minutes or more. Combine lamb, onion, cilantro, garlic, cumin, coriander, salt, cayenne, paprika, pepper, ground ginger, allspice, and cinnamon in a medium bowl and blend well. Form mixture into sausage shapes, about 3 inches in length, and place 3 on each skewer. Lightly flatten them so they will cook evenly.

To Prepare Kebabs on an Outdoor Grill Over moderately hot coals, place lamb kebabs on a grill coated with a nonstick vegetable spray. Cover grill and cook for 10 to 12 minutes, turning kebabs frequently.

To Prepare Kebabs on an Indoor Grill Place lamb kebabs on a preheated grill over moderately high heat and cook for 25 minutes, turning kebabs frequently.

Oriental Butterflied Leg of Lamb

The Asian spices and smoky flavor from the grill imbue the lamb with a wonderfully subtle flavor. Serve with Acorn Squash with Fruited Wild Rice (page 336).

3	tablespoons oyster sauce	1	teaspoon minced garlic
3	tablespoons hoisin sauce	½	teaspoon crushed red pepper
1½	tablespoons rice wine	1	butterflied leg of lamb
1½	tablespoons soy sauce		(1½ pounds)
1	teaspoon minced fresh ginger		

To Make Marinade Combine oyster sauce, hoisin sauce, rice wine, soy sauce, ginger, garlic, and crushed red pepper in a resealable plastic bag and blend. Add lamb and turn to coat all over. Refrigerate for several hours or overnight, turning lamb at least once.

To Prepare Lamb on an Outdoor Grill Remove lamb from marinade. Over moderately hot coals, place lamb on a grill coated with a nonstick vegetable spray. Sear lamb for 1 minute on each side. Cover grill and cook for 25 to 30 minutes or until a meat thermometer registers 150 degrees for medium-rare or 160 degrees for medium, turning lamb every 10 minutes. Allow lamb to sit for 5 minutes before carving into thin slices.

To Prepare Lamb on an Indoor Grill Remove lamb from marinade. Place lamb on a preheated grill over moderately high heat and cook for 40 to 50 minutes or until a meat thermometer registers 150 degrees for medium-rare or 160 degrees for medium, turning lamb every 10 minutes. Allow lamb to sit for 5 minutes before carving into thin slices.

Savory Marinated Butterflied Leg of Lamb

SERVES 4

Fresh ginger, cilantro, and garlic combined with an array of spices embolden the characteristic flavor of lamb. Serve with Pat's Vegetable Byriani (recipe below).

Marinade
2 tablespoons fresh lemon juice
1 tablespoon extra virgin olive oil
1 ¼-inch-thick piece fresh ginger, halved
1 tablespoon minced cilantro leaves
1 large clove garlic, minced
1 teaspoon cumin
1 teaspoon turmeric
⅛ teaspoon cayenne
1 butterflied leg of lamb (1½ pounds)

Pat's Vegetable Byriani
1 tablespoon canola oil
½ cup golden raisins
1 Bermuda onion, thinly sliced
½ cup slivered almonds
1 cup long-grain rice
¼ teaspoon salt
2 carrots, peeled and thinly sliced
½ cup frozen peas

To Make Marinade Combine 2 tablespoons cold water, lemon juice, olive oil, ginger, cilantro, garlic, cumin, turmeric, and cayenne in a resealable plastic bag and blend. Add lamb and turn to coat all over. Refrigerate for several hours or overnight, turning lamb at least once.

To Prepare Lamb on an Outdoor Grill Remove lamb from marinade. Over moderately hot coals, place lamb on a grill coated with a nonstick vegetable spray. Sear lamb for 1 minute on each side. Cover grill and cook for 25 to 30 minutes or until a meat thermometer registers 150 degrees for medium-rare or 160 degrees for medium, turning lamb every 10 minutes. Allow lamb to sit for 5 minutes before carving into thin slices.

To Prepare Lamb on an Indoor Grill Remove lamb from marinade. Place lamb on a preheated grill over moderately high heat and cook for 40 to 50 minutes or until a meat thermometer registers 150 degrees for medium-rare or 160 degrees for medium, turning lamb every 10 minutes. Allow lamb to sit for 5 minutes before carving into thin slices.

To Make Byriani While grilling the lamb, line a baking sheet with two layers of paper towels and preheat oven to 150 degrees.

Heat canola oil in a large frying pan over moderate heat. Add raisins and sauté for 4 minutes or until raisins begin to turn brown. Transfer raisins to a corner of the paper-lined baking sheet and place it in the oven. To the same frying pan, add onion and sauté over moderate to moderately high heat for 15 to 20 minutes or until onion slices begin to brown, turning occasionally. Transfer onions to a different corner of the paper-lined baking sheet and place it in the oven. Add almonds to the same frying pan and sauté over moderate heat for 2 minutes or until almonds begin to brown. Transfer almonds to a different corner of the paper-lined baking sheet and place it in the oven.

Place 2 cups water, rice, and salt in a large saucepan over moderately high heat and bring to a boil. Add carrots and peas, reduce heat to low, and cook, covered, for 20 minutes. Blend well.

Place rice on a platter and make a well in the center. Fill with raisins, onions, and almonds and blend well.

Lamb Shish Kebabs in Red Wine Marinade

SERVES 4

Red wine, rosemary, orange marmalade, and other spices create lamb shish kebabs that will qualify as an elegant feast. Start the meal by offering Chilled and Spicy Grilled Red Pepper Soup and then serve the shish kebabs with Savory Wild Rice (page 120) and Grilled Polenta (page 322).

½ cup dry red wine	½ teaspoon ground ginger
¼ cup orange marmalade	1 clove garlic, minced
1 tablespoon red wine vinegar	1 leg of lamb (1½ pounds), cut into 1¼-inch cubes
1 tablespoon extra virgin olive oil	8 shiitake mushrooms
1 tablespoon rosemary	8 firm cherry tomatoes
½ tablespoon marjoram	1 orange bell pepper, cut into 8 pieces
½ tablespoon oregano	
½ teaspoon seasoned salt	

To Make Marinade Combine red wine, orange marmalade, red wine vinegar, olive oil, rosemary, marjoram, oregano, seasoned salt, ground ginger, and garlic in a resealable plastic bag and blend. Add cubed lamb and turn to coat all over. Refrigerate for several hours or overnight, turning lamb at least once.

To Prepare Kebabs on an Outdoor Grill Soak bamboo skewers in water for 30 minutes or more. Remove cubed lamb from marinade. Alternate lamb, shiitake mushrooms, tomatoes, and orange pepper on skewers. Over moderately hot coals, place the lamb kebabs on a grill coated with a nonstick vegetable spray. Cover grill and cook for 12 to 16 minutes or until a meat thermometer registers 150 degrees for medium-rare or 160 degrees for medium, turning kebabs every 6 minutes.

To Prepare Kebabs on an Indoor Grill Soak bamboo skewers in water for 30 minutes or more. Remove cubed lamb from marinade. Alternate lamb, shiitake mushrooms, tomatoes, and orange pepper on skewers. Place them on a preheated grill over moderately high heat and cook for 25 to 30 minutes or until a meat thermometer registers 150 degrees for medium-rare or 160 degrees for medium, turning kebabs every 8 minutes.

Marinated Butterflied Leg of Lamb

SERVES 4

A hint of the East permeates the lamb, as flavors from the marinade become intensified during the grilling. Serve with a combination of sautéed Chinese pea pods, red bell pepper slivers, and water chestnuts.

¼	cup soy sauce	1	teaspoon freshly ground
2	tablespoons canola oil		Szechwan peppercorns (or
2	tablespoons rice wine vinegar		freshly ground pepper)
2	tablespoons rice wine	3	cloves garlic, minced
2	teaspoons oriental sesame oil	1	butterflied leg of lamb
½	teaspoon salt		(1½ pounds)

To Make Marinade Combine soy sauce, canola oil, rice wine vinegar, rice wine, sesame oil, salt, Szechwan peppercorns, and garlic in a resealable plastic bag and blend. Add lamb and turn to coat all over. Refrigerate for several hours or overnight, turning lamb at least once.

To Prepare Lamb on an Outdoor Grill Remove lamb from marinade. Over moderately hot coals, place lamb on a grill coated with a nonstick vegetable spray. Sear lamb for 1 minute on each side. Cover grill and cook for 25 to 30 minutes or until a meat thermometer registers 150 degrees for medium-rare or 160 degrees for medium, turning lamb every 10 minutes. Allow lamb to sit for 5 minutes before carving into thin slices.

To Prepare Lamb on an Indoor Grill Remove lamb from marinade. Place it on a preheated grill over moderately high heat and cook for 40 to 50 minutes or until a meat thermometer registers 150 degrees for medium-rare or 160 degrees for medium, turning lamb every 8 minutes. Allow lamb to sit for 5 minutes before carving into thin slices.

4

PORK

Pork is extremely well suited to the grill. It melds easily with many different sauces and marinades. Like beef, pork is being bred leaner today. Choose pork that has a pale pink color, which indicates that it comes from a younger animal. The popular cuts of pork are pork loin chops and spareribs.

PORK LOIN CHOPS

These chops are the most tender and come from the loin section. Other cuts from the loin section that make excellent grilling include the rib chop, top loin chop, butterfly chop, sirloin chop, tenderloin, country-style ribs, and baby back ribs.

SPARERIBS

Spareribs are found beneath the loin in the pork belly. Both the lean and fatty portions of the belly are removed and sold as bacon and salt pork. Spareribs are the remaining "bones." There is no better way to prepare spareribs than on a grill, either as the total cooking process or as the final step after being partially precooked.

HELPFUL GUIDELINES FOR PREPARING PORK

- When grilling pork chops on an outdoor grill, sear the pork for 1 minute on each side. If the chop is ¾ inch thick, continue cooking it for 4 to 5 minutes on each side, and if 1½ inches thick, 8 to 10 minutes on each side.
- When grilling pork chops on an indoor grill, cook ones that are ½ to ¾ inch thick for 25 to 40 minutes, turning occasionally.
- Although most recipes suggest cooking pork until a meat thermometer registers 160 degrees, I prefer to cook it until it registers 150 to 155 degrees, because at this temperature the meat is safely cooked but remains more tender and juicy.

Chinese Pork Tenderloin

Chinese Five Spice powder, used in combination with other Asian ingredients in a marinade or rub, imbues pork with a marvelous, aromatic flavor. Serve with Jasmine Rice (page 158).

¼ cup granulated sugar
2 tablespoons soy sauce
1 tablespoon white miso
1 tablespoon oyster sauce
½ teaspoon sesame paste
¼ teaspoon Chinese Five Spice powder
¼ teaspoon salt
1 pork tenderloin (1½ pounds)

To Make Marinade Combine sugar, soy sauce, white miso, oyster sauce, sesame paste, Chinese Five Spice powder, and salt in a resealable plastic bag and blend. Add pork tenderloin and turn to coat all over. Refrigerate for several hours or overnight, turning pork at least once.

To Prepare Pork on an Outdoor Grill Place a drip pan in the center of the lower grate and place an equal number of briquettes on both sides. When coals are hot, remove pork tenderloin from marinade, reserving marinade. Place the pork tenderloin over coals on a grill coated with a nonstick vegetable spray. Sear the pork for 1 minute on each side. Move the pork tenderloin directly over the drip pan. Cover grill and cook for 20 to 30 minutes or until a meat thermometer registers 150 to 155 degrees, turning pork every 15 minutes and brushing with reserved marinade. Allow the pork to sit for 5 minutes before carving into thin slices.

To Prepare Pork on an Indoor Grill Remove the pork tenderloin from marinade, reserving marinade. Place the pork tenderloin on a preheated grill over moderately high heat and cook for 30 to 40 minutes or until a meat thermometer registers 150 to 155 degrees, turning pork frequently and brushing with reserved marinade. Allow the pork to sit for 5 minutes before carving into thin slices.

Pork Tenderloin with Spicy Rub

SERVES 8

Coating pork tenderloin with a spicy rub not only adds flavor but also tenderizes the meat. The pork is delicious served thinly sliced and can be accented with your favorite barbecue sauce. It also makes a delicious filling for fajitas. Serve with Mary's Tortilla Soup (recipe below) and Garlic-Basted Grilled Corn on the Cob (page 317).

Rub
½ cup packed dark brown sugar
¼ cup celery salt
2 tablespoons paprika
1 tablespoon chili powder
1 tablespoon freshly ground pepper
1 teaspoon dried lemon peel
½ teaspoon garlic salt
¼ teaspoon cinnamon
⅛ teaspoon cayenne
1 pork tenderloin (3 pounds)

Mary's Tortilla Soup
6 (6-inch) corn tortillas
3 cups canola oil
Salt, to taste
3 tablespoons extra virgin olive oil

1 medium onion, chopped
1 can (4 ounces) diced mild green chiles
3 cloves garlic, minced
1 can (10¾ ounces) beef broth
1 can (10¾ ounces) chicken broth
1½ cups tomato juice
1 large tomato, chopped
1½ tablespoons chopped cilantro or parsley
1½ teaspoons steak sauce
1¼ teaspoons chili powder
1 teaspoon Worcestershire sauce
1 teaspoon cumin
1 teaspoon salt
⅛ teaspoon freshly ground pepper
1 large ripe avocado, diced
¼ cup shredded cheddar cheese
¼ cup shredded Monterey Jack cheese

To Make Rub Combine brown sugar, celery salt, paprika, chili powder, pepper, lemon peel, garlic salt, cinnamon, and cayenne in a covered jar and shake well.

Press the spicy rub all over pork tenderloin. Place the pork tenderloin in a nonmetal dish and cover with a piece of plastic wrap. Refrigerate for several hours or overnight.

To Prepare Soup Stack the corn tortillas together and trim the sides to form a square. Cut into 1½ × ½-inch strips. Heat canola oil to 350 degrees in a large, heavy saucepan over moderately high heat. Fry the tortilla strips, a few at a time, for 1 to 2 minutes or until light brown. Remove tortilla strips from oil with a slotted spoon and place them on paper towels. Season with salt while warm. Store the tortilla strips in an airtight container until ready to use.

Heat olive oil in a large pot over moderate heat. Add onion, chiles, and garlic and sauté for 5 minutes, stirring occasionally. Add beef broth, chicken broth, tomato juice, 1½ cups cold water, tomato, cilantro, steak sauce, chili powder, Worcestershire sauce, cumin, salt, and pepper and blend. Bring to a boil, reduce heat, and simmer, covered, for 1 hour and 30 minutes.

When ready to serve the soup, divide the tortilla strips, diced avocado, and cheeses in each of six soup bowls. Ladle hot soup over each.

To Prepare Pork on an Outdoor Grill Place a drip pan in the center of the lower grate and place an equal number of briquettes on both sides. When coals are hot, place the pork tenderloin over coals on a grill coated with a nonstick vegetable spray. Sear the pork for 1 minute on each side. Move the pork directly over the drip pan. Cover grill and cook for 20 to 30 minutes or until a meat thermometer registers 150 to 155 degrees, turning pork every 15 minutes. Allow the pork tenderloin to sit for 5 minutes before carving into thin slices.

To Prepare Pork on an Indoor Grill Place the pork tenderloin on a preheated grill over moderately high heat and cook for 30 to 40 minutes or until a meat thermometer registers 155 degrees, turning pork every 10 minutes. Allow the pork tenderloin to sit for 5 minutes before carving into thin slices.

Santa Fe Pork Chops with Gazpacho Salsa

SERVES 4

It is hard to resist marinating almost any meat in Southwestern marinades! In this recipe, the pork's flavor becomes especially vibrant when marinated and grilled. The spicy gazpacho salsa then adds color, texture, and an additional bite. Serve with Garlic-Basted Grilled Corn on the Cob (page 317) and Mexican Rice (page 170).

¼ cup fresh lime juice	½ teaspoon chili powder
1 tablespoon extra virgin olive oil	½ teaspoon salt
2 tablespoons chopped cilantro leaves	⅛ teaspoon cayenne
1 clove garlic, minced	4 butterflied pork chops (6 ounces each) (see note)
1 teaspoon cumin	Gazpacho Salsa (page 38)

To Make Marinade Combine lime juice, olive oil, cilantro, garlic, cumin, chili powder, salt, and cayenne in a resealable bag and blend. Add the pork chops and turn to coat all over. Refrigerate for several hours or overnight, turning the pork chops at least once.

To Prepare Pork on an Outdoor Grill Remove pork chops from marinade. Over moderately hot coals, place the pork chops on a grill coated with a nonstick vegetable spray. Sear pork chops for 1 minute on each side. Cover grill and cook for 4 to 5 minutes on each side or until a meat thermometer registers 150 to 155 degrees.

To Prepare Pork on an Indoor Grill Remove pork chops from marinade. Place them on a preheated grill over moderately high heat and cook for 25 to 35 minutes or until a meat thermometer registers 150 to 155 degrees, turning the pork chops every 7 minutes.

To Serve Arrange a Santa Fe pork chop on each of four dinner plates. Spoon gazpacho salsa over each and garnish with a sprig of cilantro.

Note Butterflied pork chops are center-cut boneless loin chops that are sliced down the center, cut almost—but not completely—through. The halves are carefully opened flat to resemble a butterfly.

Greek Pork Tenderloin

This is a wonderful summer dish. Invite friends over for a barbecue, and start the evening off by serving a platter laden with stuffed grape leaves, followed by Greek pork tenderloin slices, Rice Pilaf with Toasted Almonds and Raisins (page 44), Greek Salad (page 40), and warmed pita breads. To finish off the evening, pass around a tray of baklava and offer a glass of ouzo.

¼	cup dry white wine	2	tablespoons chopped green onions
¼	cup fresh lemon juice	2	tablespoons chopped parsley
1	tablespoon extra virgin olive oil	1½	teaspoons Greek oregano
3	large cloves garlic, minced	1	pork tenderloin (1½ pounds)
2	tablespoons dried dill weed		

To Make Marinade Combine wine, lemon juice, olive oil, garlic, dill weed, green onions, parsley, and oregano in a resealable plastic bag and blend. Add pork tenderloin and turn to coat all over. Refrigerate for several hours or overnight, turning pork at least once.

To Prepare Pork on an Outdoor Grill Remove the pork tenderloin from marinade, reserving marinade. Over moderately hot coals, place the pork tenderloin on a grill coated with a nonstick vegetable spray. Sear the pork for 1 minute on each side. Cover grill and cook for 18 to 24 minutes or until a meat thermometer registers 150 to 155 degrees, turning pork frequently and brushing with reserved marinade. Allow the pork to sit for 5 minutes before carving into thin slices.

To Prepare Pork on an Indoor Grill Remove the pork tenderloin from marinade, reserving marinade. Place the pork tenderloin on a preheated grill and cook over moderately high heat for 30 to 40 minutes or until a meat thermometer registers 150 to 155 degrees, turning pork frequently and brushing with reserved marinade. Allow the pork to sit for 5 minutes before carving into thin slices.

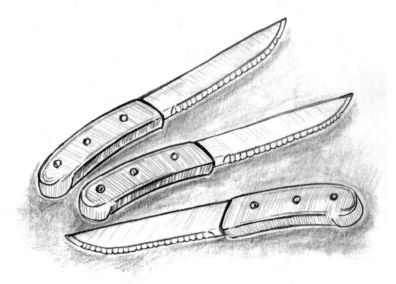

Mary's Maytag Bleu–Stuffed Iowa Chops

SERVES 4

Maytag Bleu is an award-winning cheese made in Newton, Iowa, close to my home in Iowa City. One Christmas, I gave gifts of Maytag Bleu cheese to friends and family. One of the recipients was my neighbor, who was kind enough to share this special recipe with me. Serve with Tossed Salad with Dijon Mustard Vinaigrette (recipe below) and Sautéed New Potatoes (page 186).

Tossed Salad with Dijon Mustard Vinaigrette

⅓ cup Dijon mustard

2 tablespoons white wine vinegar

¾ teaspoon freshly ground pepper

¼ teaspoon salt

½ cup extra virgin olive oil

1 large head romaine lettuce, torn into bite-size pieces

3 plum tomatoes, quartered

1 jar (6½ ounces) quartered marinated artichoke hearts, drained

1 can (2.4 ounces) sliced black olives, drained

1 small Bermuda onion, thinly sliced

2 cups croutons

Maytag Bleu Filling

3 tablespoons butter

¼ cup onion, finely chopped

½ cup fresh mushrooms, thinly sliced

6 ounces bleu cheese (Maytag, if you want to be authentic), crumbled

¾ cup fine bread crumbs
Salt and freshly ground pepper, to taste

6 Iowa chops, 1¼ inches thick (see note)

To Make Salad Combine Dijon mustard, white wine vinegar, pepper, and salt in the work bowl of a food processor fitted with a metal blade and process until blended. Add olive oil in a slow steady stream and process until well blended. Set aside the vinaigrette.

When ready to serve the salad, combine romaine lettuce, tomatoes, artichoke hearts, olives, Bermuda onion, and croutons in a large salad bowl. Add Dijon mustard vinaigrette and toss.

To Make Filling Melt butter in a medium saucepan over moderate heat. Add onion and mushrooms and sauté for 5 minutes, stirring occasionally. Remove saucepan from heat and add bleu cheese, bread crumbs, salt, and pepper and blend well.

Create a pocket by cutting along the length of the pork chop or make a small pocket by making an incision at one end and rotating the blade inside the chop, keeping the opening no wider than 1 inch. Stuff some bleu cheese mixture into each pork chop, dividing evenly. The membrane on the inside of the loin will shrink during cooking and hold the filling in place.

To Prepare Pork on an Outdoor Grill Over moderately hot coals, place the pork chops on a grill coated with a nonstick vegetable spray. Sear pork chops for 1 minute on each side. Cover the grill and cook for 8 to 10 minutes on each side or until a meat thermometer registers 155 degrees.

To Prepare Pork on an Indoor Grill Place the pork chops on a preheated grill over moderately high heat and cook for 35 to 45 minutes or until a meat thermometer registers 155 degrees, turning the pork chops every 10 minutes.

Note Iowa chops are the loin cut of a bone-in pork loin chop and are usually cut 1¼ to 1½ inches thick.

Orange-Glazed Baby Back Pork Ribs

SERVES 4

Baby back ribs are smaller, less fatty, and have more meat than spareribs. Coating them first with the spicy barbecue rub and later with the sweeter orange glaze adds a sensational richness to this all-American specialty. Serve with Grilled New Potatoes (page 342).

Orange Glaze

- 2 navel oranges
- 1 cup granulated sugar
- ¼ cup garlic chili sauce
- 2 tablespoons soy sauce
- 2 tablespoons fresh lime juice
- 1 tablespoon honey

Rub

- ¼ cup freshly ground pepper
- ¼ cup packed dark brown sugar

- ¼ cup paprika
- 2 teaspoons celery salt
- 2 teaspoons oregano
- 2 teaspoons salt
- 2 teaspoons thyme
- 2 teaspoons garlic salt
- 1¼ teaspoons cayenne

- 2 slabs baby back pork ribs (3 pounds each) (see note)

To Make Glaze Both the orange peel and juice will be used in this recipe. Peel oranges, leaving most of the white part on the oranges; set aside the oranges. Place the peel in a small saucepan and add enough water to cover. Bring to a boil over moderately high heat and boil for 1 minute. Drain. Combine 1 cup water, sugar, and orange peel in a small saucepan and bring to a boil. Reduce heat to moderate and simmer for 30 minutes. Place a sieve over another small saucepan and strain the mixture. Discard the orange peel. Return the mixture in the saucepan to low heat.

Squeeze enough orange juice from reserved oranges to yield 1 cup. Add orange juice, garlic chili sauce, soy sauce, lime juice, and honey to the mixture in the saucepan and blend. Bring to a boil and simmer over moderate heat for 30 minutes or until mixture becomes syrupy. Cool to room temperature. The orange glaze can be used at room temperature or transferred to a covered container and refrigerated for up to 5 days.

To Make Rub Combine pepper, brown sugar, paprika, celery salt, oregano, salt, thyme, garlic salt, and cayenne in a small bowl and blend well.

To Prepare Pork on an Outdoor Grill Press a thick layer of barbecue rub on both sides of ribs if you like spicy food, or apply a thin layer of the rub to make it less spicy. Over moderately hot coals, place ribs on a grill coated with a nonstick vegetable spray. Cover grill and cook for 45 minutes or until a meat thermometer registers 150 to 155 degrees, turning ribs occasionally. Brush both sides of ribs with orange glaze the last 5 to 10 minutes, turning occasionally to prevent burning.

To Prepare Pork on an Indoor Grill Bring water to a boil in a large pot over moderately high heat. Add the ribs and boil for 10 minutes. Drain well. Press a thick layer of barbecue rub on both sides of ribs if you like spicy food, or apply a thin layer of the rub to make it less spicy. Place the ribs on a preheated grill over moderately high heat and cook for 1 hour and 10 to 20 minutes or until a meat thermometer registers 155 to 160 degrees, brushing both sides of ribs with orange glaze the last 5 to 10 minutes, turning occasionally to prevent burning. Additional sauce can be served on the side.

Note Ask your butcher to remove any thick layers of fat and to cut away both the membrane and the flap, or skirt, on the underside of the ribs. The ribs will become dry if overcooked. When done, the meat should easily pull apart when you pull ribs in opposite directions or you should be able to easily insert a skewer between the bones. To tenderize the ribs, prick the meat between the bones with a fork before applying the rub.

Oriental Pork Kebabs

These kebabs, with their array of unique Asian flavors, are absolutely delicious hot off the grill! Serve with Jasmine Rice (page 158) and Grilled Pineapple Rings (page 330).

⅓ cup finely chopped
   cilantro leaves

3 tablespoons fresh lime juice

2 tablespoons soy sauce

2 tablespoons canola oil

4 large garlic cloves, chopped

2 tablespoons chopped
   fresh ginger

1 pork tenderloin (1½ pounds),
   cut into 1¼-inch cubes

8 shiitake mushrooms,
   stems trimmed

1 red bell pepper, cut into
   8 squares

4 large green onions, cut into
   8 (2-inch) pieces

To Make Marinade Combine cilantro, lime juice, soy sauce, canola oil, 2 tablespoons cold water, garlic, and ginger in a resealable plastic bag and blend. Add cubed pork and turn to coat all over. Refrigerate for several hours or overnight, turning pork at least once.

To Prepare Kebabs on an Outdoor Grill Soak bamboo skewers in water for 30 minutes or more. Remove cubed pork from marinade. Alternate pork, shiitake mushrooms, red pepper, and green onions on skewers. Over moderately hot coals, place pork kebabs on a grill coated with a nonstick vegetable spray. Cover grill and cook for 8 to 10 minutes or until a meat thermometer registers 150 to 155 degrees, turning skewers every 6 minutes.

To Prepare Kebabs on an Indoor Grill Soak bamboo skewers in water for 30 minutes or more. Remove cubed pork from marinade. Alternate pork, shiitake mushrooms, red pepper, and green onions on skewers. Place the kebabs on a preheated grill over moderately high heat and cook for 20 to 25 minutes or until a meat thermometer registers 150 to 155 degrees, turning skewers every 8 minutes.

Pork Chops in Savory Marinade

SERVES 4

These flavorful pork chops are exceptionally delicious when grilled. They are fabulous topped with a dollop of Green Pepper Jelly (page 160), but they can also be enjoyed unadorned. Serve with Grilled Spicy Yams (page 347) and Grilled Apple Rings (page 343).

½ cup dry white wine
¼ cup packed dark brown sugar
2 tablespoons Worcestershire sauce
2 tablespoons soy sauce
1 tablespoon rice wine vinegar
1 tablespoon extra virgin olive oil

1 tablespoon Sriracha hot chili sauce
1 teaspoon salt
½ teaspoon freshly ground pepper
¼ teaspoon cinnamon
¼ teaspoon nutmeg
¼ teaspoon thyme
4 pork loin chops (6 ounces each)

To Make Marinade Combine wine, brown sugar, Worcestershire sauce, soy sauce, rice wine vinegar, olive oil, Sriracha hot chili sauce, salt, pepper, cinnamon, nutmeg, and thyme in a resealable plastic bag and blend. Add pork chops and turn to coat all over. Refrigerate for several hours or overnight, turning pork at least once.

To Prepare Pork on an Outdoor Grill Remove pork chops from marinade. Over moderately hot coals, place the pork chops on a grill coated with a nonstick vegetable spray. Sear pork for 1 minute on each side. Cover grill and cook for 4 to 5 minutes on each side or until a meat thermometer registers 150 to 155 degrees.

To Prepare Pork on an Indoor Grill Remove pork chops from marinade. Place them on a preheated grill over moderately high heat and cook pork for 25 to 30 minutes or until a meat thermometer registers 150 to 155 degrees, turning the pork every 10 minutes.

Tex-Mex Pork Tenderloin with Corn and Black Bean Salsa

SERVES 4

Tex-Mex pork tenderloin is delicious served thinly sliced with corn and black bean salsa on the side. The pork is equally delectable when made into fajitas—just provide warmed tortillas, Jo Gail's Guacamole (page 86), shredded cheese, salsa, and sour cream.

¼ cup fresh lime juice	½ teaspoon chili powder
1 tablespoon extra virgin olive oil	½ teaspoon salt
1 large clove garlic, minced	⅛ teaspoon cayenne
1½ teaspoons cumin	1 pork tenderloin (1½ pounds)
½ teaspoon coriander	Corn and Black Bean Salsa (page 150)

To Make Marinade Combine lime juice, olive oil, garlic, cumin, coriander, chili powder, salt, and cayenne in a resealable plastic bag and blend. Add pork tenderloin and turn to coat both sides. Refrigerate for several hours or overnight, turning pork at least once.

To Prepare Pork on an Outdoor Grill Place a drip pan in the center of the lower grate and place an equal number of briquettes on both sides. When coals are moderately hot, remove the pork tenderloin from marinade, reserving marinade. Place the pork tenderloin over coals on a grill coated with a nonstick vegetable spray. Sear the pork for 1 minute on each side. Move the pork tenderloin directly over the drip pan. Cover grill and cook for 20 to 30 minutes or until a meat thermometer registers 150 to 155 degrees, turning pork every 15 minutes and brushing with reserved marinade.

To Prepare Pork on an Indoor Grill Remove pork tenderloin from marinade, reserving marinade. Place pork on a preheated grill over moderately high heat and cook for 30 to 40 minutes or until a meat thermometer registers 150 to 155 degrees, turning pork frequently and brushing with reserved marinade.

To Serve Thinly slice pork tenderloin and serve with corn and black bean salsa on the side.

Thai-Style Pork Chops with Ginger-Peach Salsa

SERVES 6

The recipe comes from the National Pork Producers, culinary experts when it comes to preparing a succulent pork dish. Serve with Basmati Rice (page 72).

Marinade
½ cup Sweet Ginger Sesame Hibachi Grill Sauce (or other teriyaki sauce)
4 green onions (all of the white part and some of the green), chopped
4 tablespoons minced cilantro leaves
2 tablespoons fresh lime juice
6 America's Cut pork chops (1¼ inches thick)

Ginger-Peach Salsa
4 ripe peaches (see note)
2 green onions (all of the white part and some of the green), minced
2 tablespoons Sweet Ginger Sesame Hibachi Grill Sauce (or other teriyaki sauce)
2 tablespoons firmly packed dark brown sugar
¼ teaspoon crushed red pepper
4 tablespoons minced cilantro leaves

To Make Marinade Combine Sweet Ginger Sesame Hibachi Grill Sauce, green onions, cilantro, and lime juice in a resealable bag and blend well. Add the pork chops and turn to coat all over. Refrigerate for 6 to 24 hours, turning the pork chops occasionally.

To Make Salsa Bring 6 cups water to a boil in a large saucepan. Add the peaches and cook for 1 minute. Drain. When the peaches are cool enough to handle, remove the skins and pits and coarsely chop the peaches.

In a small bowl, combine green onions, Sweet Ginger Sesame Hibachi Grill Sauce, brown sugar, and crushed red pepper and blend. Add the peaches and blend. Serve immediately, or let stand at room temperature for up to an hour. Add cilantro just before serving and blend well.

To Prepare Pork on an Outdoor Grill Remove pork chops from marinade. Over hot coals, place the pork chops on a grill coated with a nonstick vegetable spray. Sear the pork chops for 1 minute on each side. Cover the grill and cook for 8 minutes on each side or until a meat thermometer registers 150 to 155 degrees.

To Prepare Pork on an Indoor Grill Remove pork chops from marinade. Place them on a preheated grill over moderately high heat and cook for 25 to 40 minutes or until a meat thermometer registers 150 to 155 degrees, turning the pork chop every 10 minutes.

To Serve Place a pork chop on each of six dinner plates and spoon some ginger-peach salsa on top or beside each chop.

Note If you wish, 1 can (29 ounces) peach slices, drained and chopped, may be substituted for fresh peaches.

Oriental Marinated Pork Tenderloin

This is a simple but elegant way to serve pork tenderloin. The marinade gives this dish a flavorful sparkle and at the same time makes the pork tender and moist. Serve with Lemon-Glazed Carrots (recipe below) and Grilled Fruit Kebabs (page 341).

Marinade

⅓ cup soy sauce
2 tablespoons packed dark brown sugar
2 tablespoons rice wine vinegar
1 tablespoon minced fresh ginger
1 clove garlic, minced
1 pork tenderloin (1½ pounds)

Lemon-Glazed Carrots

8 carrots, peeled and thinly sliced on the diagonal
6 tablespoons butter
6 tablespoons packed dark brown sugar
3 tablespoons fresh lemon juice

To Make Marinade Combine soy sauce, brown sugar, rice wine vinegar, ginger, and garlic in a resealable plastic bag and blend. Add pork tenderloin and turn to coat all over. Refrigerate for several hours or overnight, turning pork at least once.

To Prepare Pork on an Outdoor Grill Remove pork tenderloin from marinade. Over moderately hot coals, place the pork on a grill coated with a nonstick vegetable spray. Sear pork for 1 minute on each side. Cover grill and cook for 18 to 24 minutes or until a meat thermometer registers 150 to 155 degrees, turning pork every 8 minutes. Allow the pork to sit for 5 minutes before carving into thin slices.

To Prepare Pork on an Indoor Grill Remove pork tenderloin from marinade. Place pork on a preheated grill over moderately high heat and cook pork for 30 to 40 minutes or until a meat thermometer registers 150 to 155 degrees, turning the pork every 10 minutes. Allow the pork to sit for 5 minutes before carving into thin slices.

To Make Carrots While grilling the pork, cook carrots for 10 minutes in a large saucepan filled with boiling water over moderately high heat. Drain well. Return carrots to saucepan.

Melt butter in a medium saucepan over moderately low heat. Add brown sugar and lemon juice and bring to a boil over moderate heat, stirring occasionally. Pour sauce over carrots and blend well.

Pork Tenderloin in Lemongrass and Soy Sauce Marinade

SERVES 4

Lemongrass is a Southeast Asian herb. Its fibrous outer layer is removed to reveal the inner stalk, which is the culinary heart of the plant. It has a delicate lemony flavor, which seems to embrace food with a subtle, citrus perfume. Look for fresh lemongrass stalks that are pale to medium green and firm and have a white bulb. Serve this dish with Jasmine Rice (page 158) and Asparagus with Lemon Crumbs (page 228).

2	tablespoons granulated sugar	1	tablespoon garlic chili sauce
2	tablespoons soy sauce	2	cloves garlic, minced
2	tablespoons rice wine vinegar	½	teaspoon freshly ground Szechwan pepper (or freshly ground pepper)
2	tablespoons canola oil		
2	tablespoons rice wine		
2	stalks lemongrass, chopped	1	pork tenderloin (1½ pounds)

To Make Marinade Combine sugar, soy sauce, rice wine vinegar, canola oil, rice wine, lemongrass, garlic chili sauce, garlic, and Szechwan pepper in a resealable plastic bag and blend. Add pork tenderloin and turn to coat all over. Refrigerate for several hours or overnight, turning pork at least once.

To Prepare Pork on an Outdoor Grill Place a drip pan in the center of the lower grate and place an equal number of briquettes on both sides. When coals are hot, remove the pork tenderloin from marinade, reserving marinade. Place the pork tenderloin over coals on a grill coated with a nonstick vegetable spray. Sear the pork for 1 minute on each side. Move the pork tenderloin directly over the drip pan. Cover grill and cook for 20 to 30 minutes or until a meat thermometer registers 150 to 155 degrees, turning pork every 15 minutes and brushing with reserved marinade. Allow the pork to sit for 5 minutes before carving into thin slices.

To Prepare Pork on an Indoor Grill Remove pork tenderloin from marinade, reserving marinade. Place the pork tenderloin on a preheated grill over moderately high heat and cook for 30 to 40 minutes or until a meat thermometer registers 150 to 155 degrees, turning pork frequently and brushing with reserved marinade. Allow the pork to sit for 5 minutes before carving into thin slices.

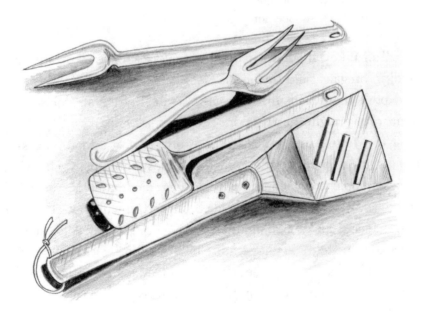

Applejack Pork Chops

Applejack (or Calvados) imparts a wonderful, subtle apple flavor to pork chops. They are delicious when served with Grilled Apple Rings (page 343) and Tangy Applesauce (recipe below) on the side.

Marinade

- 6 tablespoons applejack or Calvados
- 2 tablespoons extra virgin olive oil
- 2 tablespoons white wine vinegar
- 2 teaspoons oregano
- 2 teaspoons thyme
- 4 butterflied pork loin chops (6 ounces each) (see note)

Tangy Applesauce

- 1½ pounds McIntosh apples, peeled, cored, and quartered
- ¼ cup granulated sugar
- 1 (3-inch) vanilla bean, split into 2 pieces
- 1 (3-inch) cinnamon stick
- 2 tablespoons white horseradish

To Make Marinade Combine applejack, olive oil, white wine vinegar, oregano, and thyme in a resealable plastic bag and blend. Add pork chops and turn to coat all over. Refrigerate for several hours or overnight, turning pork chops at least once.

To Make Applesauce In the work bowl of a food processor fitted with a metal blade, process apples until finely chopped. Transfer apples to a medium saucepan over moderately low heat and add sugar, ¼ cup cold water, vanilla bean, and cinnamon stick. Cover saucepan and cook for 25 minutes, stirring occasionally. Allow applesauce to come to room temperature before removing cinnamon stick and vanilla bean. Add horseradish and blend well. Refrigerate the tangy applesauce, covered, until ready to serve.

To Prepare Pork on an Outdoor Grill Remove pork chops from marinade. Over moderately hot coals, place the pork chops on a grill coated with a nonstick vegetable spray. Sear pork chops for 1 minute on each side. Cover grill and cook for 4 to 5 minutes on each side or until a meat thermometer registers 155 degrees.

To Prepare Pork on an Indoor Grill Remove pork chops from marinade. Place them on a preheated grill over moderately high heat and cook for 20 to 30 minutes or until a meat thermometer registers 155 degrees, turning the pork chops every 10 minutes.

Note Butterflied pork chops are center-cut boneless loin chops that are sliced down the center, cut almost—but not completely—through. The halves are carefully opened flat to resemble a butterfly.

Note The pork chops are also delicious topped with a creamy applejack sauce. Combine ½ cup applejack, ½ cup apple jelly, ½ cup heavy cream, and ¼ cup Dijon mustard in a small saucepan over moderate heat and bring to a boil, stirring occasionally. Boil for 7 to 8 minutes or until sauce begins to thicken, stirring occasionally. Spoon some applejack sauce over each pork chop.

Barbecued Baby Back Pork Ribs

This past Fourth of July, my son had a friend from Ireland visiting us. We could think of no better way to give him a taste of the holiday and the United States than to serve barbecued ribs, Dill and Basil Potato Salad (page 130), and Garlic-Basted Grilled Corn on the Cob (page 317). Dessert was a triple-layer lemon cake topped with blueberries and strawberries. What a great food-filled celebration!

Barbecue Sauce

- 1½ cups ketchup
- ¼ cup apple cider vinegar
- ⅓ cup firmly packed dark brown sugar
- 2 tablespoons butter
- 2 cloves garlic, chopped
- 1 tablespoon Worcestershire sauce
- 2 teaspoons steak sauce
- 1½ teaspoons honey
- 1 teaspoon yellow mustard
- ½ teaspoon cayenne

Rub

- ¼ cup coarse ground pepper
- ¼ cup packed dark brown sugar
- ¼ cup paprika
- 2 teaspoons celery salt
- 2 teaspoons oregano
- 2 teaspoons salt
- 2 teaspoons thyme
- 2 teaspoons garlic salt
- 1¼ teaspoons cayenne

- 2 slabs baby back pork ribs (3 pounds each) (see note)

To Make Barbecue Sauce Combine ketchup, cider vinegar, ¼ cup cold water, brown sugar, butter, garlic, Worcestershire sauce, steak sauce, honey, mustard, and cayenne in a medium saucepan over moderate heat and blend well. Bring to a simmer. Reduce heat to moderately low and cook for 15 to 20 minutes or until sauce thickens, stirring frequently. The barbecue sauce can be made ahead and refrigerated in a covered container until ready to use.

To Make Rub Combine pepper, brown sugar, paprika, celery salt, oregano, salt, thyme, garlic salt, and cayenne in a small bowl and blend well.

To Prepare Pork on an Outdoor Grill Press a thick layer of barbecue rub on both sides of ribs if you like spicy food, or apply a thin layer of the rub to make it less spicy. Place a grilling pan filled with water off to one side on the grilling grate. Place briquettes on the other half and light them. When coals are moderately hot, place ribs on a grill coated with a nonstick vegetable spray over the grilling pan and away from the heat. Cover grill, leaving vents slightly open, and cook for 4 to 5 hours or until a meat thermometer registers 150 to 155 degrees. The ribs can be served with the barbecue sauce on the side, or the ribs can be brushed with barbecue sauce on both sides the last 5 minutes of cooking time, with additional sauce served on the side.

To Prepare Pork on an Indoor Grill Bring water to a boil in a large pot over moderately high heat. Add ribs and boil for 10 minutes. Drain. Press a thick layer of barbecue rub on both sides of ribs if you like spicy food, or apply a thin layer of the rub to make it less spicy. Place the ribs on a preheated grill over moderately high heat and cook for 1 hour and 10 to 20 minutes or until a meat thermometer registers 150 to 155 degrees, turning the ribs every 8 minutes. The ribs can be served with the barbecue sauce on the side, or the ribs can be brushed with barbecue sauce on both sides the last 5 minutes of cooking time, with additional sauce served on the side.

Note Ask your butcher to remove any thick layers of fat and to cut away both the membrane and the flap, or skirt, on the underside of the ribs. The ribs will become dry if overcooked. When done, the meat should easily pull apart when you pull ribs in opposite directions or you should be able to easily insert a skewer between the bones. To tenderize the ribs, prick the meat between the bones with a fork before applying the rub.

Pork Tenderloin in Orange Marmalade Marinade

Marmalade is a preserve traditionally made with bitter oranges. The rind of the fruit is visually found in pieces throughout the preserve. Because of its intense flavor, it makes a marvelous marinade for pork, duck, and other meats. Serve with Green Bean and Mozzarella Salad (recipe below) and Savory Wild Rice (page 120).

Marinade

- ½ cup fresh orange juice
- ¼ cup orange marmalade
- 2 tablespoons minced cilantro leaves
- 2 cloves garlic, minced
- 1½ tablespoons extra virgin olive oil
- 1 teaspoon Sriracha hot chili sauce
- ½ teaspoon allspice
- ⅛ teaspoon salt
- 1 pork tenderloin (1½ pounds)

Green Bean and Mozzarella Salad

- 2 cups fresh green beans, cooked just until fork-tender
- 8 ounces mozzarella cheese, cut into ½-inch cubes
- ½ cup bottled spicy Italian dressing
- 6 plum tomatoes, sliced
- ⅓ cup chopped fresh basil
- ⅛ teaspoon freshly ground pepper

To Make Marinade Combine orange juice, marmalade, cilantro, garlic, olive oil, Sriracha hot chili sauce, allspice, and salt in a resealable plastic bag and blend. Add pork tenderloin and turn to coat all over. Refrigerate for several hours or overnight, turning pork at least once.

To Make Salad Combine green beans, mozzarella cheese, Italian dressing, tomatoes, basil, and pepper in a large bowl and blend well. Cover bowl and refrigerate the green bean and mozzarella salad for several hours or overnight. Stir before serving.

To Prepare Pork on an Outdoor Grill Place a drip pan in the center of the lower grate and place an equal number of briquettes on both sides. When coals are hot, remove the pork tenderloin from marinade, reserving the marinade. Place the pork tenderloin over coals on a grill coated with a nonstick vegetable spray. Sear the pork for 1 minute on each side. Move the pork tenderloin directly over the drip pan. Cover grill and cook for 20 to 30 minutes or until a meat thermometer registers 150 to 155 degrees, turning pork every 15 minutes and brushing with reserved marinade. Allow the pork to sit for 5 minutes before carving into thin slices.

To Prepare Pork on an Indoor Grill Remove pork tenderloin from marinade, reserving marinade. Place the pork tenderloin on a preheated grill over moderately high heat and cook for 30 to 40 minutes or until a meat thermometer registers 150 to 155 degrees, turning pork frequently and brushing with reserved marinade. Allow the pork to sit for 5 minutes before carving into thin slices.

Pork Tenderloin with Orange and Mustard Glaze

SERVES 8

Orange marmalade and Dijon mustard are truly a winning combination when used to glaze a pork tenderloin. Serve with Asparagus with Lemon Crumbs (recipe below).

Marinade
- ½ cup orange marmalade
- ¼ cup Dijon mustard
- 2 tablespoons Worcestershire sauce
- ½ teaspoon salt
- ½ teaspoon freshly ground pepper
- 1 pork tenderloin (3 pounds)

Asparagus with Lemon Crumbs
- 2½ pounds asparagus
- 8 tablespoons (1 stick) butter
- ½ cup bread crumbs
- Grated peel of 2 lemons
- Salt and freshly ground pepper, to taste

To Make Marinade Combine marmalade, Dijon mustard, Worcestershire sauce, salt, and pepper in a resealable plastic bag and blend. Add pork tenderloin and turn to coat all over. Refrigerate for several hours or overnight, turning pork at least once.

To Prepare Pork on an Outdoor Grill Place a drip pan in the center of the lower grate and place an equal number of briquettes on both sides. When coals are moderately hot, remove the pork tenderloin from marinade, reserving marinade. Place the pork tenderloin over coals on a grill coated with a nonstick vegetable spray.

Sear the pork for 1 minute on each side. Move the pork tenderloin directly over the drip pan. Cover grill and cook for 20 to 30 minutes or until a meat thermometer registers 150 to 155 degrees, turning pork every 15 minutes and brushing with reserved marinade. Allow the pork to sit for 5 minutes before carving into thin slices.

To Prepare Pork on an Indoor Grill Remove pork tenderloin from marinade, reserving marinade. Place the pork tenderloin on a preheated grill over moderately high heat and cook for 30 to 40 minutes or until a meat thermometer registers 150 to 155 degrees, turning pork frequently and brushing with reserved marinade. Allow the pork to sit for 5 minutes before carving into thin slices.

To Make Asparagus Immediately after the pork is removed from the grill, cook asparagus in a steamer for 7 minutes. Drain well.

While asparagus is cooking, melt butter in a small saucepan over moderate heat. Add bread crumbs and sauté for 2 minutes, stirring frequently. Add grated lemon peel and blend. Season with salt and pepper.

To Serve Arrange hot asparagus spears in a serving dish and sprinkle lemon crumbs on top.

Sherry-Marinated
Pork Tenderloin

SERVES 4

A pork tenderloin can be so easy to prepare. All it needs is a marinade—then you can sit back and relax and let the grill do the rest. Serve with Grilled Red Pepper Flan (page 350) and Mixed Baby Greens with Kiwi Fruit, Red Onion, and Praline Pecans (page 272).

¼ cup medium-dry sherry
2 tablespoons oyster sauce
2 tablespoons honey
1 tablespoon soy sauce
2 tablespoons minced cilantro
1 tablespoon chopped fresh ginger

1½ teaspoons oriental sesame oil
1 teaspoon Sriracha hot chili sauce
2 cloves garlic, minced
1 pork tenderloin (1½ pounds)

To Make Marinade Combine sherry, oyster sauce, honey, soy sauce, cilantro, ginger, sesame oil, Sriracha hot chili sauce, and garlic in a resealable plastic bag and blend. Add pork tenderloin and turn to coat all over. Refrigerate for several hours or overnight, turning pork at least once.

To Prepare Pork on an Outdoor Grill Remove pork tenderloin from marinade, reserving marinade. Over moderately hot coals, place pork on a grill coated with a nonstick vegetable spray. Sear pork for 1 minute on each side. Cover grill and cook for 18 to 24 minutes or until a meat thermometer registers 150 to 155 degrees, turning pork every 8 minutes and brushing with reserved marinade occasionally. Allow the pork to sit for 5 minutes before carving into thin slices.

To Prepare Pork on an Indoor Grill Remove pork tenderloin from marinade, reserving marinade. Place pork on a preheated grill over moderately high heat and cook pork for 30 to 40 minutes or until a meat thermometer registers 150 to 155 degrees, turning the pork every 10 minutes and brushing with reserved marinade occasionally. Allow the pork to sit for 5 minutes before carving into thin slices.

Southwestern Butterflied Pork Chops with Mango Salsa

SERVES 4

The Southwestern flavors in the marinade are highlighted in the pork when grilled and then are accented when topped with the cool sweetness of mango salsa. Serve with Sweet Potato Hash (page 82) and Grilled Polenta (page 322).

Marinade

½   cup fresh lime juice
¼   cup granulated sugar
1   tablespoon extra virgin olive oil
1   tablespoon dried thyme
1½ teaspoons cumin
1½ teaspoons freshly ground pepper
1   teaspoon cinnamon
1   teaspoon chili powder
1   teaspoon Mexican oregano
½   teaspoon salt
4   butterflied pork loin chops (6 ounces each) (see note)

Mango Salsa

1   mango, peeled, pitted, and diced
¼   cup chopped cilantro leaves
2   tablespoons fresh lime juice
2   tablespoons diced red onion
1   tablespoon minced jalapeño chile (see note)
1   tablespoon minced fresh ginger
½   teaspoon cumin

To Make Marinade Combine lime juice, sugar, olive oil, thyme, cumin, pepper, cinnamon, chili powder, oregano, and salt in a resealable plastic bag and blend. Add the pork chops and turn to coat all over. Refrigerate for several hours or overnight, turning the pork chops at least once.

To Make Salsa Combine mango, cilantro, lime juice, red onion, jalapeño chile, ginger, and cumin in a small dish and blend well. The mango salsa can be refrigerated in a covered container for 2 to 3 hours.

To Prepare Pork on an Outdoor Grill Remove pork chops from marinade. Over moderately hot coals, place the pork chops on a grill coated with a nonstick vegetable spray. Sear pork chops for 1 minute on each side. Cover the grill and cook for 4 to 5 minutes on each side or until a meat thermometer registers 150 to 155 degrees.

To Prepare Pork on an Indoor Grill Remove pork chops from marinade. Place them on a preheated grill over moderately high heat and cook for 20 to 30 minutes or until a meat thermometer registers 150 to 155 degrees, turning the pork chops every 7 minutes.

Note Butterflied pork chops are center-cut boneless loin chops that are sliced down the center, cut almost—but not completely—through. The halves are carefully opened flat to resemble a butterfly.

Note The seeds of a jalapeño chile are very hot. To avoid burning your skin, wear rubber or latex gloves when removing the seeds. Immediately wash the knife, cutting surface, and gloves when finished.

Pork Tenderloin with Honey and Mustard Glaze

SERVES 4

It is no wonder that honey and mustard are so often made together—the contrast in flavor and texture is remarkably delicious. Further testimony to this exquisite combination is in how well it glazes pork tenderloins, chicken, and seafood. Serve this pork tenderloin with Savory Wild Rice (page 120) and Mixed Baby Greens with Kiwi Fruit, Red Onion, and Praline Pecans (page 272).

¼ cup fresh lime juice
2 tablespoons honey
2 tablespoons extra virgin olive oil
2 tablespoons minced cilantro leaves
1 tablespoon Dijon mustard

1 tablespoon Sriracha hot chili sauce
1 teaspoon cumin
1 large clove garlic, minced
1 pork tenderloin (1½ pounds)

To Make Marinade Combine lime juice, honey, olive oil, cilantro, Dijon mustard, Sriracha hot chili sauce, cumin, and garlic in a resealable plastic bag and blend. Add pork tenderloin and turn to coat both sides. Refrigerate, covered, for several hours or overnight, turning pork at least once.

To Prepare Pork on an Outdoor Grill Remove the pork tenderloin from marinade, reserving marinade. Over moderately hot coals, place the pork tenderloin on a grill coated with a nonstick vegetable spray. Sear the pork for 1 minute on each side. Cover grill and cook for 18 to 24 minutes or until a meat thermometer registers 150 to 155 degrees, turning pork frequently and brushing with reserved marinade. Allow the pork to sit for 5 minutes before carving into thin slices.

To Prepare Pork on an Indoor Grill Remove the pork tenderloin from marinade, reserving marinade. Place the pork tenderloin on a preheated grill over moderately high heat and cook for 30 to 40 minutes or until a meat thermometer registers 150 to 155 degrees, turning pork frequently and brushing with reserved marinade. Allow the pork to sit for 5 minutes before carving into thin slices.

Teriyaki Butterflied Pork Chops

This fabulous teriyaki marinade can be used with poultry or beef or just about anytime you want a dominating flavor that is a showstopper. It really shines in this recipe! Serve with Grilled Pineapple Rings (page 330) and Saffron Rice (page 264).

¼ cup soy sauce
¼ cup rice wine vinegar
2 tablespoons medium-dry sherry
1 tablespoon canola oil
2 teaspoons oriental sesame oil

6 cloves garlic, chopped
1 ½ inch-thick piece fresh ginger, peeled, and coarsely chopped
4 butterflied pork loin chops (6 ounces each) (see note)

To Make Marinade Combine soy sauce, rice wine vinegar, sherry, canola oil, sesame oil, garlic, and ginger in a resealable plastic bag and blend. Add pork chops and turn to coat all over. Refrigerate for several hours or overnight, turning pork at least once.

To Prepare Pork on an Outdoor Grill Remove pork chops from marinade. Over moderately hot coals, place the pork chops on a grill coated with a nonstick vegetable spray. Sear the pork chops for 1 minute on each side. Cover the grill and cook for 4 to 5 minutes on each side or until a meat thermometer registers 150 to 155 degrees.

To Prepare Pork on an Indoor Grill Remove pork chops from marinade. Place them on a preheated grill over moderately high heat and cook for 20 to 30 minutes or until a meat thermometer registers 150 to 155 degrees, turning the pork chops every 7 to 10 minutes.

Note Butterflied pork chops are center-cut boneless loin chops that are sliced down the center, cut almost—but not completely—through. The halves are carefully opened flat to resemble a butterfly.

Spicy Butterflied Pork Chops

SERVES 4

Spicy pork chops are certain to become one of your favorite quick-and-easy dishes. The marinade is so easy to put together and adds a wonderful flavor to the pork. The pork chops are delicious served with Cranberry Chutney (page 74) or topped with Mango Salsa (page 232).

3	tablespoons soy sauce	1	tablespoon freshly ground
1	tablespoon firmly packed dark		pepper
	brown sugar	4	butterflied pork loin chops
2	cloves garlic, minced		(6 ounces each) (see note)
1	tablespoon coriander		

To Make Marinade Combine soy sauce, brown sugar, garlic, coriander, and pepper in a resealable plastic bag and blend. Add the pork chops and turn to coat all over. Refrigerate for 1 to 2 hours or overnight, turning the pork chops at least once.

To Prepare Pork on an Outdoor Grill Remove pork chops from marinade. Over moderately hot coals, place the pork chops on a grill coated with a nonstick vegetable spray. Sear the pork chops for 1 minute on each side. Cover grill and cook for 4 to 5 minutes on each side or until a meat thermometer registers 150 to 155 degrees.

To Prepare Pork on an Indoor Grill Remove pork chops from marinade. Place them on a preheated grill over moderately high heat and cook for 20 to 30 minutes or until a meat thermometer registers 150 to 155 degrees, turning the pork chops every 7 minutes.

Note Butterflied pork chops are center-cut boneless loin chops that are sliced down the center, cut almost—but not completely—through. The halves are carefully opened flat to resemble a butterfly.

5

SEAFOOD

The thought of grilled seafood prompts visions of fresh-caught fish prepared on a shoreside grill. While you may not have a trout stream running through your backyard or kitchen, the abundance and variety of fresh seafood at most markets makes these denizens of the deep a wonderful choice for grilling.

FRESHWATER AND SALTWATER FISH

Fish cooked on a grill is a real treat. Not only does the smoky aroma from a grill imbue fish with added flavor, but a real bonus is that the fish remains succulent and tender. Moreover, fish is a healthy way to dine. It is renowned for being low in fat and cholesterol yet high in several critical vitamins and minerals. Another positive feature is that many fish have a high content of health-promoting omega-3 fatty acids. This is especially true of salmon, tuna, mackerel, and sardines.

Fish is quick and easy to grill, but you must avoid overcooking it. A good rule of thumb for an outdoor grill is that a ¾-inch-thick serving of fish usually requires eight minutes total cooking time, and a one-inch portion requires ten minutes or less. The time required for indoor grilling will vary, depending on the type of equipment you use, but it is generally longer. To check for doneness, insert a fork into the thickest part of the fish and determine if the flesh is flaky and no longer translucent. If using a meat thermometer, the fish should have an internal temperature of 140 degrees.

With such an overwhelming abundance of fish available to us, I have chosen to discuss a few specific examples that are exceptionally delicious when grilled. Using the list as a starting point, I hope you will explore your local seafood purveyor and experiment with many other varieties.

COD

Cod is a mild-flavored, lean, firm white-fleshed fish that is available year-round. Because of its abundance and good quality, it also known as the "beef of the sea" or "the poor man's friend." The best-known members of the cod family are the haddock and pollock. Cod is sold as filets or steaks.

ESCOLAR

This fish has a white, meaty flesh with a very mild flavor. Escolar is also high in omega-3 fatty acids. Because of the similarity in taste and texture, sea bass is a good substitution in recipes calling for escolare. Escolar is sold as a filet.

FLOUNDER

Flounder is similar to sole, both being a lean, firm white-fleshed fish with a subtly sweet flavor. It is the name for combined three families of flatfish. Flounder is sold whole or as a filet.

GROUPER

The grouper is a member of the sea bass family. It is a meaty, dense, firm white-fleshed fish with a very mild flavor. It is available year-round and is sold as steaks or filets.

HALIBUT

Halibut is a mild-flavored, white-fleshed flatfish. The three common varieties are the Pacific (Alaska or northern halibut), Atlantic (called chicken halibut if it weighs less than 20 pounds), and California (southern or bastard halibut). The majority of halibut available is the Pacific variety. Don't even think about buying an entire fish, since an adult can weigh up to 700 pounds. For this reason, halibut is usually sold as steaks.

MACKEREL

Mackerel is a soft, gray or pink firm-fleshed fish. It is related to the tuna, which can be substituted in recipes when mackerel is unavailable. It is more oily than most other fish and is rich in omega-3 fatty acids. The best-known mackerels are the Atlantic mackerel (Boston mackerel), Pacific mackerel (chub, American, or blue mackerel), Spanish mackerel, and king mackerel. Mackerel is sold whole or as filets.

MAHI MAHI

Mahi mahi, otherwise known as dolphinfish, is a sweet-flavored, firm, pink-fleshed fish that turns white when grilled. Dolphinfish is not to be confused with the seagoing mammal, the dolphin. If mahi mahi is unavailable, snapper, flounder, halibut, and catfish are good substitutes. Mahi mahi is sold as filets.

MARLIN

Marlin is a prized fish with lean, firm flesh. It has a mild flavor and is similar in taste to swordfish. Although a marlin can weigh as much as 2,000 pounds, the best-tasting selections come from those that are 150 pounds or less. Marlin is sold as steaks.

MONKFISH

A monkfish is one of the ugliest fish, yet its firm, white flesh is exceptionally sweet and delicious, very similar to that of lobster. Monkfish is sold as filets.

RED SNAPPER

With 200 species of snapper, only one species can correctly be called red snapper. The red snapper, with its bright red skin, is a lean, firm white-fleshed fish with a sweet flavor. It is sold whole or as filets or steaks.

ROCKFISH

Rockfish is a lean, mild-flavored, white-fleshed fish. It is also known as tilefish on the East Coast. It is found in rocky coasts and rocky sea bottoms. Rockfish is sold as filets.

SALMON

Salmon is a firm, pink-fleshed fish with a delicate, butter-smooth flavor and texture. It is sold as either Atlantic salmon or Pacific salmon, the former being the tastier, especially if caught in Scotland or Ireland. Pacific salmon are usually harvested wild, so they are available only during the spring and summer months. Among the five species of Pacific salmon, the king salmon is the biggest and best tasting. It is excellent when grilled. Sockeye salmon and silver salmon are also good on the grill, but chum and pink salmon are usually not prepared this way. Salmon is sold as steaks or filets.

SEA BASS

Sea bass has a white, meaty flesh with a very sweet flavor. It is found in the Pacific Ocean and is very similar to the grouper or escolar. Sea bass is sold as filets or steaks.

SHARK

Shark is a mild-flavored, dense-textured, white-fleshed fish found in the Atlantic and Pacific Oceans. The mako, thresher, soupfin, and angel shark are popular on the Pacific Coast, while the mako is the most highly regarded variety on the Atlantic Coast. Shark is similar in taste to halibut and swordfish and is sold as filets or steaks.

SOLE

There are five species of true sole found in the U.S. Atlantic, but none are as tasty as those from Europe. Dover sole, found in the Atlantic off the shores of England, is considered the best because of its firm-textured, white flesh and its delicate flavor. Sole is sold whole or as filets.

SWORDFISH

Swordfish is a deep-sea fish with a firm, fine-textured white flesh and a subtle beef flavor. Its upper jaw and snout are flat and shaped like a sword, hence its name. If swordfish is unavailable, you can substitute shark, tuna, or salmon. It is sold as steaks.

TROUT

Trout is available year-round, thanks to the proliferation of trout farms. As is true of salmon grown in fish hatcheries, wild trout are considered by many to be more flavorful. Practically speaking, all trout available at the market is hatchery-raised, so if your taste runs to wild trout, you'll have to catch it yourself. Trout has a soft, white flesh. It is sold whole and grilled that way.

TUNA

Tuna is a mild-flavored, firm, fatty, deep red–fleshed fish found in the Mediterranean Sea and also in the warm waters of the Pacific, Indian, and Atlantic Oceans. Among the more familiar tuna are the yellowfin, bigeye, blackfin, bluefin, and Atlantic bonito. Tuna is sold as steaks.

HELPFUL GUIDELINES FOR SELECTING WHOLE FISH

- To determine the freshness of a whole fish, look for eyes that are clear, bright, and bulging. Any fish with cloudy or sunken eyes should not be purchased.
- Feel the flesh to be sure that it is firm to the touch and resilient.
- Avoid fish with brown or gray gills. Look for gills that are bright red.
- Fish should have a sea smell rather than a fish odor.
- Look for fish with firm, glossy scales.

HELPFUL GUIDELINES FOR SELECTING FILETS AND STEAKS

- The flesh of the fish should be moist and have a glossy sheen. Avoid any fish with brown edges.

- Fish should have a translucent appearance.
- The fish should have a sea smell rather than a fish odor.
- The flesh should be firm and the edges clean and even.

HELPFUL GUIDELINES FOR PREPARING FISH

- All fish should be kept refrigerated in the coldest part of the refrigerator.
- When fish is marinated in a mixture that contains lemon juice, the marinating time should be no more than 30 minutes. If marinated longer than this, the lemon juice will initiate a chemical change in the fish similar to cooking.
- Before putting the grate on an indoor or outdoor grill, coat it with a nonstick vegetable spray or oil.
- Do not turn fish with a fork, since piercing it might allow natural juices to run out.
- When calculating grilling time, remember that fish will continue to cook for a couple of minutes after it has been removed from the grill.
- Do not overcook tuna, or it will become dry. It should be rare to medium-rare.
- Fish filets or steaks that are cut at least 1 inch to 1½ inches thick tend to remain more moist and succulent when grilled.

SHELLFISH

Shellfish are aquatic animals with an external covering consisting of a shell or an interior shell component. One group, the crustaceans, have a hard external shell, a segmented body, and two jointed legs. Their flesh is white, firm, and sweet, with a hint of fishy flavor. Lobsters and shrimp are examples of crustaceans. The other group, mollusks, are found both in the sea and on land. Mollusks are either univalves, bivalves, or cephalopods. Univalves have one shell, either spiral shaped or ear shaped, while the bivalve has two shells. Cephalopods carry their shells within the flesh of their bodies, such as the long pen inside the squid or the hard beak of an octopus.

Shellfish cook quickly on both an outdoor and an indoor grill. When the flesh of crustaceans, such as a lobster, changes from translucent to opaque, it is done. Mollusks, cooked in their shell, are done when the shells open. If cooked without their shell, mollusks should be considered done when the meat becomes firm and opaque.

CLAMS

Clams are bivalve mollusks with a two-part, hinged shell. Hard-shell clams (or quahogs, as they are called on the East Coast) are most abundant on the East Coast. The three kinds of hard-shell clams found on the East Coast are the littleneck, cherrystone, and chowder. The Pacific Coast has Pacific littlenecks and Manilas. Soft-shell clams have thin shells that do not completely close because of a neck of flesh that reaches out beyond the edges of the shell. The steamer is the best-known soft-shell clam on the East Coast, while razor clams and geoducks are Pacific varieties. The geoduck is so large that steaks large enough to grill can be gotten from a single clam.

CRABS

Rock, stone, and blue crabs are found on the East Coast, the Dungeness variety is found on the West Coast, and the king crab comes from Alaska. Look for large crabs that are active, with claws and limbs intact. They turn bright orange when cooked, and their meat is very tender, flaky, and sweet.

LOBSTER

The best-known lobsters are from the North Atlantic waters of Europe and America. They should be active, with claws and limbs intact. Lobsters that are alive until just before grilling taste the best. They turn bright orange when cooked, and their meat is very sweet.

MUSSELS

Like clams, mussels are bivalve mollusks. Fresh mussels should close up securely when tapped and should feel somewhat heavy. The shells should be scrubbed with a brush and the beard (fibers that hang out of the shell) pulled out before grilling.

OYSTERS

Of the many different kinds of oysters, the Tomales Bay, Walapa, and bluepoint are best known. They are graded according to their size. Look for oysters with tightly closed shells. If they do not close when tapped, it is an indication that the oyster is dead and should be discarded. Oysters should be scrubbed with a brush and rinsed under water before grilling.

SCALLOPS

Sea scallops and bay scallops are another form of bivalve mollusk. As the scallop swims, it snaps its shell together. As a result of this constant motion, the muscle that controls the shell becomes very large. This muscle, called the "eye," is the white, plump part of the scallop that is eaten. It has a sweet, nutty flavor. Bay scallops are considerably smaller and more tender than sea scallops, but unfortunately they are less suited to being cooked on the grill, unless carefully skewered and exposed to a brief cooking time.

SHRIMP AND PRAWNS

The term *prawn* officially refers to a species of crustacean separate from shrimp, but it has come to be used to describe any jumbo shrimp. Therefore, there is no difference between shrimp and prawns at the supermarket, except their size. Both jumbo and medium-size shrimp are excellent when grilled, whereas smaller varieties are more prone to overcooking and drying. Shrimp have a very sweet flesh. Look for firm, moist shrimp with tight-fitting shells. Avoid any shrimp with black discoloration along the head or belly or that have an ammonia odor. Shrimp should also be deveined before cooking. This is done by using a sharp knife to make a shallow cut down the back and then removing the vein. Shrimp can be grilled with or without their shells. They turn bright orange when fully cooked.

Orange-Glazed Sea Bass

This glaze is one of my favorites to use on seafood. It can be made several days ahead and used as needed. Serve with Saffron Rice (page 264) and Mixed Baby Greens with Kiwi Fruit, Red Onion, and Praline Pecans (page 272).

2   sea bass filets
    (12 ounces each)
    Orange Glaze (page 210)

To Prepare Sea Bass on an Outdoor Grill Brush one side of each sea bass filet with orange glaze. Over moderately hot coals, place sea bass filets, glazed side down, on a grill coated with a non-stick vegetable spray. Brush tops of filets with orange glaze and cover grill. Cook for 6 minutes. Turn sea bass filet over and brush with orange glaze. Cook an additional 6 to 8 minutes or until flesh is no longer translucent when a knife is inserted into the thickest part, brushing occasionally with glaze. Divide each sea bass filet in half.

To Prepare Sea Bass on an Indoor Grill Brush one side of each sea bass filet with orange glaze. Place sea bass filets, glazed side down, on a preheated grill over moderately high heat. Brush tops of filets with orange glaze and cook for 15 minutes. Turn sea bass filet over and brush with orange glaze. Cook an additional 15 minutes or until sea bass is no longer translucent when a knife is inserted into the thickest part, brushing occasionally with glaze. Divide each sea bass filet in half.

Basil-Coated Mahi Mahi with Lemon Butter

Mahi mahi is the Hawaiian name for the dolphinfish. Because the dolphinfish is commonly confused with Flipper, our favorite aquatic mammal (a dolphin), the Hawaiian name is preferred to the English term. You can also use this recipe with other firm-fleshed fish, such as grouper, sea bass, or halibut, if mahi mahi is not available. Serve with Zucchini and Yellow Squash Soufflé (page 302).

Lemon Butter

8 tablespoons (1 stick) butter, at room temperature
¼ teaspoon freshly ground pepper
2 tablespoons fresh lemon juice

Basil Coating

2 tablespoons extra virgin olive oil
2 tablespoons minced fresh basil
4 mahi mahi filets (6 ounces each)

To Make Lemon Butter Combine butter and pepper in a small dish. Add lemon juice, a drop at a time, and blend well. Cover dish and set aside at room temperature.

To Make Basil Coating Combine olive oil and basil in a non-metal dish. Add mahi mahi, one at a time, and coat both sides. Cover dish and refrigerate for 30 minutes.

To Prepare Mahi Mahi on an Outdoor Grill Over moderately hot coals, place mahi mahi on a grill coated with a nonstick vegetable spray. Cover grill and cook for 10 to 12 minutes or until mahi mahi is no longer translucent when a knife is inserted into the thickest part.

To Prepare Mahi Mahi on an Indoor Grill Place mahi mahi on a preheated grill over moderately high heat and cook for 15 minutes on each side or until mahi mahi is no longer translucent when a knife is inserted into the thickest part.

To Serve Place a mahi mahi filet on each of four dinner plates and immediately top with a spoonful of lemon butter. Garnish each serving with a sprig of fresh basil leaves.

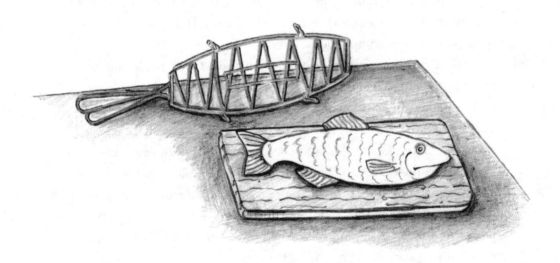

Shrimp Kebabs

Although these shrimp kebabs are easy to prepare, you will be pleasantly surprised at how appealing to the eye and delectable in taste they are. Serve with Jasmine Rice (page 158) and a fresh fruit salad.

¼	cup rice wine	1½	pounds medium shrimp, peeled and deveined
¼	cup mushroom soy sauce (or soy sauce)	8	pineapple chunks
2	tablespoons canola oil	8	shiitake mushrooms
1	teaspoon ground ginger	1	red bell pepper, cut into 8 pieces
1	clove garlic, minced		

To Make Marinade Combine rice wine, mushroom soy sauce, canola oil, ground ginger, and garlic in a resealable plastic bag and blend. Add shrimp and turn to coat all over. Refrigerate for 2 to 3 hours, turning shrimp at least once.

To Prepare Kebabs on an Outdoor Grill Soak bamboo skewers in water for 30 minutes or more. Alternate shrimp, pineapple, shiitake mushrooms, and red pepper on skewers and place over moderately hot coals on a grill coated with a nonstick vegetable spray (see note). Cover grill and cook for 3 minutes on each side.

To Prepare Kebabs on an Indoor Grill Soak bamboo skewers in water for 30 minutes or more. Alternate shrimp, pineapple, shiitake mushrooms, and red pepper on skewers and place on a preheated grill over moderate heat (see note). Cook them for 15 minutes, turning shrimp every 4 minutes.

Note The skewers will be easier to turn if you thread the shrimp, vegetables, and fruit onto two bamboo skewers that are parallel to each other, about 1 inch apart.

Grilled Butterflied Shrimp Kebabs

The Sriracha hot chili sauce in the marinade makes these shrimp kebabs exceptionally spicy and flavorful. Serve with Grilled Pineapple Rings (page 330) and Saffron Rice (page 264).

½ cup mushroom soy sauce or soy sauce

¼ cup granulated sugar

2 tablespoons Sriracha hot chili sauce

2 teaspoons ground ginger

1 teaspoon rice wine

1½ pounds medium shrimp, peeled and deveined

To Make Marinade Combine mushroom soy sauce, sugar, Sriracha hot chili sauce, ground ginger, and rice wine in a resealable plastic bag and blend.

Using a sharp knife, make a slit along the back of each shrimp, cutting almost through the shrimp. Gently open the shrimp so that when it lies flat it resembles a butterfly.

Gently combine marinade and shrimp in a nonmetal dish. Turn shrimp to coat both sides. Cover dish and refrigerate for 1 to 2 hours.

To Prepare Shrimp on an Outdoor Grill Soak bamboo skewers in water for 30 minutes or more. Thread the shrimp on skewers and place over moderately hot coals on a grill coated with a nonstick vegetable spray. Cover grill and cook for 3 minutes on each side.

To Prepare Shrimp on an Indoor Grill Soak bamboo skewers in water for 30 minutes or more. Thread the shrimp on skewers. Place them on a preheated grill over moderate heat and cook for 15 minutes, turning shrimp every 4 minutes.

Southwestern Salmon with Corn Salsa

Coating salmon filets with a savory rub before grilling adds a hint of the Southwest. When topped with Corn Salsa (recipe below), it is the ultimate combination. I like to make extra corn salsa to spoon over grilled hot dogs or to serve with other Southwestern dishes.

Corn Salsa

- 3 cups cooked corn kernels (about 4 large ears of corn)
- 1 red bell pepper, diced
- ½ cup diced red onion
- 3 tablespoons chopped cilantro leaves
- 2 jalapeño chiles, seeded and minced (see note)
- 2 tablespoons fresh lime juice
- 1 tablespoon extra virgin olive oil
- ½ teaspoon sherry vinegar
- ¼ teaspoon salt
- ¼ teaspoon freshly ground pepper

Rub

- 2 tablespoons dark brown sugar
- 1 tablespoon cumin
- 2 teaspoons coriander
- 2 teaspoons dry mustard
- 1 teaspoon freshly ground pepper
- ½ teaspoon salt
- ½ teaspoon cayenne
- 4 salmon filets (6 ounces each), skin removed

To Make Corn Salsa Combine corn, red pepper, red onion, cilantro, jalapeño chiles, lime juice, olive oil, sherry vinegar, salt, and pepper in a medium bowl and blend well. Refrigerate the corn salsa, covered, for several hours.

To Make Rub Combine brown sugar, cumin, coriander, dry mustard, pepper, salt, and cayenne in a small bowl and blend. Press rub on both sides of each salmon filet.

To Prepare Salmon on an Outdoor Grill Over moderately hot coals, place salmon filets on a grill coated with a nonstick vegetable spray. Cover grill and cook for 10 minutes or until salmon is no longer red when a knife is inserted into the thickest part.

To Prepare Salmon on an Indoor Grill Place salmon filets on a preheated grill over moderately high heat and cook for 15 minutes on each side or until salmon is no longer red when a knife is inserted into the thickest part.

To Serve Place a salmon filet on each of four dinner plates and spoon some corn salsa over the top or to the side of each filet. Garnish with a sprig of cilantro.

Note The seeds of jalapeño chiles are very hot. To avoid burning your skin, wear rubber or latex gloves when removing the seeds. Immediately wash the knife, cutting surface, and gloves when finished.

Papaya-Glazed Salmon

SERVES 6

Papayas are known for being rich in antioxidants, and I can't think of a more delicious way to incorporate them into your diet than this recipe! The papaya glaze is excellent on other seafood as well. Serve with Saffron Rice (page 264).

Glaze

1 papaya, peeled and seeded (see note)
¼ cup papaya nectar (see note)
¼ cup Dijon mustard
2 tablespoons honey
2 tablespoons fresh lime juice
1 teaspoon Sriracha hot chili sauce
  Dash of salt

Basil Coating

2 tablespoons extra virgin olive oil
2 tablespoons minced fresh basil
  Salt and freshly ground pepper, to taste
6 salmon filets (6 ounces each), skin removed

Papaya slices, for garnish

To Make Glaze Place papaya in the work bowl of a food processor fitted with a metal blade and process until pureed. Add papaya nectar, Dijon mustard, honey, lime juice, Sriracha hot chili sauce, and salt and process until smooth.

Transfer papaya mixture to a heavy, medium saucepan and place over moderate heat. Bring to a simmer. Reduce heat to moderately low and cook for 30 minutes, stirring occasionally. Allow papaya glaze to come to room temperature. Transfer papaya glaze to a covered container and refrigerate for several hours or overnight.

To Make Basil Coating Combine olive oil, basil, salt, and pepper in a shallow dish. Press both sides of each salmon filet in the mixture, making sure salmon filets are completely coated.

To Prepare Salmon on an Outdoor Grill Over moderately hot coals, place salmon filets on a grill coated with a nonstick vegetable spray and brush with a thick layer of papaya glaze. Cover grill and cook for 10 minutes or until salmon is no longer red when a knife is inserted into the thickest part.

To Prepare Salmon on an Indoor Grill Place salmon on a preheated grill over moderately high heat and cook for 15 minutes. Turn salmon filets over to the other side and brush with a thick layer of papaya glaze. Cook an additional 15 minutes or until salmon is no longer red when a knife is inserted into the thickest part.

To Serve Place a salmon filet on each of six dinner plates. Garnish each salmon filet with 2 thin slices of papaya and a sprig of basil or watercress.

Note For a slight variation, try a mango and mango nectar in place of the papaya and papaya nectar.

Cumin-Marinated Escolar Kebabs with Banana Salsa

SERVES 4

Although this marinade recipe works very well with swordfish or other fleshy fish, I prefer the flavor of escolar. The addition of Banana Salsa (recipe below) brings out its full, rich flavor. Serve with Sweet Potato Hash (page 82).

Banana Salsa

- 2 bananas, diced
- ½ cup minced red bell pepper
- 2 tablespoons minced cilantro leaves
- 2 tablespoons fresh lime juice
- 1 teaspoon honey
- 2 jalapeño chiles, seeded and minced (see note)

Marinade

- ½ cup rice vinegar
- 3 tablespoons soy sauce
- 1 tablespoon dry white wine
- ¾ teaspoon cumin
- ⅛ teaspoon salt
- 2 escolar filets (12 ounces each), cut into 1¼-inch cubes

Kebabs

- 1 red bell pepper, cut into 8 pieces
- 4 green onions, cut into 8 pieces
- 8 shiitake mushrooms, stems removed

To Make Banana Salsa Combine bananas, red pepper, cilantro, lime juice, honey, and jalapeño chiles in a dish and blend well. Cover and refrigerate banana salsa for 1 to 2 hours.

To Make Marinade Combine rice vinegar, soy sauce, wine, cumin, and salt in a resealable plastic bag and blend. Add cubed escolar and gently turn to coat all over. Refrigerate for 30 to 60 minutes.

To Prepare Kebabs on an Outdoor Grill Soak bamboo skewers in water for 30 minutes or more. Alternate escolar, red pepper, green onions, and shiitake mushrooms on skewers. Over moderately hot coals, place escolar kebabs on a grill coated with a nonstick vegetable spray (see note). Cover grill and cook for 5 to 6 minutes on each side or until escolar is no longer translucent when a knife is inserted into the thickest part.

To Prepare Kebabs on an Indoor Grill Soak bamboo skewers in water for 30 minutes or more. Alternate escolar, red pepper, green onions, and shiitake mushrooms on skewers (see note). Place escolar kebabs on a preheated grill over moderately high heat and cook for 10 minutes on each side or until escolar is no longer translucent when a knife is inserted into the thickest part.

To Serve Arrange cumin-marinated escolar kebabs on four dinner plates and place banana salsa beside each serving. Garnish the banana salsa with a sprig of cilantro.

Note The seeds of jalapeño chiles are very hot. To avoid burning your skin, wear rubber or latex gloves when removing the seeds. Immediately wash the knife, cutting surface, and gloves when finished.

Note The skewers will be easier to turn if you thread the escolar and vegetables on two bamboo skewers that are parallel to each other, about 1 inch apart.

Grilled Halibut Kebabs

Halibut is the largest flatfish of the sea. Despite its enormous size, it has a very rich flavor. Serve these halibut kebabs with Lemon Rice and Capers (page 266) and Lemon-Glazed Carrots (page 218).

¼ cup Dijon mustard
4 tablespoons butter, melted
2 tablespoons honey
2 tablespoons fresh lemon juice
⅛ teaspoon salt
⅛ teaspoon freshly ground pepper

6 halibut filets (5 ounces each), cut into 1¼-inch cubes
1 red bell pepper, cut into 8 pieces
8 fresh mushrooms
1 star fruit, cut out into 8 stars

To Make Marinade Combine Dijon mustard, butter, honey, lemon juice, salt, and pepper in a resealable plastic bag and blend. Add cubed halibut and turn to coat all over. Refrigerate for 30 minutes, turning halibut at least once.

To Prepare Kebabs on an Outdoor Grill Soak bamboo skewers in water for 30 minutes or more. Remove halibut from marinade, reserving marinade. Alternate halibut, red pepper, mushrooms, and star fruit on skewers (see note). Over moderately hot coals, place halibut kebabs on a grill coated with a nonstick vegetable spray. Cover grill and cook for 8 to 10 minutes or until halibut is no longer translucent when a knife is inserted into flesh, turning skewers every 4 minutes and brushing with reserved marinade.

To Prepare Kebabs on an Indoor Grill Soak bamboo skewers in water for 30 minutes or more. Remove halibut from marinade, reserving marinade. Alternate halibut, red pepper, mushrooms, and star fruit on skewers. Place halibut kebabs on a preheated grill over moderate heat and cook for 25 to 30 minutes or until halibut is no longer translucent when a knife is inserted into flesh, turning skewers every 4 minutes and brushing with reserved marinade (see note).

Note The skewers will be easier to turn if you thread the halibut, vegetables, and star fruit on two bamboo skewers that are parallel to each other, about 1 inch apart.

Seafood

Tuna with Grilled Red Pepper Rouille

SERVES 4

Traditional rouille is a red pepper sauce. However, when it is made with grilled red peppers, it becomes much more flavorful. This rouille would complement most seafood, but it is exceptional on tuna. Serve with Grilled Bermuda Onions (page 331).

Grilled Red Pepper Rouille
- 2 red bell peppers
- 2 cloves garlic, chopped
- ⅛ teaspoon saffron threads
- 2 tablespoons mayonnaise
- ¼ teaspoon salt
- ⅛ teaspoon cayenne

Marinade
- ½ cup fresh lemon juice
- 1½ tablespoons extra virgin olive oil
- 2 teaspoons oregano
- ½ teaspoon crushed red pepper
- 2 cloves garlic, minced
- 4 yellowfin tuna steaks (6 ounces each)

To Prepare Peppers on an Outdoor Grill Over moderately hot coals, place the red peppers on a grill coated with a nonstick vegetable spray. Cover grill and cook for 14 to 20 minutes or until skins are charred all over, turning the peppers as skins blacken. Once grilled, place the peppers in a plastic bag and allow to steam for 15 minutes. When they are cool enough to handle, peel away the skins and remove the tops and seeds (do not rinse the peppers).

To Prepare Peppers on an Indoor Grill Place the red peppers on a preheated grill over high heat and cook for 20 to 30 minutes or until skins are charred all over, turning the peppers as skins blacken. Once grilled, place the peppers in a plastic bag and allow to steam for 15 minutes. When they are cool enough to handle, peel away the skins and remove the tops and seeds (do not rinse the peppers).

To Make Rouille Combine garlic, 1½ tablespoons cold water, and saffron in a small saucepan over low heat and cook for 2 minutes.

In the work bowl of a food processor fitted with a metal blade, process grilled red peppers until pureed. Add saffron mixture and process until blended. Add mayonnaise, salt, and cayenne and process with on/off pulses until just blended. Transfer grilled red pepper rouille to a dish, cover, and refrigerate for several hours.

To Make Marinade Combine lemon juice, olive oil, oregano, crushed red pepper, and garlic in a resealable plastic bag and blend. Add tuna steaks and turn to coat all over. Refrigerate for 30 minutes, turning tuna at least once.

To Prepare Tuna on an Outdoor Grill Remove tuna steaks from marinade. Over moderately hot coals, place the tuna steaks on a grill coated with a nonstick vegetable spray. Cover grill and cook for 5 minutes on each side or until tuna is no longer red when a knife is inserted into the thickest part.

To Prepare Tuna on an Indoor Grill Remove tuna steaks from marinade. Place them on a preheated grill over moderately high heat and cook for 15 minutes on first side and 12 to 15 minutes on other side or until tuna is no longer red when a knife is inserted into the thickest part.

To Serve Place a tuna steak on each of four dinner plates and spoon some grilled red pepper rouille on top of each tuna steak. Garnish with a sprig of parsley or watercress.

Grilled Salmon with Basil and Tomato Sauce

SERVES 4

This eye-appealing dish features fresh basil, which is used both to add flavor to the tomato sauce and to coat the salmon. The richly flavored red sauce, spooned over the top of the basil-speckled salmon, looks and tastes spectacular! The sauce also nicely complements grilled tuna and swordfish. Serve with Saffron Rice (recipe below) and Grilled Artichokes (page 332).

Basil and Tomato Sauce

3½ tablespoons butter

4 ripe plum tomatoes, peeled, seeded, and coarsely chopped

¼ teaspoon granulated sugar

1 large clove garlic, minced

1 tablespoon chopped fresh basil

¼ teaspoon freshly ground pepper

⅛ teaspoon salt

Saffron Rice

2 tablespoons canola oil

1 medium Vidalia onion or other sweet onion, diced

1 clove garlic, minced

1 cup long-grain rice

1 can (14½ ounces) chicken broth

2 teaspoons saffron threads

½ teaspoon freshly ground pepper

¼ teaspoon salt

1 cup frozen peas and carrots, defrosted

Basil Coating

2 tablespoons extra virgin olive oil

2 tablespoons coarsely chopped fresh basil

¼ teaspoon salt

¼ teaspoon freshly ground pepper

4 salmon filets (6 ounces each), skin removed

To Make Sauce Melt 1½ tablespoons butter in a medium saucepan over moderately low heat. Add tomatoes and sugar and cook for 15 minutes, stirring occasionally. Add garlic and remaining 2 tablespoons butter, 1 tablespoon at a time, and cook for 3 to 4 minutes or until sauce thickens, stirring frequently. Add basil, pepper, and salt and blend well. Loosely cover the basil and tomato sauce with a piece of aluminum foil and allow it to come to room temperature before serving.

To Make Saffron Rice Heat canola oil in a medium saucepan over moderate heat for 2 minutes. Add onion and garlic and sauté for 5 minutes, stirring occasionally. Add rice and sauté for 3 minutes, stirring occasionally. Add chicken broth, saffron, pepper, and salt and bring to a boil. Boil for 5 minutes. Reduce heat to low, cover saucepan, and cook for 15 minutes. Distribute the peas and carrots on top of rice, cover, and cook an additional 5 minutes or until vegetables are fork-tender. Blend well. Cover and keep warm at room temperature.

To Make Basil Coating Combine olive oil, basil, salt, and pepper in a dish. Add the salmon and turn to coat all over.

To Prepare Salmon on an Outdoor Grill Over moderately hot coals, place salmon filets on a grill coated with a nonstick vegetable spray. Cover grill and cook for 10 minutes or until salmon is no longer red when a knife is inserted into the thickest part.

To Prepare Salmon on an Indoor Grill Place salmon on a preheated grill over moderately high heat and cook for 15 minutes on each side or until salmon is no longer red when a knife is inserted into the thickest part.

To Serve Arrange a salmon filet off to one side on each of four dinner plates. Spoon a vertical stripe of the basil and tomato sauce over the salmon and place a serving of saffron rice beside the salmon. Garnish the salmon with two baby basil leaves.

Joyce's Pecan-Crusted Salmon

The original recipe for this delightful salmon entree required baking the fish in a 450-degree oven for 10 to 12 minutes. However, cooking this fabulous salmon on the grill is equally as delicious. Serve with Lemon Rice and Capers (recipe below).

Lemon Rice and Capers

3   tablespoons butter
1   cup long-grain rice
1   can (14½ ounces) chicken broth
½   teaspoon freshly ground pepper
¼   teaspoon salt
1   tablespoon fresh lemon juice
2   tablespoons minced parsley
2   teaspoons capers

Pecan Coating

2   tablespoons Dijon mustard
2   tablespoons butter, melted
1½ tablespoons honey
1   teaspoon fresh lemon juice
¼   cup bread crumbs
¼   cup finely chopped pecans
2   teaspoons minced parsley
4   salmon filets (6 ounces each), skin removed

To Make Rice Melt butter in a medium saucepan over moderate heat. Add rice and sauté for 5 minutes, stirring occasionally. Add chicken broth, pepper, and salt and bring to a boil. Reduce heat to low, cover, and cook for 25 minutes or until all the chicken broth is absorbed. Add lemon juice, parsley, and capers and blend well. Cover and keep rice warm at room temperature until ready to serve.

To Make Pecan Coating Combine Dijon mustard, butter, honey, and lemon juice in a small bowl and blend well. Combine bread crumbs, pecans, and parsley in another small bowl and blend well.

Brush Dijon mustard mixture over each salmon filet and press pecan mixture on top of each filet.

To Prepare Salmon on an Outdoor Grill Over moderately hot coals, place salmon filets on a grill coated with a nonstick vegetable spray. Cover grill and cook for 10 to 12 minutes or until salmon is no longer red when a knife is inserted into the thickest part.

To Prepare Salmon on an Indoor Grill Place salmon on a preheated grill over moderately high heat and cook for 15 minutes on one side. Turn salmon over and brush with Dijon mustard mixture and press pecan mixture on top. Cook for 15 minutes or until salmon is no longer red when a knife is inserted into the thickest part.

Salmon with Dill Sauce

Dill and salmon are a perfect culinary match. The grilled salmon is highlighted by a creamy, speckled Dill Sauce (recipe below) and is delicately garnished with just a sprig of fresh dill. Serve with Lemon Rice and Capers (page 266).

Dill Sauce

1 large shallot, finely chopped
½ cup dry white wine
½ cup white wine vinegar
1 cup heavy cream
¼ teaspoon freshly ground pepper
⅛ teaspoon salt
6 tablespoons butter, at room temperature
2 tablespoons minced fresh dill

Dill Coating

2 tablespoons extra virgin olive oil
2 tablespoons minced fresh dill
   Salt and freshly ground pepper, to taste
4 salmon filets (6 ounces each), skin removed

To Make Sauce Bring shallot, wine, and white wine vinegar to a boil over high heat. Boil for 6 minutes or until mixture is reduced to about 2 tablespoons. Add heavy cream, pepper, and salt and boil on moderately high heat for 8 minutes or until mixture thickens. Reduce heat to low and add butter, 1 tablespoon at a time, stirring frequently. Place a sieve over a small saucepan and strain the sauce. Discard the shallots in the strainer. Return the saucepan to heat. Add dill and blend well. Keep the dill sauce warm over very low heat until ready to serve.

To Make Dill Coating Combine olive oil, dill, salt, and pepper in a dish. Press both sides of each salmon filet in the mixture, making sure salmon is completely coated.

To Prepare Salmon on an Outdoor Grill Over moderately hot coals, place salmon filets on a grill coated with a nonstick vegetable spray. Cover grill and cook for 10 minutes or until salmon is no longer red when a knife is inserted into the thickest part.

To Prepare Salmon on an Indoor Grill Place salmon filets on a preheated grill over moderately high heat and cook for 15 minutes on each side or until salmon is no longer red when a knife is inserted into the thickest part.

To Serve Place a salmon filet on each of four dinner plates, and spoon some of the dill sauce around the salmon or spoon the sauce on top of the salmon. Garnish with a sprig of fresh dill.

Seafood

269

Santa Fe Mahi Mahi with Avocado and Papaya Salsa

SERVES 4

Mahi mahi has a subtle kick when enhanced with the flavorful marinade in this recipe. Pairing it with Avocado and Papaya Salsa is a natural. Serve with Garlic-Basted Grilled Corn on the Cob (page 317) and Mexican Rice (page 170).

Avocado and Papaya Salsa

- 1 avocado, peeled (reserve pit) and diced
- 1 papaya, peeled, seeded, and diced
- 1 red bell pepper, seeded and diced
- 3 green onions, thinly sliced
- 1 jalapeño chile, minced (see note)
- 1½ tablespoons minced cilantro leaves
- 1 tablespoon fresh lime juice
- 1 tablespoon rice wine vinegar
- ½ teaspoon salt

Marinade

- ¾ cup minced cilantro leaves
- ⅓ cup fresh lime juice
- 2 tablespoons extra virgin olive oil
- ½ teaspoon crushed red pepper
- 4 mahi mahi filets (6 ounces each)

Papaya slices (from 1 to 2 papayas), for garnish

To Make Salsa Combine avocado, papaya, red pepper, green onions, jalapeño chile, cilantro, lime juice, rice wine vinegar, and salt in a medium bowl and blend well. If not serving the salsa within an hour, place the reserved avocado pit in the salsa to prevent the avocado from turning brown. Cover the bowl and refrigerate the avocado and papaya salsa until ready to serve.

To Make Marinade Combine cilantro, lime juice, olive oil, and crushed red pepper in a resealable plastic bag and blend. Add mahi mahi filets and turn to coat all over. Refrigerate for 30 minutes, turning mahi mahi at least once.

To Prepare Mahi Mahi on an Outdoor Grill Over moderately hot coals, place mahi mahi filets on a grill coated with a non-stick vegetable spray. Cover grill and cook for 10 to 12 minutes or until mahi mahi is no longer translucent when a knife is inserted into the thickest part.

To Prepare Mahi Mahi on an Indoor Grill Place mahi mahi filets on a preheated grill over moderately high heat and cook for 15 minutes on each side or until mahi mahi is no longer translucent when a knife is inserted into the thickest part.

To Serve Arrange mahi mahi filets slightly off to one side on four dinner plates and spoon some avocado and papaya salsa on top of each. Arrange a fan of 3 to 4 slices of papaya beside each mahi mahi filet and place a cilantro leaf at the pointed tip of each fan.

Note The seeds of a jalapeño chile are very hot. To avoid burning your skin, wear rubber or latex gloves when removing the seeds. Immediately wash the knife, cutting surface, and gloves when finished.

Kathy's Marinated Escolar

This marinade is a quick and easy way to bring out the true flavors of escolar. Serve with Acorn Squash with Fruited Wild Rice (page 336) and Mixed Baby Greens with Kiwi Fruit, Red Onion, and Praline Pecans (recipe below).

Mixed Baby Greens with Kiwi Fruit, Red Onion, and Praline Pecans

- $\frac{1}{3}$ cup canola oil
- 6 tablespoons granulated sugar
- 2 tablespoons white distilled vinegar
- 1 tablespoon honey
- $\frac{1}{2}$ tablespoon finely minced Vidalia onion or other sweet onion
- $\frac{1}{2}$ teaspoon celery seed
- $\frac{1}{2}$ teaspoon dry mustard
- $\frac{1}{2}$ teaspoon paprika
- $\frac{1}{4}$ teaspoon salt, plus $\frac{1}{2}$ teaspoon salt
- $\frac{1}{3}$ cup coarsely chopped pecans
- $\frac{1}{8}$ teaspoon cayenne
- 1 small red onion, thinly sliced
- $\frac{1}{2}$ pound mixed baby greens
- 4 kiwi fruit, peeled and thinly sliced

Marinade

- $\frac{1}{2}$ cup fresh lime juice
- 2 tablespoons canola oil
- 1 teaspoon tarragon
- 1 teaspoon onion salt
- $\frac{1}{4}$ teaspoon freshly ground pepper
- 4 escolar filets (6 ounces each)

To Make Salad Dressing Combine canola oil, 3 tablespoons sugar, white vinegar, honey, Vidalia onion, celery seed, dry mustard, paprika, and $\frac{1}{4}$ teaspoon salt in a double boiler and cook over hot water for 6 to 7 minutes or until dressing is lukewarm. Transfer dressing to the work bowl of a food processor fitted with a metal blade and process until well blended. The dressing can be served immediately or stored in a covered container in the refrigerator until ready to use.

To Make Praline Pecans Combine pecans, ½ teaspoon salt, and cayenne in a small dish and blend.

Place 3 tablespoons sugar in a heavy, small pan over moderate heat and cook for 10 minutes or until sugar melts, stirring occasionally. Cook an additional 2 minutes without stirring or until sugar turns a rich caramel color. Add the pecan mixture and blend well. Spoon praline pecans onto a sheet of aluminum foil to cool, then transfer to a cutting board and coarsely chop. The pecan praline can be served immediately or stored in a covered container for up to 2 days.

To Make Salad Combine red onion and 1 tablespoon of the dressing in a bowl and blend well. Cover bowl and set aside for 1 hour.

When ready to serve the salad, combine mixed baby greens, kiwi fruit, and reserved red onion in a salad bowl. Add just enough dressing to make greens glisten and lightly toss. Arrange salad on each of four salad plates and garnish with praline pecans.

To Make Marinade Combine lime juice, canola oil, tarragon, onion salt, and pepper in a resealable plastic bag and blend. Add escolar filets and turn to coat all over. Refrigerate for 30 minutes.

To Prepare Escolar on an Outdoor Grill Remove escolar from marinade. Over moderately hot coals, place escolar filets on a grill coated with a nonstick vegetable spray. Cover grill and cook for 10 to 12 minutes or until escolar is no longer translucent when a knife is inserted into the thickest part.

To Prepare Escolar on an Indoor Grill Remove escolar from marinade. Place them on a preheated grill over moderately high heat and cook for 15 minutes on each side or until escolar is no longer translucent when a knife is inserted into the thickest part.

Mediterranean Tuna Salad

This wonderfully light and refreshing salad is ideal summer fare. Serve with French baguettes and your favorite bottle of chardonnay.

Lemon Vinaigrette

1 clove garlic
3 tablespoons fresh lemon juice
½ tablespoon Dijon mustard
⅛ teaspoon salt
⅛ teaspoon freshly ground pepper
¼ cup extra virgin olive oil

Marinade

¼ cup fresh lemon juice
1 tablespoon extra virgin olive oil
¼ teaspoon oregano
¼ teaspoon freshly ground pepper

Salad

4 new potatoes, halved
2 eggs
1 teaspoon extra virgin olive oil
1 yellowfin tuna steak (10 ounces)
1 red bell pepper
3 cups mixed baby greens
1 tomato, cut into 8 wedges
8 Greek olives (kalamatas), pitted

To Make Vinaigrette In the work bowl of a food processor fitted with a metal blade, process garlic until chopped. Add lemon juice, Dijon mustard, salt, and pepper and process until smooth. Add olive oil in a slow, steady stream and process until well blended. Transfer to a covered container and refrigerate until ready to serve.

To Make Marinade Combine lemon juice, olive oil, oregano, and pepper in a resealable plastic bag and blend. Set aside in the refrigerator.

To Prepare Salad Soak bamboo skewers in water for 30 minutes or more. Place potatoes and eggs in a large saucepan and add enough water to cover. Bring to a boil over moderately high heat. Turn off heat, cover saucepan, and allow potatoes and eggs to come to room temperature. Remove shells from eggs; cut eggs into quarters, and transfer to a covered container. Refrigerate the eggs until ready to serve. Drain potatoes. Combine potatoes and olive oil in a plastic bag and turn potatoes to coat all over. Thread potatoes on skewers.

To Prepare Potatoes, Pepper, and Tuna on an Outdoor Grill Place tuna steak in marinade and turn to coat all over. Refrigerate for 30 minutes.

Over moderately hot coals, place the potatoes and red pepper on a grill coated with a nonstick vegetable spray. Cover the grill and cook the potatoes for 8 to 10 minutes or until brown, turning potatoes every 3 minutes. Remove potatoes to a dish and loosely cover with aluminum foil to keep warm. Cook the red pepper for 14 to 20 minutes or until skin is charred all over, turning the pepper as skin blackens. Once grilled, place the pepper in a plastic bag and allow to steam for 15 minutes. When it is cool enough to handle, peel away the skin and remove the top and seeds (do not rinse the pepper). Cut the pepper into slivers and wrap loosely with aluminum foil to keep warm.

Remove tuna from marinade and place on grill. Cover grill and cook for 5 minutes on each side or until tuna is no longer red when a knife is inserted into the thickest part. Carve the tuna into thin slices.

To Prepare Potatoes, Pepper, and Tuna on an Indoor Grill Place tuna steak in marinade and turn to coat all over. Refrigerate for 30 minutes.

Place the potatoes and red pepper on a preheated grill over high heat and cook the potatoes for 20 minutes or until brown, turning potatoes every 5 minutes. Remove potatoes to a dish and loosely cover with aluminum foil to keep warm. Cook the red pepper for 20 to 30 minutes or until skin is charred all over, turning the pepper as skin blackens. Once grilled, place the pepper in a plastic bag and allow to steam for 15 minutes. When it is cool enough to handle, peel away the skin and remove the top and seeds (do not rinse the pepper). Cut the pepper into slivers and wrap loosely with aluminum foil to keep warm.

Remove tuna from marinade. Place tuna on a preheated grill over moderate heat and cook for 15 minutes on one side and 12 to 15 minutes on the other side or until tuna is no longer red when a knife is inserted into the thickest part. Carve the tuna into thin slices.

To Serve Make a bed of mixed baby greens on two dinner plates. Center the tuna slices on the greens, and in spoke fashion, surround the tuna with tomatoes, potatoes, and eggs. Randomly distribute the red pepper slices over tuna and dot with Greek olives. Drizzle lemon vinaigrette over each serving.

Indonesian Marinated Tuna

SERVES 4

The turmeric in this marinade tints the tuna with a subtle yellow hue while also contributing to the mild oriental flavor of the marinade. Pairing the marinated tuna with Banana Salsa (page 258) is the ultimate way to enjoy this meal. Serve with Saffron Rice (page 264).

¼ cup fresh lime juice
½ teaspoon turmeric
3 cloves garlic, minced
2 teaspoons Sriracha hot chili sauce

1 teaspoon kecap manis (sweet soy sauce)
⅛ teaspoon salt
4 yellowfin tuna steaks (6 ounces each)

To Make Marinade Combine lime juice, turmeric, garlic, Sriracha hot chili sauce, kecap manis, and salt in a resealable plastic bag and blend. Add tuna steaks and turn to coat all over. Refrigerate for 30 minutes, turning tuna at least once.

To Prepare Tuna on an Outdoor Grill Remove tuna from marinade. Over moderately hot coals, place tuna on a grill coated with a nonstick vegetable spray. Cover grill and cook for 5 minutes on each side or until tuna is no longer red when a knife is inserted into the thickest part.

To Prepare Tuna on an Indoor Grill Remove tuna from marinade. Place tuna on a preheated grill over moderately high heat and cook for 15 minutes on one side and 12 to 15 minutes on other side or until tuna is no longer red when a knife is inserted into the thickest part.

Morel-Coated Salmon Filets with Grilled Red Pepper Sauce

SERVES 4

This is an exquisite dish that is both appealing to the eye and delicious. Although dried morels can be pricey, you will enjoy having this recipe in your special collection. Serve the salmon on top of Grilled Red Pepper Sauce (recipe below) and arrange spears of steamed asparagus radiating out from under the fish, with a sprig of watercress on top as a garnish.

Grilled Red Pepper Sauce

4 red bell peppers
9 tablespoons butter
2 cloves garlic, minced
½ teaspoon granulated sugar
2 tablespoons chopped basil
¼ teaspoon salt
¼ teaspoon freshly ground pepper

Morel Coating

2 packages (½ ounce each) dried morels
2 tablespoons extra virgin olive oil
   Salt and freshly ground pepper, to taste
4 salmon filets (6 ounces each), skin removed

To Prepare Peppers on an Outdoor Grill Over hot coals, place the red peppers on a grill coated with a nonstick vegetable spray. Cover and cook for 14 to 20 minutes or until skins are charred all over, turning the peppers as skins blacken. Once grilled, place the peppers in a plastic bag and allow to steam for 15 minutes. When they are cool enough to handle, peel away the skins and remove the tops and seeds (do not rinse the peppers). Slice the peppers into slivers.

To Prepare Peppers on an Indoor Grill Place the red peppers on a preheated grill over high heat and cook for 20 to 30 minutes or until skins are charred all over, turning the peppers as skins blacken. Once grilled, place the peppers in a plastic bag and allow to steam for 15 minutes. When they are cool enough to handle, peel away the skins and remove tops and seeds (do not rinse the peppers). Slice the peppers into slivers.

To Make Sauce Melt 3 tablespoons butter in a medium saucepan over moderately low heat. Add red pepper slivers, garlic, and sugar and cook for 10 minutes, stirring occasionally. Transfer mixture to the work bowl of a food processor fitted with a metal blade and process until pureed. Return red pepper mixture to saucepan and add remaining 6 tablespoons of butter, 1 tablespoon at a time, and cook over low heat until butter has melted, stirring frequently. Add basil, salt, and pepper and blend well. Keep grilled red pepper sauce warm over very low heat until ready to serve.

To Make Morel Coating Place morels in the clean work bowl of a food processor fitted with a metal blade and process until finely chopped.

Combine olive oil, salt, and pepper in one dish and place morels in another dish. Coat both sides of salmon in olive oil mixture first and then in morels, making sure salmon is completely coated.

To Prepare Salmon on an Outdoor Grill Over moderately hot coals, place salmon filets on a grill coated with a nonstick vegetable spray. Cover grill and cook for 10 minutes or until salmon is no longer red when a knife is inserted into the thickest part.

To Prepare Salmon on an Indoor Grill Place salmon on a preheated grill over moderately high heat and cook for 15 minutes on each side or until salmon is no longer red when a knife is inserted into the thickest part.

Orange and Ginger Tuna with Orange Butter

SERVES 6

Oranges and ginger give tuna a tangy, summertime flavor that is enhanced even more after topping it with Orange Butter (recipe below), which melts into a sauce. I like to garnish the tuna steaks with slivered candied orange peel or a touch of parsley for a colorful accent. Serve with Mashed Potatoes with Caramelized Onions (page 134).

Orange Butter

8 tablespoons (1 stick) butter, at room temperature

1 tablespoon finely grated orange peel

1½ tablespoons fresh orange juice

Orange and Ginger Marinade

½ cup fresh orange juice

2 cloves garlic, minced

2 teaspoons minced fresh ginger

1 tablespoon extra virgin olive oil

¼ teaspoon salt

⅛ teaspoon freshly ground pepper

6 yellowfin tuna steaks (6 ounces each)

To Make Orange Butter Combine butter and orange peel in a small bowl. Add orange juice, a drop at a time, and blend well. (If any orange juice has not been absorbed by the butter, pour it into a dish and, drop by drop, add it to the butter again until all of it is absorbed.) Place orange butter on a piece of plastic wrap and twist the ends to enclose it. Place the orange butter in the freezer. Allow orange butter to come to room temperature before using.

To Make Marinade Combine orange juice, garlic, ginger, olive oil, salt, and pepper in a resealable plastic bag and blend. Add tuna steaks and turn to coat all over. Refrigerate for 30 minutes, turning tuna at least once.

To Prepare Tuna on an Outdoor Grill Over moderately hot coals, place tuna on a grill coated with a nonstick vegetable spray. Cover grill and cook for 10 minutes or until tuna is no longer red when a knife is inserted into the thickest part.

To Prepare Tuna on an Indoor Grill Place tuna on a pre-heated grill over moderately high heat and cook for 15 minutes on first side and 12 to 15 minutes on other side or until tuna is no longer red when a knife is inserted into the thickest part.

To Serve Place a tuna steak on each of six dinner plates and immediately top with orange butter, dividing evenly. Garnish with a sprig of parsley or slivered candied orange peel.

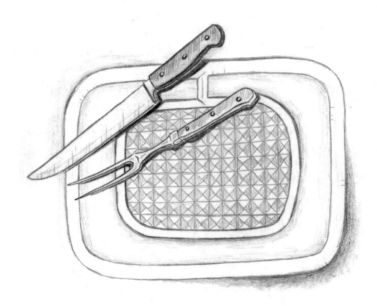

Seafood

Salmon with Creamy Orange Sauce

SERVES 4

Creamy Orange Sauce (recipe below) is so delicious, you will want to pair it with other grilled seafood. It adds a subtle orange flavor and a strong contrasting color, both of which will captivate your guests or family. Serve with Spinach and Rice (page 84) and a fresh fruit salad.

Salmon

1 tablespoon extra virgin olive oil

4 salmon filets (6 ounces each), skin removed
Salt and freshly ground pepper, to taste

Creamy Orange Sauce

¾ cup fresh orange juice

¼ cup dry white wine

4 tablespoons butter, at room temperature

2 tablespoons heavy cream

1 scant tablespoon granulated sugar

⅛ teaspoon salt
Orange segments, for garnish

To Prepare Salmon on an Outdoor Grill Brush olive oil on both sides of each salmon filet and season with salt and pepper. Over moderately hot coals, place salmon filets on a grill coated with a nonstick vegetable spray. Cover grill and cook for 10 minutes or until salmon is no longer red when a knife is inserted into the thickest part.

To Prepare Salmon on an Indoor Grill Brush olive oil on both sides of each salmon filet and season with salt and pepper. Place salmon on a preheated grill over moderately high heat and cook for 15 minutes on each side or until salmon is no longer red when a knife is inserted into the thickest part.

To Make Sauce While grilling the salmon, bring orange juice and wine to a boil in a medium saucepan over moderately high heat. Boil for 7 to 8 minutes or until mixture is reduced by half. Reduce heat to moderately low and add butter, 1 tablespoon at a time, stirring frequently. When butter has melted, add heavy cream, sugar, and salt and cook for 2 to 4 minutes or until sauce thickens.

To Serve Place a salmon filet on each of four dinner plates and spoon a vertical stripe of creamy orange sauce over the salmon. Place orange segments beside each salmon filet and garnish with watercress or parsley.

Sea Bass with Mashed Potatoes and Balsamic-Flavored Mushrooms

SERVES 4

The sweetness of sea bass is a pleasant contrast in taste to the Balsamic-Flavored Mushrooms and creamy Mashed Potatoes. Serve with sourdough bread.

Mashed Potatoes

- 2 pounds potatoes, peeled and diced
- 2 tablespoons butter, at room temperature
- ¼ teaspoon salt
- ¼ teaspoon freshly ground pepper
- ½ to ¾ cup milk

Balsamic-Flavored Mushrooms

- 2 tablespoons extra virgin olive oil
- ½ pound fresh mushrooms, thinly sliced
- 2 tablespoons balsamic vinegar
- 1 tablespoon minced parsley
- 1 teaspoon Worcestershire sauce
- 1 teaspoon freshly ground pink peppercorns

- 2 sea bass filets (12 ounces each)
  Olive oil

To Make Potatoes Place potatoes in a medium saucepan filled with boiling water. Simmer over moderately high heat for 25 to 30 minutes or until potatoes are fork-tender. Drain well. Return potatoes to saucepan and mix with a handheld beater until smooth. Add butter, salt, and pepper and mix well. Add milk, 2 tablespoons at a time, and beat until mashed potatoes are creamy. Transfer to a double boiler, cover, and keep warm over moderate heat.

To Make Mushrooms Heat olive oil in a medium pan over moderate heat for 2 minutes. Add mushrooms and sauté for 5 minutes, stirring occasionally. Add balsamic vinegar, parsley, Worcestershire sauce, and peppercorns and blend well. Cover and keep warm over very low heat.

To Prepare Sea Bass on an Outdoor Grill Brush both sides of each sea bass filet with olive oil. Over moderately hot coals, place sea bass filets on a grill coated with a nonstick vegetable spray. Cover grill and cook for 10 to 12 minutes or until flesh is no longer translucent when a knife is inserted into the thickest part. Divide each sea bass filet in half.

To Prepare Sea Bass on an Indoor Grill Brush both sides of each sea bass filet with olive oil. Place them on a preheated grill over moderately high heat and cook for 15 minutes on each side or until sea bass is no longer translucent when a knife is inserted into the thickest part. Divide each sea bass filet in half.

To Serve Make a bed of mashed potatoes on each of four dinner plates. Center a portion of sea bass on the potatoes and spoon mushrooms on top. Garnish with a sprig of parsley.

Grilled Swordfish Kebabs

Because swordfish is very meaty, it is the ideal fish to use for making kebabs. The orange and rosemary marinade adds a definite tang. It is delicious with Grapefruit, Orange, and Pineapple Salsa (page 46). Serve with Spinach and Rice (page 84) and Asparagus with Lemon Crumbs (page 228).

½ cup fresh orange juice

3 tablespoons chopped fresh rosemary

1 tablespoon finely grated orange peel

1 tablespoon extra virgin olive oil

2 cloves garlic, minced

⅛ teaspoon salt

⅛ teaspoon freshly ground pepper

2 swordfish steaks (12 ounces each), cut into 1¼-inch cubes

1 orange bell pepper, cut into 8 pieces

4 green onions, cut into 8 pieces

8 shiitake mushrooms, stems removed

8 large chunks of fresh pineapple

To Make Marinade Combine orange juice, rosemary, grated orange peel, olive oil, garlic, salt, and pepper in a resealable plastic bag and blend. Add cubed swordfish and turn to coat all over. Refrigerate for 45 minutes, turning swordfish at least once.

To Prepare Kebabs on an Outdoor Grill Soak bamboo skewers in water for 30 minutes or more. Remove swordfish from marinade, reserving marinade. Alternate swordfish, orange pepper, green onions, shiitake mushrooms, and pineapple on skewers. Over moderately hot coals, place swordfish kebabs on a grill coated with a nonstick vegetable spray. Cover grill and cook for 10 minutes, turning skewers every 4 minutes and brushing with reserved marinade (see note).

To Prepare Kebabs on an Indoor Grill Soak bamboo skewers in water for 30 minutes or more. Remove swordfish from marinade, reserving marinade. Alternate swordfish, orange pepper, green onions, shiitake mushrooms, and pineapple on skewers. Place swordfish kebabs on a preheated grill over moderate heat and cook for 25 to 30 minutes, turning skewers every 4 minutes and brushing with reserved marinade (see note).

Note The skewers will be easier to turn if you thread the swordfish, vegetables, and fruit on two bamboo skewers that are parallel to each other, about 1 inch apart.

Honey-Glazed Marlin

SERVES 4

The intermingling of honey with other flavorful ingredients accents the strong flavor of marlin. It is delicious by itself or with Banana Salsa (page 258). Serve with Grilled Fruit Kebabs (page 341) and Basmati and Wild Rice (page 144).

2 tablespoons dry white wine	½ teaspoon dry mustard
2 tablespoons soy sauce	4 marlin steaks (6 ounces each)
1 tablespoon honey	2 star fruit, cut into ⅛-inch-
1 clove garlic, minced	thick stars
1 teaspoon oriental sesame oil	

To Make Marinade Combine wine, soy sauce, honey, garlic, sesame oil, and dry mustard in a resealable plastic bag and blend. Add marlin steaks and turn to coat all over. Refrigerate for up to 1 hour, turning marlin at least once.

To Prepare Marlin on an Outdoor Grill Remove marlin from marinade, reserving marinade. Over moderately hot coals, place marlin on a grill coated with a nonstick vegetable spray. Cover grill and cook for 5 minutes on each side or until marlin is no longer red when a knife is inserted into the thickest part, brushing occasionally with reserved marinade.

To Prepare Marlin on an Indoor Grill Remove marlin from marinade, reserving marinade. Place marlin on a preheated grill over moderately high heat and cook for 15 minutes on one side and 12 to 15 minutes on the other side or until marlin is no longer red when a knife is inserted into the thickest part, brushing occasionally with reserved marinade.

To Serve Garnish marlin steaks with star fruit slices as soon as they are removed from the grill.

Shrimp and Scallop Kebabs

SERVES 4

Because shrimp and scallops provide just the right contrast in color, texture, and taste, they are a perfect match in a number of dishes. I like to use them as the sole components of a kebab, but you can add red peppers, bananas, or pineapple as a colorful and complementary variation. Serve on a bed of Jasmine Rice (page 158), with Grilled Pineapple Rings (page 330) on the side.

½ cup fresh orange juice
¼ cup soy sauce
1 tablespoon chili oil (see note)
1 tablespoon packed dark brown sugar

1 tablespoon minced ginger
¾ pound sea scallops
¾ pound medium shrimp, peeled and deveined

To Make Marinade Combine orange juice, soy sauce, chili oil, brown sugar, and ginger in a resealable plastic bag and blend. Add scallops and shrimp and turn to coat all over. Refrigerate for 30 minutes, turning shrimp and scallops at least once.

To Prepare Kebabs on an Outdoor Grill Soak bamboo skewers in water for 30 minutes or more. Alternate shrimp and scallops on skewers and place over moderately hot coals on a grill coated with a nonstick vegetable spray. Cover grill and cook for 3 to 4 minutes on each side.

To Prepare Kebabs on an Indoor Grill Soak bamboo skewers in water for 30 minutes or more. Alternate shrimp and scallops on skewers and place on a preheated grill over moderate heat. Cook them for 15 minutes, turning kebabs occasionally.

Note Chili oil is available in Asian food stores.

Sea Bass with Ginger Sauce, Spinach, and Purple Mashed Potatoes

SERVES 6

Brushing sea bass with Ginger Oil (recipe below) before grilling accentuates its uniquely sweet flavor. Combining the fish with a rich Ginger Sauce, Sautéed Spinach, and creamy Purple Mashed Potatoes (recipes below) transforms it into a striking and memorable culinary experience.

Ginger Oil
- ½ cup extra virgin olive oil
- 1 ¼-inch-thick piece fresh ginger, peeled and halved

Purple Mashed Potatoes
- 2 pounds purple potatoes (or new potatoes), peeled and quartered
- 1 quart milk
- 3 tablespoons butter
  Salt and freshly ground pepper, to taste

Ginger Sauce
- 1½ cups dry white wine
- ¾ cup diced fresh ginger
- 6 tablespoons shallots, minced

- 1½ cups heavy cream
- 12 tablespoons (1½ sticks) butter, at room temperature

Spinach
- 1 tablespoon canola oil
- 1 pound washed spinach
- 1 can (16 ounces) bamboo shoots, drained and julienned
- 3 large cloves garlic, slivered
- ½ cup chicken broth
  Salt and freshly ground pepper, to taste

- 3 sea bass filets (12 ounces each)
  Tobiko caviar, for garnish

To Make Ginger Oil Combine olive oil and ginger in a small heavy saucepan over moderate heat and bring to a boil. Remove saucepan from heat, cover, and allow to sit for 30 minutes. Pour ginger oil in a glass jar with a tight-fitting lid and store in a cool, dark place for up to 2 weeks. Use as needed.

To Make Potatoes Combine purple potatoes and milk in a large saucepan and bring to a boil over moderately high heat. Boil for 25 minutes. Place a sieve over a large bowl and drain potatoes, reserving milk. Mash the potatoes with a masher. Add butter and blend well. Add reserved milk, 2 tablespoons at a time, and beat with a handheld mixer until mashed potatoes are creamy. Season with salt and pepper. Transfer to a double boiler, cover, and keep warm over moderate heat.

To Make Ginger Sauce Combine wine, ginger, and shallots in a medium saucepan over high heat and bring to a boil. Boil for 6 to 8 minutes or until mixture is reduced by one third. Reduce heat to moderately high and add heavy cream. Boil for 6 to 8 minutes or until sauce thickens, stirring occasionally. Reduce heat to moderate and add butter, 1 tablespoon at a time, blending well after each addition. Place a sieve over a large bowl and strain ginger sauce; discard ginger and shallots in the sieve. Return ginger sauce to saucepan and keep warm over very low heat.

To Make Spinach While preparing ginger sauce, heat canola oil in a large nonstick skillet over moderate heat. Add spinach, bamboo shoots, and garlic and sauté for 5 to 10 minutes or until spinach has wilted, stirring occasionally. Add chicken broth and blend well. Season with salt and pepper. Keep warm over very low heat.

To Prepare Sea Bass on an Outdoor Grill Brush each side of the sea bass filets with 1 to 2 teaspoons of ginger oil. Over moderately hot coals, place sea bass on a grill coated with a nonstick vegetable spray. Cover grill and cook for 10 to 12 minutes or until flesh is no longer translucent when a knife is inserted into the thickest part. Divide each sea bass filet in half.

To Prepare Sea Bass on an Indoor Grill Brush each side of the sea bass filets with 1 to 2 teaspoons ginger oil. Place them on a preheated grill over moderately high heat and cook for 15 minutes on each side or until sea bass is no longer translucent when a knife is inserted into the thickest part. Divide each sea bass filet in half.

To Serve Using an ice cream scoop, mound a serving of purple mashed potatoes on each of six dinner plates. Center a portion of sea bass on the potatoes and spoon the spinach on top. Spoon some ginger sauce around the sea bass and dot the ginger sauce with tobiko caviar, if desired.

Chinese Shrimp Kebabs

SERVES 4

These flavorful shrimp kebabs have a high reward-to-effort ratio. In other words, they are extremely easy to prepare and they taste great. Serve with Jasmine Rice (page 158) and a fresh fruit salad.

¼	cup medium-dry sherry	1	tablespoon minced fresh ginger
¼	cup soy sauce	1	clove garlic, minced
1	tablespoon canola oil	1½	pounds medium shrimp, peeled and deveined
1	tablespoon Sriracha hot chili sauce		

To Make Marinade Combine sherry, soy sauce, canola oil, Sriracha hot chili sauce, ginger, and garlic in a resealable plastic bag and blend. Add shrimp and turn to coat all over. Refrigerate for up to 1 hour, turning shrimp at least once.

To Prepare Shrimp on an Outdoor Grill Soak bamboo skewers in water for 30 minutes or more. Thread shrimp on skewers and place over moderately hot coals on a grill coated with a nonstick vegetable spray. Cover grill and cook for 3 minutes on each side.

To Prepare Shrimp on an Indoor Grill Soak bamboo skewers in water for 30 minutes or more. Thread shrimp on skewers and place them on a preheated grill over moderate heat. Cook for 15 minutes, turning shrimp every 4 minutes.

Swordfish with Avocado and Cilantro Butter

SERVES 6

The savory marinade in this recipe adds a Southwestern flavor to swordfish when grilled. The Avocado and Cilantro Butter is like icing on the cake. Serve with mugs of Gazpacho (page 32) and Garlic-Basted Grilled Corn on the Cob (page 317).

Avocado and Cilantro Butter

8 tablespoons (1 stick) butter, at room temperature

1 ripe avocado, peeled and pit removed

2 tablespoons minced cilantro leaves

2 cloves garlic, minced

¼ teaspoon salt

¼ teaspoon freshly ground pepper

¼ cup fresh lime juice

Marinade

¼ cup fresh lemon juice

2 tablespoons tequila

2 tablespoons chopped cilantro leaves

2 cloves garlic, minced

1 tablespoon extra virgin olive oil

¼ teaspoon crushed red pepper

¼ teaspoon salt

¼ teaspoon freshly ground pepper

3 swordfish steaks (12 ounces each)

To Make Butter Combine butter and avocado and blend until smooth. Add cilantro, garlic, salt, and pepper and blend. Add lime juice, a drop at a time, and blend well. Place avocado and cilantro butter on a piece of plastic wrap and twist ends to enclose it. Place the avocado and cilantro butter in the freezer. Allow it to come to room temperature before using.

To Make Marinade Combine lemon juice, tequila, cilantro, garlic, olive oil, crushed red pepper, salt, and pepper in a resealable plastic bag and blend. Add swordfish steaks and turn to coat all over. Refrigerate for 30 minutes.

To Prepare Swordfish on an Outdoor Grill Remove swordfish from marinade. Over moderately hot coals, place swordfish steaks on a grill coated with a nonstick vegetable spray. Cover grill and cook for 10 minutes or until swordfish is no longer translucent when a knife is inserted into the thickest part. Divide each swordfish steak in half.

To Prepare Swordfish on an Indoor Grill Remove swordfish from marinade. Place swordfish steaks on a preheated grill over moderate heat and cook for 15 minutes on each side or until swordfish is no longer translucent when a knife is inserted into the thickest part. Divide each swordfish steak in half.

To Serve Arrange swordfish portions on six dinner plates. Immediately top each with a dollop of avocado and cilantro butter and garnish with a sprig of cilantro.

Cilantro-Coated Tuna

It takes only a few hours for the tuna to be imbued with the aromatic flavor of cilantro leaves. The flavor seems to get even stronger as the tuna cooks on the grill. Serve topped with Sonia's Tomatillo Sauce (recipe below) and Mashed Potatoes with Caramelized Onions (page 134).

Sonia's Tomatillo Sauce

- 3 tomatillos
- ½ tablespoon extra virgin olive oil
- ½ cup chopped cilantro leaves
- 2 jalapeño chiles, seeded (see note)
- 1 clove garlic, minced
- ½ cup plain yogurt
- 3 tablespoons fresh lime juice
- ¼ teaspoon salt

Cilantro Coating

- 2 tablespoons extra virgin olive oil
- ½ teaspoon salt
- ½ teaspoon freshly ground pepper
- ½ cup minced cilantro leaves
- 4 yellowfin tuna steaks (6 ounces each)

To Make Tomatillo Sauce Peel off husks and stems of tomatillos. Wash the tomatillos in hot water to remove the sticky, resinous material covering them. Thinly slice the tomatillos.

Place a small frying pan over moderately high heat for 1 minute. Add olive oil and heat for 1 minute. Add tomatillos and cook for 4 minutes, stirring frequently. Set aside.

In the work bowl of a food processor fitted with a metal blade, process cilantro, jalapeño chiles, and garlic. Add tomatillos and process until blended. Add yogurt, lime juice, and salt and process with on/off pulses until just blended. Transfer Sonia's tomatillo sauce to a covered container and refrigerate for up to 4 hours.

To Make Cilantro Coating Combine olive oil, salt, and pepper on one plate and place cilantro on another plate. Coat both sides of each tuna steak with oil mixture first and then with cilantro. Place cilantro-coated tuna in a nonmetal dish, cover, and refrigerate for up to 4 hours (or the tuna can be grilled immediately).

To Prepare Tuna on an Outdoor Grill Over moderately hot coals, place tuna on a grill coated with a nonstick vegetable spray. Cover grill and cook for 10 to 12 minutes or until tuna is no longer red when a knife is inserted into the thickest part.

To Prepare Tuna on an Indoor Grill Place tuna on a preheated grill over moderately high heat and cook for 15 minutes on one side and 12 to 15 minutes on other side or until tuna is no longer red when a knife is inserted into the thickest part.

Note The seeds of jalapeño chiles are very hot. To avoid burning your skin, wear rubber or latex gloves when removing the seeds. Immediately wash the knife, cutting surface, and gloves when finished.

Swordfish with Greek Olive and Grilled Red Pepper Relish

SERVES 6

Swordfish marinated in a zesty lemon marinade, grilled, and topped with a colorful relish is both a visual and a taste sensation. Serve with a Greek Salad (page 40) and warmed pita bread.

Greek Olive and Grilled Red Pepper Relish

- 1 red bell pepper
- 1 cup chopped Greek olives (kalamatas)
- 1 tablespoon minced parsley
- 1 tablespoon capers
- 1 tablespoon extra virgin olive oil
- 1 clove garlic, minced
- 1 teaspoon red wine vinegar

Marinade

- ½ cup fresh lemon juice
- 1½ tablespoons extra virgin olive oil
- 2 teaspoons oregano
- ½ teaspoon crushed red pepper
- 2 cloves garlic, minced
- 3 swordfish steaks (12 ounces each)

To Prepare Pepper on an Outdoor Grill Over moderately hot coals, place the red pepper on a grill coated with a nonstick vegetable spray. Cover and cook for 14 to 20 minutes or until skin is charred all over, turning the pepper as skin blackens. Once grilled, place the pepper in a plastic bag and allow to steam for 15 minutes. When it is cool enough to handle, peel away the skin and remove the top and seeds (do not rinse the pepper). Dice the pepper and set aside.

To Prepare Pepper on an Indoor Grill Place the red pepper on a preheated grill over high heat and cook for 20 to 30 minutes or until skin is charred all over, turning the pepper as skin blackens. Once grilled, place the pepper in a plastic bag and allow to steam for 15 minutes. When it is cool enough to handle, peel away the skin and remove the top and seeds (do not rinse the pepper). Dice the pepper and set aside.

To Make Relish Combine olives, diced red pepper, parsley, capers, olive oil, garlic, and red wine vinegar in a bowl and blend well. Cover bowl and refrigerate for several hours or overnight. Stir before serving.

To Make Marinade Combine lemon juice, olive oil, oregano, crushed red pepper, and garlic in a resealable plastic bag and blend. Add swordfish steaks and turn to coat all over. Refrigerate for 30 minutes, turning swordfish at least once.

To Prepare Swordfish on an Outdoor Grill Remove swordfish from marinade. Over moderately hot coals, place swordfish steaks on a grill coated with a nonstick vegetable spray. Cover grill and cook for 10 minutes or until swordfish is no longer translucent when a knife is inserted into the thickest part. Divide each swordfish steak in half.

To Prepare Swordfish on an Indoor Grill Remove swordfish from marinade. Place swordfish steaks on a preheated grill over moderate heat and cook for 15 minutes on each side or until swordfish is no longer translucent when a knife is inserted into the thickest part. Divide each swordfish steak in half.

To Serve Arrange swordfish portions on six dinner plates. Spoon some Greek olive and grilled red pepper relish on the top or to the side of each swordfish steak.

Swordfish with Mustard and Italian Vinaigrette

SERVES 4

The simplicity of this recipe belies how exquisite swordfish tastes when marinated and grilled. Serve with Valda's Pesto Tart (recipe below).

Valda's Pesto Tart

1½	cups flour
6½	tablespoons extra virgin olive oil
	Salt
1	cup thinly sliced green onions
1	container (15 ounces) ricotta cheese
4	eggs
1	container (6 ounces) pesto sauce
3	tablespoons toasted pine nuts (see note)

Marinade

1	cup bottled Italian dressing
1	tablespoon minced parsley
1	tablespoon Dijon mustard
2	swordfish steaks (12 ounces each)

To Make Tart Preheat oven to 375 degrees. Combine flour, 6 tablespoons olive oil, 2 tablespoons cold water, and dash of salt in the work bowl of a food processor fitted with a metal blade and process until mixture forms a ball. (Add additional olive oil if mixture seems dry.) Press mixture into a 9-inch pie or quiche pan and bake for 5 to 10 minutes or until crust feels dry. Do not turn oven off. Set aside.

Heat remaining ½ tablespoon olive oil in a small skillet over moderate heat for 2 minutes. Add green onions and sauté for 5 minutes, stirring occasionally. Combine ricotta cheese, green onions, eggs, and dash of salt in the clean work bowl of the food processor and process until smooth. Spoon the mixture into the pie crust and bake for 45 minutes.

When tart is removed from oven, immediately spread pesto sauce over the baked filling. Garnish the pesto tart by sprinkling pine nuts on top. Allow the pesto tart to rest a few minutes before serving. (The pesto tart can be served warm or at room temperature.)

To Make Marinade Combine Italian dressing, parsley, and Dijon mustard in a resealable plastic bag and blend. Add swordfish steaks and turn to coat all over. Refrigerate for 30 minutes, turning swordfish at least once.

To Prepare Swordfish on an Outdoor Grill Remove swordfish steaks from marinade. Over moderately hot coals, place swordfish steaks on a grill coated with a nonstick vegetable spray. Cover grill and cook for 10 minutes or until swordfish is no longer translucent when a knife is inserted into the thickest part. Divide each swordfish steak in half.

To Prepare Swordfish on an Indoor Grill Remove swordfish steaks from marinade. Place swordfish steaks on a preheated grill over moderate heat and cook for 15 minutes on each side or until swordfish is no longer translucent when a knife is inserted into the thickest part. Divide each swordfish steak in half.

Note To toast pine nuts: Preheat oven to 350 degrees. Place pine nuts in a shallow pan and bake for 10 to 15 minutes or until golden brown.

Lemon-Marinated Tuna with Grilled Red Pepper Aioli

SERVES 4

The sensational Grilled Red Pepper Aioli (recipe below) would enhance the flavor of most seafood. It contributes to a wonderful taste when layered over lemon-marinated tuna. Serve with Zucchini and Yellow Squash Soufflé (recipe below).

Grilled Red Pepper Aioli

- 1 large red bell pepper
- 2 egg yolks
- 14 tablespoons extra virgin olive oil
- ¼ cup fresh lemon juice
- ⅜ teaspoon salt
- ⅜ teaspoon freshly ground pepper

- 1 medium Vidalia onion or other sweet onion, chopped
- 1 large clove garlic, minced
- 4 eggs, lightly beaten
- ½ cup freshly grated Parmesan cheese
- ½ teaspoon salt
- ¼ teaspoon freshly ground pepper

Zucchini and Yellow Squash Soufflé

- 1 pound zucchini, thinly sliced
- 1 pound yellow squash, thinly sliced
- ¼ teaspoon salt
- 2 slices white bread, torn into bite-size pieces
- 1 cup milk
- 2 tablespoons canola oil
- 2 tablespoons butter

Marinade

- ¼ cup fresh lemon juice
- 2 tablespoons minced fresh basil
- 1 tablespoon extra virgin olive oil
- ¼ teaspoon salt
- ¼ teaspoon freshly ground pepper
- 4 yellowfin tuna steaks (6 ounces each)

To Prepare Pepper on an Outdoor Grill Over moderately hot coals, place the red pepper on a grill coated with a nonstick vegetable spray. Cover and cook for 14 to 20 minutes or until skin is charred all over, turning the pepper as skin blackens. Once grilled, place the pepper in a plastic bag and allow to steam for 15 minutes. When it is cool enough to handle, peel away the skin and remove the top and seeds (do not rinse the pepper). Slice the pepper into slivers.

To Prepare Pepper on an Indoor Grill Place the red pepper on a preheated grill over high heat and cook for 20 to 30 minutes or until skin is charred all over, turning the pepper as skin blackens. Once grilled, place the pepper in a plastic bag and allow to steam for 15 minutes. When it is cool enough to handle, peel away the skin and remove the top and seeds (do not rinse the pepper). Slice the pepper into slivers.

To Make Aioli In the work bowl of a food processor fitted with a metal blade, process egg yolks until beaten. Add olive oil in a slow, steady stream and process until well blended. Add the red pepper slivers, lemon juice, salt, and pepper and process until blended. Transfer grilled red pepper aioli to a dish, cover, and refrigerate until ready to serve.

To Make Soufflé Preheat oven to 350 degrees. Place zucchini, yellow squash, 1 cup cold water, and ¼ teaspoon salt in a large saucepan over high heat and bring to a boil. Reduce heat to moderate, cover, and cook for 10 to 15 minutes or until vegetables are fork-tender. Drain and push down with the back of a spoon to remove as much water as possible.

Combine bread and milk in a medium bowl and set aside.

Heat canola oil and butter in a medium skillet over moderate heat. When butter has melted, add onion and garlic and sauté for 5 minutes, stirring occasionally.

Transfer zucchini and yellow squash to a large bowl and mash with a potato masher. Squeeze the milk from the bread and add the bread, eggs, onion mixture, Parmesan cheese, ½ teaspoon salt, and pepper and blend well. Spoon mixture into a greased 1½-quart soufflé dish and bake for 50 minutes or until golden brown.

To Make Marinade Combine lemon juice, basil, olive oil, salt, and pepper in a resealable plastic bag and blend. Add tuna steaks and turn to coat all over. Refrigerate for 30 minutes, turning tuna at least once.

To Prepare Tuna on an Outdoor Grill Remove tuna steaks from marinade. Over moderately hot coals, place tuna on a grill coated with a nonstick vegetable spray. Cover grill and cook for 10 minutes or until tuna is no longer red when a knife is inserted into the thickest part.

To Prepare Tuna on an Indoor Grill Remove tuna steaks from marinade. Place tuna on a preheated grill over moderate heat and cook for 15 minutes on first side and 12 to 15 minutes on other side or until tuna is no longer red when a knife is inserted into the thickest part.

To Serve Place a tuna steak and a serving of zucchini and yellow squash soufflé on each of four dinner plates. Spoon some grilled red pepper aioli over each tuna steak and garnish with a sprig of parsley or watercress.

Triple-Spicy Shrimp Kebabs

A friend who knows how much my husband enjoys hot and spicy food gave me this recipe to test his tolerance for fire. He absolutely adored it. But be forewarned—it is not for the faint of heart. An extra bonus is that the shrimp do not have to be peeled before being marinated. Serve with Lemon Rice and Capers (page 266) and Grilled Pineapple Rings (page 330).

6 tablespoons fresh lemon juice	1½ teaspoons salt
1½ tablespoons chili oil (see note)	1½ teaspoons freshly ground pepper
1 tablespoon curry powder	1½ pounds medium shrimp, unpeeled
1½ teaspoons cayenne	

To Make Marinade Combine lemon juice, chili oil, curry powder, cayenne, salt, and pepper in a resealable plastic bag and blend. Add shrimp and turn to coat all over. Refrigerate for 2 to 8 hours, turning shrimp at least once.

To Prepare Kebabs on an Outdoor Grill Soak bamboo skewers in water for 30 minutes or more. Thread shrimp on skewers and place over moderately hot coals on a grill coated with a nonstick vegetable spray. Cover grill and cook for 6 minutes on each side.

To Prepare Kebabs on an Indoor Grill Soak bamboo skewers in water for 30 minutes or more. Thread shrimp on skewers and place on a preheated grill over moderate heat. Cook for 15 minutes, turning shrimp occasionally.

Note Chili oil is available in Asian food stores.

Tuna with Strawberry and Mango Salsa

Strawberry and Mango Salsa (recipe below) provides a beautiful contrast in colors and taste to tuna. In fact, this salsa would be delicious with most other seafood or poultry as well. Serve with Basmati and Wild Rice (page 144).

Strawberry and Mango Salsa

12 large strawberries, tops removed and diced
½ cup mango, peeled and diced
¼ cup yellow bell pepper, seeded and diced
1 tablespoon chopped cilantro leaves
1 jalapeño chile, minced (see note)
2 tablespoons fresh lime juice
1 tablespoon rice wine vinegar

Marinade

½ cup soy sauce
¼ cup granulated sugar
1 tablespoon minced fresh ginger
1 clove garlic, minced
4 yellowfin tuna steaks (6 ounces each)

To Make Salsa Combine strawberries, mango, yellow pepper, cilantro, jalapeño chile, lime juice, and rice wine vinegar in a non-metal bowl and blend well. Refrigerate strawberry and mango salsa, covered, for up to 2 hours.

To Make Marinade Combine soy sauce, sugar, ginger, and garlic in a resealable plastic bag and blend. Add tuna steaks and turn to coat all over. Refrigerate for up to 1 hour.

To Prepare Tuna on an Outdoor Grill Remove tuna steaks from marinade. Over moderately hot coals, place the tuna steaks on a grill coated with a nonstick vegetable spray. Cover grill and cook for 5 minutes on each side or until tuna is no longer red when a knife is inserted into the thickest part.

To Prepare Tuna on an Indoor Grill Remove tuna steaks from marinade. Place tuna on a preheated grill over moderately high heat and cook for 15 minutes on first side and 12 to 15 minutes on other side or until tuna is no longer red when a knife is inserted into the thickest part.

To Serve Place a tuna steak on each of four dinner plates and spoon some strawberry and mango salsa over it. Garnish with a sprig of cilantro.

Note The seeds of a jalapeño chile are very hot. To avoid burning your skin, wear rubber or latex gloves when removing the seeds. Immediately wash the knife, cutting surface, and gloves when finished.

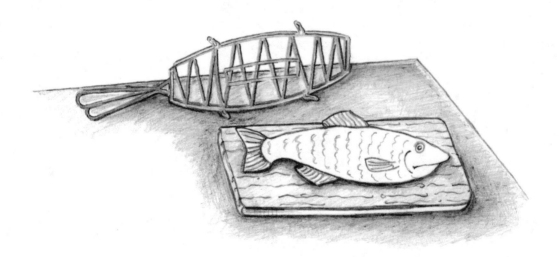

6

VEGETABLES
AND FRUIT

Grilling is one of the most satisfying ways to prepare vegetables and fruit. Grilled fruits and vegetables are not only a way to add flavor, texture, and color to your grilling creation, but also a wonderful opportunity to enhance the health benefits of your menu. Heat from the grill seals in the natural flavors and moisture of fruit and vegetables, resulting in a treat that will seem to melt in your mouth. Taking advantage of the unique smoky flavor they absorb from the grill, you can combine grilled vegetables with a host of other ingredients to create a savory ratatouille, a flavorful soup, a vegetable au gratin, a zesty appetizer . . . the possibilities are limitless. Grilled fruits that become caramelized during the grilling process are the perfect accompaniment to meats, poultry, or fish. For a simple but unusual dessert, spoon grilled apples, bananas, or pineapple over ice cream or frozen yogurt.

Most vegetables should be lightly coated with vegetable or olive oil before grilling; fruit benefits from a basting of melted butter. It is best to grill vegetables and fruit on a covered grill so they will cook evenly. Although there is no cover for an indoor grill, you will still be pleased with the tasty results when you grill vegetables and fruit in the kitchen. For fruit or vegetables that are delicate or have an unusual shape, I encourage you to use a hinged wire basket or a skewer, especially the two-pronged variety.

The vegetables and fruits described here are only a sampling of some of the more common varieties that can be prepared on a grill. Many other vegetables and fruits, some of which may be among your favorites, are good candidates for grilling. Once you have mastered the art of preparing these fruits and vegetables on the grill, you will want to experiment with others.

FRUIT

APPLE

Granny Smith, pippin, McIntosh, Cortland, Rhode Island, Gravenstein, and greening apples are all excellent on the grill because they are firm and slightly tart. They should be washed first, cored, and cut into rings, halves, or wedges. Brush them with melted butter before grilling. Cooking time will vary, but both sides of the apples should be brown and fork-tender.

BANANA

Bananas retain their wonderful, distinctive flavor when grilled. Choose firm, slightly underripe bananas. Brush the bananas with a little melted butter and grill them until brown all over.

PEAR

Bosc, Anjou, Seckel, and Bartlett pears are the best choice for the grill, because they are firm enough to withstand the heat. Cut the pears in half and remove the seeds. Brush them with melted butter and grill on both sides until lightly browned and fork-tender.

PINEAPPLE

Pineapples cooked on a grill become almost caramelized. The intensity of their sweet flavor complements fish, poultry, or pork. Choose a pineapple that is ripe and has a fresh smell. Remove the top, sides, and bottom and cut it into rings or chunks. Cook until brown all over.

STRAWBERRY

Plump strawberries cooked on a grill are a sweet taste sensation. They can be served as an accompaniment with seafood or as a topping on frozen yogurt. Cook until fork-tender.

VEGETABLES

ARTICHOKE

Artichokes are available throughout the year, but they are at their peak in flavor and quality during March, April, and May. Look for artichokes that are heavy, have compact leaves, and are free of any purple tips. Before grilling, they should be steamed or parboiled for at least 25 to 40 minutes or until a leaf near the bottom can be easily pulled away. Remove most of the stem and cut the artichoke in half. Remove *all* the fibrous strands, or choke, with a spoon or melon baller. As you finish with each artichoke, place it in a bowl filled with cold water and lemon juice (the lemon juice will prevent the artichoke from turning brown). Grill until the cut side is brown.

BELGIAN ENDIVE

Belgian endive leaves are five to six inches long and are tightly wrapped, resembling a cigar. Cut endives in half vertically, brush with oil, and grill on each side until fork-tender.

CARROT

Grilling results in a carrot that is crisp on the outside, with an intensely sweet surprise on the inside. Choose firm, unblemished, medium-size carrots that are bright orange and uniform in shape. Cook them unpeeled until brown all over.

CORN

Whether corn is grilled in its husk or without, it remains fabulously delicious and sweet. The fresher the corn, the sweeter it will be. Select corn with tightly wrapped green husks and a dry silk. When you peel back the husk, the kernels should be uniformly plump. To prepare corn in the husk, gently peel back, but do not detach, the layers of husk on each corn and remove the exposed outer threads. Remove one of the outer pieces of husk to use as a string and set it aside. Gently return the remaining husk to its original shape around the corn, twisting it at the top. Secure the twisted top by tying the reserved husk around it. Soak the corn in cold water for 10 minutes to an hour. Squeeze out the excess water before grilling. For grilling without the husk, first remove the entire husk and silk threads and baste the corn with butter. Grill until brown and fork-tender.

EGGPLANT

Eggplant is delectable when instilled with a hint of smoky flavor from a grill. My favorite variety is the Japanese eggplant, which is long and slender with a beautiful, rich purple color. The other common variety is the Western eggplant, which is deep purple, large, and pear-shaped. Larger eggplants should be salted before grilling, to remove any excess moisture and bitterness. Cut the eggplant in halves, slices, or chunks and grill until brown and fork-tender.

FENNEL

Florence fennel is a white bulbous root with heavy stalks growing from the top that resemble celery. It has a wonderful anise flavor and can be eaten raw or cooked. Trim the stalks and remove the outer leaves and end of the fennel. Cut the remaining bulb into quarters or rounds and grill until fork-tender.

LEEK

The onion flavor of leeks is accentuated and made somewhat sweeter when cooked on a grill. Select firm, thin leeks and wash them to remove any grit. Slice them in half lengthwise and gently rinse them under cold water. Grill on both sides until brown and fork-tender.

MUSHROOM

Button and portobello mushrooms as well as wild mushrooms, such as cepes (porcini), shiitake, crimini, and oyster, are excellent on the grill. Grill mushrooms until fork-tender.

ONION

Bermuda, yellow, Vidalia, Maui, and Spanish onions become very sweet when grilled. They are excellent as an accompaniment to all meats or as a component of a vegetarian meal. The onions can be peeled, halved, quartered, or cut into wedges. Cook until fork-tender.

PEPPER

Bell peppers can be found in an assortment of colors, including green, yellow, orange, red, and purple. The green bell pepper is the least sweet tasting, while the red is the sweetest. The sweetness of all varieties is enhanced when peppers are grilled. When grilling on an indoor grill-range, it is important to choose peppers that are symmetrical in shape and have flat sides. This will ensure that the skins of the peppers get evenly charred. My favorite way to prepare peppers on the grill is to cook them over moderately hot coals on an outdoor grill for 14 to 20 minutes or on an indoor grill over high heat for 20 to 30 minutes. Turn the peppers as the skins blacken or until skins are charred all over. Once peppers are grilled, place them in a plastic bag and allow to steam for 15 minutes. When they are cool enough to handle, peel away the skin and remove the top and seeds. Peppers can also be grilled halved, quartered, or cut into chunks; cook until brown and fork-tender.

Milder chile peppers, such as the Anaheim, banana, pasilla, and poblano peppers, are also delicious when grilled. They are prepared the same way as bell peppers.

POTATO

Potatoes prepared on the grill are a delicious accompaniment to any meal. They can be brushed with oil and grilled whole, halved, quartered, or cut into chunks. Cook the potatoes until brown all over and fork-tender. A whole potato can also be cooked by wrapping it in aluminum foil and placing it on the grill.

SQUASH

Summer squash and some winter squash are excellent on the grill. Summer squash include zucchini, yellow or crookneck squash, and pattypan squash. The skin should not be removed before grilling. Summer squash can be grilled whole, halved, quartered, or cut into chunks until fork-tender.

The best winter squash for grilling are the acorn, buttercup, banana, butternut, and hubbard. Acorn squash should be halved, buttercup and hubbard should be cut into chunks, and butternut should be halved or cut into rounds. Cook the squash until fork-tender.

SWEET POTATO AND YAM

These two vegetables are frequently confused, because they are very similar in size, shape, texture, flavor, and appearance. Although sweet potatoes and yams are both tubers, they belong to different botanical families. The sweet potato originated in the Western Hemisphere and has either a dark red skin with a moist, deep-orange flesh or a tan skin with a dry, yellow flesh. True yams originated in Asia and Africa, and it is believed that the African slaves introduced them to the New World. Yams have a rough, brown skin with either yellow, white, or purple flesh. Cooked on the grill, yams and sweet potatoes are equally delicious. They can be sliced lengthwise into ovals or sliced into rounds or chunks. Cook until fork-tender.

TOMATO

The tomato is actually a fruit, although most people think of it as a vegetable. Grilled tomatoes provide a striking visual contrast to most meat entrees, and the extra bonus is the marvelous, smoky flavor they contribute. Firm beefsteak tomatoes are excellent for grilling. They should be cut into thick slices. Roma or plum tomatoes can be halved or skewered, while cherry tomatoes should be skewered. Cook until slightly brown.

Garlic-Basted Grilled Corn on the Cob

SERVES 4

These succulent and flavorful ears of corn received rave reviews, even from those who didn't think they liked corn on the cob. Be prepared to field requests for second helpings.

Savory Basting Butter

6 tablespoons butter, melted

2 cloves garlic, minced

¼ teaspoon hot pepper sauce

1 teaspoon thyme

1 teaspoon salt

4 ears of corn, husks and silk removed

To Make Basting Butter Combine butter, garlic, hot pepper sauce, thyme, and salt in a small dish and blend.

To Prepare Corn on an Outdoor Grill Over moderately hot coals, place corn on a grill coated with a nonstick vegetable spray. Cover grill and cook for 15 to 20 minutes or until ears are fork-tender, turning corn frequently and brushing with savory basting butter.

To Prepare Corn on an Indoor Grill Place corn on a preheated grill over moderately high heat and cook for 30 to 35 minutes or until ears are fork-tender, turning corn frequently and brushing with savory basting butter.

Marinated Vegetables

These savory marinated vegetables, in combination with the smoky flavor from the grill, are fabulous. They can be served as an accompaniment, intermingled with fresh pasta, or spooned into warmed pita bread halves and topped with a yogurt or tahini sauce.

3 tablespoons extra virgin olive oil	1 to 2 ears of corn, husks removed and cut into 8 (1-inch) slices
3 tablespoons fresh lemon juice	8 fresh mushrooms
5 large cloves garlic, minced	1 red bell pepper, seeded and cut into 8 pieces
1½ teaspoons thyme	1 yellow bell pepper, seeded and cut into 8 pieces
1½ teaspoons basil	1 red onion, cut into 8 pieces and secured with a toothpick
1½ teaspoons oregano	
¼ heaping teaspoon crushed red pepper	
8 new potatoes	

To Make Marinade Combine olive oil, lemon juice, garlic, thyme, basil, oregano, and crushed red pepper in a resealable plastic bag and blend.

Place potatoes in a large saucepan with enough water to cover. Bring to a boil over high heat. Turn heat off, cover saucepan, and allow potatoes to come to room temperature. (This method for cooking potatoes can also be used to make hard-boiled eggs.) When potatoes are cool, drain well. Cut potatoes in half.

Place potatoes, corn, mushrooms, red pepper, yellow pepper, and red onion in marinade and turn to coat all over. Marinate for several hours or overnight, turning vegetables at least once.

To Prepare Vegetables on an Outdoor Grill Soak bamboo skewers in water for 30 minutes or more. Remove toothpicks from onion and alternate potatoes, corn, mushrooms, red pepper, yellow pepper, and red onion on skewers (see note). Over moderately hot coals, place vegetables on a grill coated with a nonstick vegetable spray. Cover grill and cook for 8 to 12 minutes or until vegetables are well browned, turning vegetable kebabs every 4 minutes.

To Prepare Vegetables on an Indoor Grill Soak bamboo skewers in water for 30 minutes or more. Remove toothpicks from onion and alternate potatoes, corn, mushrooms, red pepper, yellow pepper, and red onion on skewers (see note). Place vegetables on a preheated grill over moderately high heat and cook for 20 to 30 minutes, turning vegetable kebabs every 8 minutes.

Note If vegetables are uneven in size and shape, thread the vegetables onto two bamboo skewers that are parallel to each other, about 1 inch apart. This will make it easier to turn the skewers and it will keep the vegetables secure.

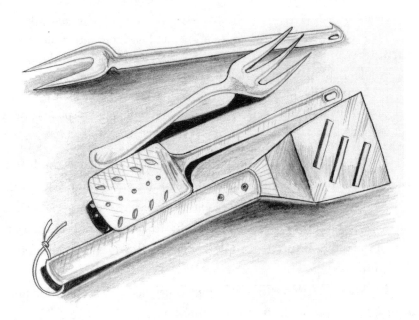

Pasta with Grilled Vegetables and Pesto Sauce

SERVES 4

Pesto is an Italian sauce that transforms a simple dish into a culinary prize. It achieves the ultimate perfection when combined with fresh pasta and grilled vegetables. Serve with crusty Italian bread.

Pesto Sauce

- 2½ cups packed fresh basil, washed and drained
- ¼ cup pine nuts
- 1 tablespoon chopped garlic
- ¼ teaspoon salt
- 6 tablespoons extra virgin olive oil, plus olive oil as needed
- ¼ cup freshly grated pecorino cheese

Marinade

- 1 eggplant (12 to 16 ounces), cut horizontally into ¼-inch-thick slices
  Salt
- 1½ tablespoons balsamic vinegar
- 1½ tablespoons extra virgin olive oil
- 6 large cloves garlic, minced
- ½ teaspoon salt
- ½ teaspoon freshly ground pepper
- 1 zucchini (8 ounces), cut horizontally into ¼-inch-thick slices
- 2 red bell peppers, seeded and each cut into 4 pieces
- 1 large portobello mushroom
- 1 package (9 ounces) fresh red bell pepper, spinach, or other flavor fettuccine

To Make Pesto In the work bowl of a food processor fitted with a metal blade, process basil, pine nuts, garlic, and salt until finely chopped. Add 6 tablespoons olive oil and puree. Add pecorino cheese and blend well. Transfer pesto to a container and pour enough olive oil on top to completely cover. Refrigerate pesto, covered, until ready to use.

To Make Marinade Place eggplant slices in a colander and sprinkle with salt. Set aside for 30 minutes.

Combine balsamic vinegar, olive oil, garlic, salt, and pepper in a resealable plastic bag and blend. Add eggplant, zucchini, red peppers, and portobello mushroom and turn to coat all over. Set aside for 2 to 3 hours, turning vegetables occasionally.

To Prepare Vegetables on an Outdoor Grill Remove eggplant, zucchini, red peppers, and portobello mushroom from marinade. Over moderately hot coals, place vegetables on a grilling grid coated with a nonstick vegetable spray. Cover grill and cook for 10 to 12 minutes or until vegetables are brown and fork-tender, turning frequently. Cut vegetables into thin slices and set aside.

To Prepare Vegetables on an Indoor Grill Remove eggplant, zucchini, red peppers, and portobello mushroom from marinade. Place a grilling grid coated with a nonstick vegetable spray on an indoor grill and preheat grill. Place vegetables on grid over moderately high heat and cook the mushroom for 16 minutes and the remaining vegetables for 20 to 24 minutes or until brown and fork-tender, turning frequently. Cut vegetables into thin slices and set aside.

To Serve While grilling the vegetables, combine 2 tablespoons water and ½ cup pesto in a small dish and blend well. Prepare fettuccine according to package directions. Drain well.

Place fettuccine and pesto in a large serving bowl and blend well. Distribute the grilled vegetables over fettuccine and garnish with fresh basil. Alternatively, the fettuccine, pesto, and vegetables can be combined together in a large serving bowl.

Note To garnish individual servings, cook 4 small plum tomatoes in boiling water for 1 minute. Drain. Remove skins and cut each tomato in half. Place 2 tomato halves, cut side down and with the slender tops slightly overlapping each other, beside the pasta on the plate. Partially tuck 2 to 3 fresh basil leaves under the slender tops of the tomatoes.

Grilled Polenta

The jalapeño pepper and green onions, along with the smoky aroma from the grill, give a wonderful Southwestern flavor to polenta. Serve it with everything!

2 tablespoons butter
2 green onions, thinly sliced
1 jalapeño chile, seeded
   and minced (see note)

1 can (14½ ounces)
   chicken broth
1 cup yellow cornmeal
½ teaspoon salt

To Make Polenta Melt butter in a small pan over moderate heat. Add green onions and jalapeño chile and sauté for 3 minutes, stirring occasionally.

Place chicken broth and 2 cups cold water in a medium saucepan and bring to a boil over moderately high heat. Slowly add cornmeal and salt, stirring rapidly with a wooden spoon. Reduce heat to moderately low and cook, stirring frequently, for 25 to 35 minutes or until the mixture is very thick and begins to pull away from the sides of the saucepan. Add green onion mixture and blend well. Spread polenta in an 8-inch square pan coated with a nonstick vegetable spray and allow it to come to room temperature. Cover pan and refrigerate polenta overnight. Cut polenta into 6 pieces.

To Prepare Polenta on an Outdoor Grill Over hot coals, place polenta pieces on a grilling grid heavily coated with a nonstick vegetable spray. Cook polenta, covered, for 12 to 15 minutes on each side or until polenta pieces are golden brown.

To Prepare Polenta on an Indoor Grill Place the polenta pieces (see note) on a preheated grill over moderately high heat and cook for 25 minutes on each side or until polenta pieces are golden brown.

Note The seeds of a jalapeño chile are very hot. To avoid burning your skin, wear rubber or latex gloves when removing the seeds. Immediately wash the knife, cutting surface, and gloves when finished.

Note If you have a grilling grid to use on an indoor grill, coat it with a nonstick vegetable spray and cook the polenta pieces on it.

Grilled Portobello Sandwiches

A friend gave me her secret recipe for marinating portobello mushrooms: Newman's Own Olive Oil and Vinegar Dressing. It adds a savory flavor to mushrooms, transforming them into delicious fillings for a variety of sandwiches.

½ cup Newman's Own Olive Oil and Vinegar Dressing (or bottled Italian dressing)

2 large portobello mushrooms, stems removed

2 small red bell peppers

8 slices jalapeño cheese bread (or other dense bread), cut into ½-inch-thick slices

4 ounces goat cheese (such as Montrachet), at room temperature (see note)

1 cup mixed baby greens

To Marinate Combine Newman's Own Olive Oil and Vinegar Dressing and portobello mushrooms in a resealable plastic bag and turn mushrooms to coat all over. Refrigerate for 2 to 4 hours, turning mushrooms at least once.

To Prepare Peppers and Mushrooms on an Outdoor Grill Over moderately hot coals, place the red peppers on a grill coated with a nonstick vegetable spray. Cover and cook for 20 to 24 minutes or until skins are charred all over, turning the peppers as skins blacken. Once grilled, place the peppers in a plastic bag and allow to steam for 15 minutes. When they are cool enough to handle, peel away the skins and remove the tops and seeds (do not rinse the peppers). Cut the red peppers into slivers.

Remove mushrooms from dressing. Place them on a grill coated with a nonstick vegetable spray. Cover grill and cook for 5 minutes on each side or until mushrooms are brown and fork-tender. Cut mushrooms into slices.

To Prepare Peppers and Mushrooms on an Indoor Grill Place the red peppers on a preheated grill over high heat and cook for 20 to 24 minutes or until skins are charred all over, turning the peppers as skins blacken. Once grilled, place the peppers in a plastic bag and allow to steam for 15 minutes. When they are cool enough to handle, peel away the skins and remove the tops and seeds (do not rinse the peppers). Cut the red peppers into slivers.

Remove mushrooms from dressing. Place them on a preheated grill over moderately high heat and cook for 14 to 16 minutes or until mushrooms are brown and fork-tender, turning every 4 minutes. Cut mushrooms into slices.

To Serve Toast one side of eight slices of bread on grill or under a broiler. Spread goat cheese on four untoasted sides of bread and arrange a thin layer of mushrooms, red pepper slivers, and mixed baby greens over cheese. Top with remaining bread, untoasted side down, and cut each sandwich in half.

Note As a variation, substitute Gorgonzola butter for the goat cheese. Combine 2 ounces Gorgonzola cheese with 1 tablespoon butter (both at room temperature) in a small bowl and blend well. (The Gorgonzola butter can be made a day ahead and refrigerated in a covered container. Bring to room temperature before using.) Use French bread in place of the cheese bread and drizzle Newman's dressing on the sandwiches.

Garlic Mashed Potatoes with Grilled Vegetables

SERVES 4

This dish is a vegetarian's wish come true. Even if you are not a vegetarian, you will love the combination of garlic mashed potatoes and grilled vegetables, topped with a rich wild mushroom sauce. Need I say more?

Vegetables and Marinade

1 eggplant, cut horizontally into ¼-inch-thick slices
Salt for sprinkling, plus ½ teaspoon salt

2 tablespoons balsamic vinegar

2 tablespoons extra virgin olive oil

4 large cloves garlic, minced

½ teaspoon freshly ground pepper

1 large red bell pepper, seeded and cut into 4 pieces

1 zucchini (about 8 ounces), cut horizontally into ¼-inch-thick slices

Mushroom Sauce

2½ tablespoons butter

½ pound shiitake mushrooms, thinly sliced

2 tablespoons flour

2 cups milk

¼ teaspoon salt

¼ teaspoon freshly ground pepper

Garlic Mashed Potatoes (page 78)

To Make Marinade Place eggplant slices in a colander and sprinkle with salt. Set aside for 30 minutes.

Combine balsamic vinegar, olive oil, garlic, salt, and pepper in a resealable plastic bag and blend. Add eggplant, red pepper, and zucchini and turn to coat all over. Set aside for 2 hours, turning vegetables occasionally.

To Make Sauce Melt butter in a medium saucepan over moderate heat. Add mushrooms and sauté for 5 minutes, stirring occasionally. Add flour and sauté for 1 minute, stirring frequently. Gradually add milk, salt, and pepper and cook for 5 to 10 minutes or until sauce thickens, stirring frequently. Cover and keep warm over very low heat.

To Prepare Vegetables on an Outdoor Grill Remove eggplant, red pepper, and zucchini from marinade. Over moderately hot coals, place vegetables on a grilling grid. Cover grill and cook for 10 to 12 minutes or until vegetables are brown and fork-tender, turning occasionally. Cut vegetables into slivers.

To Prepare Vegetables on an Indoor Grill Remove eggplant, red pepper, and zucchini from marinade. Place vegetables on a preheated grill over moderately high heat and cook for 16 to 24 minutes or until vegetables are brown and fork-tender, turning every 4 minutes. Cut vegetables into slivers.

To Serve Using an ice cream scoop, mound two scoops of garlic mashed potatoes on top of each other on each of four dinner plates. Surround the potatoes with vegetables, dividing evenly. Spoon mushroom sauce over each serving.

Grilled Accordion Potatoes

You won't have any trouble understanding how the recipe got its name. Thin vertical slices are made three-fourths of the way through each potato. When they are done grilling, the partially flayed potatoes take on the appearance of an accordion. Listen carefully as they grill—you may hear a few bars of "Lady of Spain"!

6 baking potatoes	½ teaspoon freshly ground
12 tablespoons (1½ sticks)	pepper
butter, melted	¾ to 1 cup freshly grated sharp
1 tablespoon canola oil	cheddar cheese
¾ teaspoon salt	

To Season Potatoes Make very thin vertical cuts three-fourths through the potato, making sure to leave the bottom of the potato intact.

Combine butter and canola oil in a dish and blend. Roll each potato in butter mixture, completely coating them. Place each potato on a piece of aluminum foil and pour any remaining butter over each, dividing evenly. Season potatoes with salt and pepper. Enclose the potatoes in aluminum foil and wrap securely.

To Prepare Potatoes on an Outdoor Grill Over moderately hot coals, place potatoes on a grill. Cover grill and cook for 60 minutes or until potatoes are soft when lightly squeezed, turning potatoes occasionally. Remove potatoes from grill and open the top of aluminum foil. Spoon cheese over potatoes and loosely cover with aluminum foil to allow cheese to melt (see note).

To Prepare Potatoes on an Indoor Grill Place potatoes on a preheated grill over high heat and cook for 1 hour and 30 minutes or until potatoes are soft when lightly squeezed, turning potatoes occasionally. Remove potatoes from grill and open the top of aluminum foil. Spoon cheese over potatoes and loosely cover with aluminum foil to allow cheese to melt (see note).

Note The accordion potatoes can be served without the cheese.

Grilled Pineapple Rings

This recipe will become one of your favorite ways to serve this tropical fruit. The pineapple rings become deliciously caramelized as they cook and make a great addition to poultry, pork, and seafood.

1 ripe pineapple

To Assemble Pineapple Remove top, bottom, and sides of pineapple with a sharp knife. Cut the pineapple into 1-inch-thick slices.

To Prepare Pineapple on an Outdoor Grill Place the pineapple rings on a grilling grid coated with a nonstick vegetable spray and cook over moderately hot coals for 4 to 6 minutes on each side or until pineapple rings are golden brown.

To Prepare Pineapple on an Indoor Grill Place the pineapple rings on a preheated grill over high heat and cook for 10 to 12 minutes or until pineapple rings are golden brown, turning once.

Grilled Bermuda Onions

Grilling Bermuda onions enhances their sweetness. Serve with beef or pork.

4	Bermuda onions
2	to 4 tablespoons butter, at room temperature

Salt and freshly ground pepper, to taste

To Assemble Onions Do not remove skins from Bermuda onions. Rub butter all over onions and wrap each in aluminum foil, making sure they are completely enclosed.

To Prepare Onions on an Outdoor Grill Over moderately hot coals, place Bermuda onions on the grill. Cover grill and cook for 40 to 45 minutes or until onions are soft when lightly squeezed.

To Prepare Onions on an Indoor Grill Place Bermuda onions on a preheated grill over high heat and cook for 1 hour or until onions are soft when lightly squeezed, turning occasionally.

To Serve Remove aluminum foil and top onions with a pat of butter. Season with salt and pepper.

Grilled Artichokes

Artichokes are at their peak in flavor and quality during March, April, and May. Look for those that are heavy, have compact leaves, and are free of any purple tips.

4 artichokes
2 tablespoons fresh lemon juice

Lemon Basting Butter

3 tablespoons butter, melted
2 tablespoons fresh lemon juice
1 clove garlic, minced
⅛ teaspoon salt
⅛ teaspoon freshly ground pepper

To Parboil Artichokes Steam the artichokes for 25 to 40 minutes or until a leaf near the bottom can be easily pulled away. Drain. Remove most of the stem and cut the artichokes in half. Remove all the fibrous strands with a spoon or melon baller. As you finish with each artichoke, place it in a bowl filled with enough cold water to cover and lemon juice (the lemon juice will prevent the artichokes from turning brown).

To Make Basting Butter Combine the butter, lemon juice, garlic, salt, and pepper in a small bowl and blend.

To Prepare Artichokes on an Outdoor Grill Brush inside of artichokes with lemon basting butter. Over moderately hot coals, place artichokes, buttered side down, on a grill coated with a nonstick vegetable spray. Cover grill and cook for 8 to 10 minutes or until artichokes are tender when gently pierced with a skewer. Remove artichokes from grill and brush with additional basting butter.

To Prepare Artichokes on an Indoor Grill Brush inside of artichokes with lemon basting butter. Place artichokes, buttered side down, on a preheated grill over moderately high heat and cook for 20 to 25 minutes or until artichokes are tender when gently pierced with a skewer. Remove artichokes from grill and brush with additional basting butter.

Grilled Eggplant and Red Pepper Sandwiches

SERVES 4

These sandwiches are brought to a new dimension of spicy flavor when accented with grilled red pepper mayonnaise. Make extra mayonnaise and serve it as a dip with an array of fresh vegetables. Serve the grilled eggplant and red pepper sandwiches with an assortment of fresh melon slices.

5 red bell peppers

Grilled Red Pepper Mayonnaise

2 large cloves garlic
½ teaspoon red wine vinegar
¼ teaspoon cayenne
½ cup mayonnaise

Grilled Eggplant and Red Pepper Sandwiches

1 eggplant, cut horizontally into ¼-inch-thick slices
Salt
2 tablespoons Newman's Own Olive Oil and Vinegar Dressing (or bottled Italian dressing)
1 loaf French bread
1 cup fresh spinach, washed, dried, and stems removed

To Prepare Peppers on an Outdoor Grill Over moderately hot coals, place the red peppers on a grill coated with a nonstick vegetable spray. Cover and cook for 20 to 24 minutes or until skins are charred all over, turning the peppers as skins blacken. Once grilled, place the peppers in a plastic bag and allow to steam for 15 minutes. When they are cool enough to handle, peel away the skins and remove the tops and seeds (do not rinse the peppers). Use two peppers for mayonnaise and three peppers for sandwiches.

To Prepare Peppers on an Indoor Grill Place the red peppers on a preheated grill over high heat and cook for 30 to 40 minutes or until skins are charred all over, turning the peppers as skins blacken. Once grilled, place the peppers in a plastic bag and allow to steam for 15 minutes. When they are cool enough to handle, peel away the skins and remove the tops and seeds (do not rinse the peppers). Use 2 peppers for mayonnaise and 3 peppers for sandwiches.

To Make Mayonnaise In the work bowl of a food processor fitted with a metal blade, process garlic until finely chopped. Add 2 grilled red peppers and puree. Add red wine vinegar and cayenne and process until blended. Add mayonnaise and process with on/off pulses until just blended. Transfer red pepper mayonnaise to a container, cover, and refrigerate until ready to serve.

To Prepare Eggplant on an Outdoor Grill Place eggplant slices in a colander and sprinkle with salt. Set aside for 30 minutes. Pat eggplant dry with a paper towel and brush each side with Newman's Own Olive Oil and Vinegar Dressing. Over moderately hot coals, place eggplant on a grill coated with a nonstick vegetable spray. Cover and cook for 5 to 6 minutes on each side or until slices are brown and fork-tender, turning frequently.

To Prepare Eggplant on an Indoor Grill Place eggplant slices in a colander and sprinkle with salt. Set aside for 30 minutes. Pat eggplant dry with a paper towel and brush each side with Newman's Own Olive Oil and Vinegar Dressing. Place eggplant on a preheated grill over moderately high heat and cook for 16 to 20 minutes or until slices are brown and fork-tender, turning eggplant every 4 minutes.

To Serve While grilling the eggplant, cut the remaining 3 grilled red peppers into thin slices. Cut the French bread in half horizontally, lightly brush each side with olive oil, and place on grill oil-side down or under a preheated broiler oil-side up until lightly toasted. Arrange a layer each of spinach, eggplant slices, and red peppers on bottom half of bread. Spread a thick layer of grilled red pepper mayonnaise on top half of bread and place on top of vegetables. Cut the bread on the diagonal into four sandwiches.

Acorn Squash with Fruited Wild Rice

When preparing acorn squash on an indoor grill, it is best to prebake it. The squash is delicious filled with Fruited Wild Rice (recipe below), but it can also be served alone with just the brown sugar and butter glaze.

Squash

- 2 tablespoons butter, melted
- 2 tablespoons packed dark brown sugar
- 2 acorn squash (1 pound each), cut in half and seeds removed

Fruited Wild Rice

- ¾ cup wild rice, rinsed with cold water
- 1½ tablespoons butter
- 1 medium Vidalia onion or other sweet onion, minced
- 6 tablespoons minced, mixed dried fruit, such as apples, apricots, peaches, and raisins
- 3 tablespoons toasted almonds (see note)
- ⅜ teaspoon salt
- ⅜ teaspoon freshly ground pepper

To Prepare Squash on an Outdoor Grill Combine butter and brown sugar in a small dish and blend well. Brush mixture all over the inside of the acorn squash. Place acorn squash, cut side down, over moderately hot coals on a grill coated with a nonstick vegetable spray. Cover grill and cook for 20 minutes. Turn squash over and brush with additional butter mixture. Cover grill and cook for another 20 minutes or until squash is fork-tender.

To Prepare Squash on an Indoor Grill Preheat oven to 350 degrees. Place acorn squash, cut side down, in a shallow pan and bake for 25 minutes. Combine butter and brown sugar in a small dish and blend well. Brush mixture all over the inside of the acorn squash. Place acorn squash, buttered side down, on a preheated grill over moderate heat and cook for 25 minutes or until squash is fork-tender. Remove squash from grill and brush with remaining melted butter mixture.

To Make Rice While grilling the acorn squash, place rice in a medium saucepan over moderately high heat and add enough water to come at least 2 inches above the rice. Bring to a boil and simmer for 30 minutes or until the grains begin to open.

While wild rice is cooking, melt butter in a small pan over moderate heat. Add onion and sauté for 3 minutes, stirring occasionally.

Drain the wild rice. Transfer wild rice to a bowl and add the onion, dried fruit, almonds, salt, and pepper to drained wild rice and blend well.

To Serve Spoon wild rice into acorn squash halves and serve while hot.

Note To toast almonds: Preheat oven to 350 degrees. Place almonds in a shallow pan and bake for 10 to 15 minutes or until golden brown.

Chilled and Spicy Grilled Red Pepper Soup

SERVES 4

Although this soup is served chilled, it is hot and spicy in taste. The grilled red peppers provide the distinctive taste, while the combination of spices provides the "heat." This soup is sure to become one of your favorites!

Grilled Red Pepper Soup

- 4 red bell peppers
- 5 teaspoons chopped garlic
- 5 teaspoons chopped fresh ginger
- 1 teaspoon cumin
- ½ teaspoon allspice
- ½ teaspoon turmeric
- ¼ teaspoon crushed red pepper
- 2 large onions, coarsely chopped
- 3 cans (14½ ounces each) chicken broth
- ½ teaspoon freshly ground pepper
- ¼ teaspoon salt

Saffron Cream

- ⅛ teaspoon saffron threads
- ¾ teaspoon finely minced garlic
- ¾ teaspoon finely minced fresh ginger
- ½ cup sour cream

- 1 cup cooked corn kernels

To Prepare Peppers on an Outdoor Grill Over moderately hot coals, place the red peppers on a grill coated with nonstick vegetable spray. Cover and cook for 20 to 24 minutes or until skins are charred all over, turning the peppers as skins blacken. Once grilled, place the peppers in a plastic bag and allow to steam for 15 minutes. When they are cool enough to handle, peel away the skins and remove the tops and seeds. Do not rinse the peppers (see note).

To Prepare Peppers on an Indoor Grill Place the red peppers on a preheated grill over high heat and cook for 30 to 40 minutes or until skins are charred all over, turning the peppers as skins blacken. Once grilled, place the peppers in a plastic bag and allow to steam for 15 minutes. When they are cool enough to handle, peel away the skins and remove the tops and seeds; do not rinse the peppers (see note).

To Make Soup In the work bowl of a food processor fitted with a metal blade, process garlic and ginger until finely chopped. Add ⅓ cup cold water, cumin, allspice, turmeric, and crushed red pepper and process the spice mixture until well blended.

Coat a large saucepan with a nonstick vegetable spray and place over moderately low heat for 2 minutes. Add onions, cover, and cook for 15 minutes, stirring occasionally. Increase heat to moderately high, add spice mixture, and cook uncovered for 5 minutes, stirring frequently. Add chicken broth, pepper, and salt and bring to a boil. Cook for 25 minutes. Allow the soup to cool for 15 minutes.

In a large, clean work bowl of the food processor, process the grilled red peppers until pureed. Add the cooled soup mixture and process until smooth. Transfer soup to a large bowl, cover, and refrigerate for several hours or overnight.

To Make Saffron Cream Dissolve saffron threads in 2 tablespoons warm water. Coat a small saucepan with a nonstick vegetable spray and place over moderate heat for 1 minute. Add garlic and ginger and sauté for 1 minute, stirring frequently. Add saffron mixture and cook for 1 minute. Remove saucepan from heat and add sour cream. Blend well. Transfer the saffron cream to a covered container and refrigerate for several hours or overnight.

To Serve Spoon some corn into each of four soup bowls and ladle soup over corn. Place saffron cream in a pastry bag fitted with a small tip and pipe a decorative design on top of the soup.

Note For an added touch, prepare 1 to 2 Anaheim chiles on the grill, following the directions for grilling red peppers. After the skin, top, and seeds have been removed, dice the grilled chiles. (The diced Anaheim chiles can be refrigerated in a covered container until ready to serve.) Garnish the soup by sprinkling some diced Anaheim chiles in the center of the saffron cream design.

Grilled Eggplant Dip

MAKES 4 CUPS

This spicy Mediterranean eggplant dip will disappear fast when served at a party. The smoky aroma from the grill encases the eggplant as it cooks; combined with the other exotic components, it becomes addictive! Although the smoky flavor may be less intense when the eggplant is prepared on an indoor grill, the dip remains delicious. Serve with sesame pita breads cut into bite-size pieces.

2 pounds Japanese eggplants, halved	½ cup tahini paste
3 tablespoons extra virgin olive oil	7 tablespoons fresh lemon juice
4 large cloves garlic	2 tablespoons sour cream
2 tablespoons chopped parsley	1 tablespoon soy sauce
	1 tablespoon honey
	¼ teaspoon salt

To Prepare Eggplants on an Outdoor Grill Combine eggplants and olive oil in a resealable plastic bag and turn eggplants to coat all over. Over moderately hot coals, place eggplants on a grill coated with a nonstick vegetable spray. Cover grill and cook for 5 minutes on each side or until eggplants are golden brown.

To Prepare Eggplants on an Indoor Grill Combine eggplants and olive oil in a resealable plastic bag and turn eggplants to coat all over. Place eggplants on a preheated grill over moderately high heat and cook for 16 to 24 minutes or until eggplants are golden brown, turning eggplants every 4 minutes.

To Make Dip In the work bowl of a food processor fitted with a metal blade, process garlic and parsley until finely chopped. Add grilled eggplants and process until pureed. Add tahini paste, lemon juice, sour cream, soy sauce, honey, and salt and process until smooth. Transfer grilled eggplant dip to a dish, cover, and refrigerate until ready to serve.

Grilled Fruit Kebabs

SERVES 4

Fruit kebabs are very easy to make on the grill. Choose your favorite fruits to put on the skewers. They can be grilled plain or marinated in a combination of pineapple juice, brown sugar, and a dash of cinnamon or nutmeg.

8   firm strawberries
1   pineapple, cut into 8 chunks

2   bananas, cut into 8 chunks
2   apples, cut into 8 wedges

To Prepare Kebabs on an Outdoor Grill Soak bamboo skewers in water for 30 minutes or more. Alternate strawberries, pineapple, bananas, and apples on skewers. Over moderately hot coals, place skewers on a grill coated with a nonstick vegetable spray. Cover grill and cook for 3 to 5 minutes on each side or until fruit kebabs are lightly browned.

To Prepare Kebabs on an Indoor Grill Soak bamboo skewers in water for 30 minutes or more. Alternate strawberries, pineapple, bananas, and apples on skewers. Place them on a preheated grill over moderately high heat and cook for 20 minutes or until fruit kebabs are lightly browned, turning occasionally.

Grilled New Potatoes

These potatoes are so easy to make. They can be precooked and marinated early in the day and quickly grilled just before serving. They are a great accompaniment to Barbecued Baby Back Pork Ribs (page 224).

2½	pounds new potatoes	½	teaspoon freshly ground
3	tablespoons extra virgin		pepper
	olive oil	½	teaspoon rosemary
½	teaspoon salt	¼	teaspoon paprika

To Marinate Potatoes Place potatoes in a large saucepan with enough water to cover and place over moderate heat. Bring to a boil. Turn off heat, cover saucepan, and allow the potatoes to come to room temperature. Drain and halve the potatoes. Combine olive oil, salt, pepper, rosemary, and paprika in a resealable plastic bag and blend. Add potatoes and turn to coat all over. Set aside for several hours, turning potatoes at least once.

To Prepare Potatoes on an Outdoor Grill Soak bamboo skewers in water for 30 minutes or more. Remove potatoes from marinade and thread them on skewers. Over moderately hot coals, place potatoes on a grill coated with a nonstick vegetable spray. Cover grill and cook for 6 to 8 minutes on each side or until potatoes are well browned.

To Prepare Potatoes on an Indoor Grill Soak bamboo skewers in water for 30 minutes or more. Remove potatoes from marinade and thread them on skewers. Place potatoes on a preheated grill over moderately high heat and cook for 20 to 30 minutes or until potatoes are well browned, turning potatoes every 10 minutes.

Grilled Apple Rings

These apple rings are delicious when served with grilled pork or poultry.

4   firm apples, cored and cut
     ½ inch thick
2   to 4 tablespoons butter, melted

To Prepare Apples on an Outdoor Grill Brush both sides of apple rings with melted butter. Over moderately hot coals, place apples on a grilling grid coated with a nonstick vegetable spray. Cover grill and cook for 4 to 5 minutes on each side or until apples are golden brown.

To Prepare Apples on an Indoor Grill Brush both sides of apple rings with melted butter. Place them on a preheated grill and cook over high heat for 4 to 6 minutes on each side or until apples are fork-tender, turning apples after 4 minutes.

Grilled Poblano Soup

Poblano chiles are dark green, about four to five inches long and three to four inches around. Although they are medium to hot on the heat scale, grilling them tends to make them sweeter. They are delicious when made into a soup and adorned with tortilla strips, shredded cheese, and diced avocado.

6	poblano chiles	1	teaspoon chopped fresh savory leaves
2	tablespoons extra virgin olive oil	½	teaspoon salt
1	potato (8 ounces), diced	½	teaspoon freshly ground pepper
1	medium onion, chopped	¼	teaspoon garlic salt
1	carrot, diced	1	large ripe avocado, cubed and lightly sprinkled with lemon juice
2½	tablespoons flour		
3	cans (14½ ounces each) chicken broth		
8	(6-inch) corn tortillas	6	tablespoons freshly grated sharp cheddar cheese
3	cups canola oil		
	Salt, to taste	6	tablespoons freshly grated Monterey Jack cheese
1½	tablespoons chopped cilantro leaves		

To Prepare Chiles on an Outdoor Grill Over moderately hot coals, place the poblano chiles on a grill coated with a nonstick vegetable spray. Cover and cook for 16 to 20 minutes or until skins are charred all over, turning the peppers as skins blacken. Once grilled, place the peppers in a plastic bag and allow to steam for 15 minutes. When they are cool enough to handle, peel away the skin and remove the top and seeds (do not rinse the peppers).

To Prepare Chiles on an Indoor Grill Place the poblano chiles on a preheated grill over high heat and cook for 15 to 20 minutes or until skins are charred all over, turning the peppers as skins blacken. Once grilled, place the peppers in a plastic bag and allow to steam for 15 minutes. When they are cool enough to handle, peel away the skin and remove the top and seeds (do not rinse the peppers).

To Make Soup Heat olive oil in a large pot over moderate heat for 2 minutes. Add potato, onion, and carrot and sauté for 5 minutes, stirring occasionally. Add flour and cook for 1 minute. Add chicken broth and bring to a boil. Reduce heat to low and cook, covered, for 30 minutes. Allow soup to cool for 10 minutes.

While soup is cooking, stack corn tortillas together and trim the sides to form a square. Cut into 1½ × ½-inch strips. Heat canola oil to 350 degrees in a heavy saucepan over moderately high heat. Add tortilla strips, a handful at a time, and cook for 1 to 2 minutes or just until light brown. Remove strips with a slotted spoon and drain on paper towels. Lightly season tortilla strips with salt while they're still warm.

In a large work bowl of a food processor fitted with a metal blade, process cilantro until chopped. Add poblano chiles and process until pureed. Add soup, one half at a time, and process until smooth. Return soup to pot and add savory, ½ teaspoon salt, pepper, and garlic salt and blend well. Keep warm over low heat.

To Serve Divide tortilla strips, avocado, and cheeses among six soup bowls and ladle grilled poblano soup on top.

Grilled Potatoes

Grilled potatoes are delicious topped with butter or sour cream. The cooked potatoes can also be scooped out of the shell (leaving the shell intact), mixed with cheddar cheese and sour cream, spooned back into the potato shell, and reheated in a 425-degree oven for 15 to 20 minutes. Serve with a topping of your favorite salsa.

4   baking potatoes
    Canola oil

To Prepare Potatoes on an Outdoor Grill Prick potatoes all over with a fork and coat with canola oil. Enclose each potato in a piece of aluminum foil. Over hot coals, place potatoes on a grill. Cover grill and cook for 45 to 55 minutes or until potatoes are soft when lightly squeezed, turning potatoes occasionally.

To Prepare Potatoes on an Indoor Grill Prick potatoes all over with a fork and coat with canola oil. Enclose each potato in a piece of aluminum foil. Place potatoes on a preheated grill over high heat and cook for 1 hour and 30 minutes or until potatoes are soft when lightly squeezed, turning potatoes occasionally.

Grilled Spicy Yams

SERVES 4

This recipe will become a favorite of anyone who craves spicy foods. It will definitely add zest to any meal!

3	yams	½	teaspoon freshly ground
3	tablespoons canola oil		pepper
½	teaspoon oregano	⅛	teaspoon paprika
½	teaspoon basil	⅛	teaspoon cayenne
½	teaspoon rosemary	⅛	teaspoon cinnamon
½	teaspoon thyme	⅛	teaspoon salt

To Spice Yams Preheat oven to 400 degrees. Prick yams all over with a fork. Bake for 25 minutes or until yams are slightly tender when gently squeezed. Allow the yams to cool, then remove skins and cut into large wedges.

Combine canola oil, oregano, basil, rosemary, thyme, pepper, paprika, cayenne, cinnamon, and salt in a resealable plastic bag and blend. Add the yams and gently turn to coat all over.

To Prepare Yams on an Outdoor Grill Soak bamboo skewers in water for 30 minutes or more. Thread the yams about ½ inch apart on pairs of skewers that are parallel to each other. Over hot coals, place yams on a grill coated with a nonstick vegetable spray. Cover grill and cook for 10 to 15 minutes or until yams are brown and fork-tender, turning yams occasionally.

To Prepare Yams on an Indoor Grill Soak bamboo skewers in water for 30 minutes or more. Thread the yams about ½ inch apart on pairs of skewers that are parallel to each other. Place yams on a preheated grill over moderate heat and cook for 25 to 30 minutes or until yams are brown and fork-tender, turning yams occasionally.

Grilled Red Pepper Dip

MAKES 2 CUPS

I had this dip at a friend's house and was immediately impressed. Once you have tasted it, you'll think twice before making any other kind of dip. It can be made the day before and brought to room temperature just before serving. Serve with blue corn chips.

2 red bell peppers
8 green onions, white part only
¼ cup chopped cilantro leaves
2 cloves garlic, chopped
⅔ cup marinated sun-dried tomatoes in olive oil, drained

1 package (8 ounces) cream cheese, at room temperature
2 teaspoons cumin
¼ teaspoon salt

To Prepare Peppers on an Outdoor Grill Over moderately hot coals, place the red peppers on a grill coated with a nonstick vegetable spray. Cover and cook for 20 to 24 minutes or until skins are charred all over, turning the peppers as skins blacken. Once grilled, place the peppers in a plastic bag and allow to steam for 15 minutes. When they are cool enough to handle, peel away the skins and remove the tops and seeds (do not rinse the peppers).

To Prepare Peppers on an Indoor Grill Place the red peppers on a preheated grill over high heat and cook for 30 to 40 minutes or until skins are charred all over, turning the peppers as skins blacken. Once grilled, place the peppers in a plastic bag and allow to steam for 15 minutes. When they are cool enough to handle, peel away the skins and remove the tops and seeds (do not rinse the peppers).

To Make Dip In the work bowl of a food processor fitted with a metal blade, process the green onions, cilantro, and garlic until finely chopped. Add the grilled red peppers and sun-dried tomatoes and process just until blended. Add the cream cheese, cumin, and salt and process until smooth. Transfer grilled red pepper dip to a serving dish. The grilled red pepper dip can be served immediately or it can be refrigerated, covered, for several hours or overnight. Allow it to come to room temperature before serving.

Vegetables and Fruit

Grilled Red Pepper Flan

SERVES 4

This special flan is made with smoke-flavored grilled red peppers. The contrast of the colors—beautiful red-colored flan garnished with baby basil leaves in a white custard dish—makes a striking presentation. Serve with any of your favorite beef or pork dishes.

4 large red bell peppers	⅛ teaspoon cayenne
½ teaspoon salt	½ cup heavy cream
½ teaspoon thyme	2 eggs

To Prepare Peppers on an Outdoor Grill Over moderately hot coals, place the red peppers on a grill coated with a nonstick vegetable spray. Cover and cook for 20 to 24 minutes or until skins are charred all over, turning the peppers as skins blacken. Once grilled, place the peppers in a plastic bag and allow to steam for 15 minutes. When they are cool enough to handle, peel away the skins and remove the tops and seeds (do not rinse the peppers).

To Prepare Peppers on an Indoor Grill Place the red peppers on a preheated grill over high heat and cook for 30 to 40 minutes or until skins are charred all over, turning the peppers as skins blacken. Once grilled, place the peppers in a plastic bag and allow to steam for 15 minutes. When they are cool enough to handle, peel away the skins and remove the tops and seeds (do not rinse the peppers).

To Make Flan In the work bowl of a food processor fitted with a metal blade, process grilled red peppers until pureed. Transfer pureed peppers to a heavy, medium saucepan over low heat and add salt, thyme, and cayenne. Cook for 15 minutes, stirring occasionally. Allow red pepper puree to come to room temperature.

Preheat oven to 400 degrees. In the same work bowl of the food processor, combine red pepper puree, heavy cream, and eggs and process until well blended. Divide red pepper puree among four ½-cup custard molds that have been coated with a nonstick vegetable spray. Place molds in a large pan filled with enough hot water to come halfway up the sides of the custard cups. Bake for 40 to 45 minutes or until a knife inserted into the center of the flan comes out clean. (If the flans should puff out, they will flatten when inverted onto plates, or they can be lightly flattened with a knife.)

To Serve Run a knife around each flan and place a plate on top; invert and remove custard cup. Garnish each serving with 2 baby basil leaves or a sprig of parsley or watercress. The flan can also be served in the custard cups.

Veggie Burgers

These burgers are from my cookbook The Lowfat Grill. *They are chock-full of wholesome vegetables and grains and are wonderful topped with lettuce, thinly sliced Vidalia onions, tomatoes, green pepper, and alfalfa sprouts. The entire creation can be nestled in whole-wheat buns or pita bread. Serve with mugs of Grilled Poblano Soup (page 344).*

½ cup bulgur
¾ cup boiling water
¼ cup quinoa
4 shallots
1 can (19 ounces) cannellini beans, drained
1 cup bread crumbs
¾ cup packed chopped spinach
½ cup chopped carrots

¼ cup packed chopped parsley
2 tablespoons chopped celery
2 tablespoons chopped walnuts
2 fresh mushrooms, chopped
½ tablespoon Worcestershire sauce
½ teaspoon freshly ground pepper

To Assemble Burgers Place bulgur in a large mixing bowl and pour boiling water over it. Cover bowl with plastic wrap and allow to sit for 15 minutes. Transfer bulgur to a sieve lined with cheesecloth and squeeze out all the liquid. Return bulgur to mixing bowl and set aside.

In a small saucepan, bring ½ cup water to a boil over moderately high heat. Add quinoa, reduce heat, cover, and cook for 20 minutes. Add quinoa to bulgur.

In the work bowl of a food processor fitted with a metal blade, process shallots until finely chopped. Add cannelloni beans and finely chop. Add bread crumbs, spinach, carrots, parsley, celery, walnuts, mushrooms, Worcestershire sauce, and pepper and blend well. Form the mixture into 8 patties.

To Prepare Burgers on an Outdoor Grill Over moderately hot coals, place veggie burgers on a grill coated with a nonstick vegetable spray. Cover grill and cook for 8 to 12 minutes, turning burgers every 3 minutes.

To Prepare Burgers on an Indoor Grill Place veggie burgers on a preheated grill and cook over moderately high heat for 25 minutes, turning burgers every 6 to 8 minutes.

Grilled Red Pepper Hollandaise

SERVES 6

Hollandaise, a wonderful French sauce, is made with egg yolks and butter combined with fresh lemon juice. Adding grilled red peppers intensifies its flavor and adds a beautiful contrasting color when spooned over vegetables or seafood. I like to serve it over steamed asparagus spears.

2	red bell peppers	¼	teaspoon salt
4	egg yolks, at room temperature	⅛	teaspoon freshly ground pepper
1½	tablespoons fresh lemon juice	2	tablespoons butter, melted

To Prepare Peppers on an Outdoor Grill Over moderately hot coals, place the red peppers on a grill and cook for 20 to 24 minutes or until skins are charred all over, turning the peppers as skins blacken. Once grilled, place the peppers in a plastic bag and allow to steam for 15 minutes. When they are cool enough to handle, peel away the skins and remove the tops and seeds (do not rinse the peppers).

To Prepare Peppers on an Indoor Grill Place the red peppers on a preheated grill over high heat and cook for 30 to 40 minutes or until skins are charred all over, turning the peppers as skins blacken. Once grilled, place the peppers in a plastic bag and allow to steam for 15 minutes. When they are cool enough to handle, peel away the skins and remove the tops and seeds (do not rinse the peppers).

To Make Hollandaise In the work bowl of a food processor fitted with a metal blade, process grilled red peppers until pureed. Transfer to a small bowl.

In the clean work bowl of a food processor fitted with a metal blade, process egg yolks, lemon juice, salt, and pepper until blended. Add butter in a slow, steady stream and process until smooth. Add red pepper puree and process until blended.

Grilled Vegetable Kebabs

SERVES 4

The smoky flavor of these grilled vegetables makes this an excellent side dish to accompany any of your favorite grilled specialties. The vegetables can also be incorporated into a vegetarian main course by serving them as a topping on pasta or brown rice, stuffing them in pita bread with feta cheese, or placing them on focaccia and making it a pizza.

3	tablespoons extra virgin olive oil	1	yellow squash, sliced into ¼-inch-thick rounds
2	cloves garlic, minced	1	large red onion, cut into 8 pieces and secured with toothpicks
1	teaspoon oregano		
1	teaspoon freshly ground pepper	1	large red bell pepper, seeded and cut into 8 pieces
½	teaspoon salt		
1	Japanese eggplant, sliced into ¼-inch-thick rounds	1	large portobello mushroom, cut into 8 pieces

To Make Marinade Combine olive oil, 1 tablespoon cold water, garlic, oregano, pepper, and salt in a large resealable plastic bag and blend. Add eggplant, yellow squash, red onion, red pepper, and portobello mushroom and turn to coat all over. Set aside for several hours, turning vegetables occasionally.

To Prepare Vegetables on an Outdoor Grill Soak bamboo skewers in water for 30 minutes or more. Remove toothpicks from onion and alternate eggplant, yellow squash, red onion, red pepper, and portobello mushroom on skewers (see note). Over moderately hot coals, place vegetables on a grill coated with a nonstick vegetable spray. Cover grill and cook for 8 to 12 minutes or until vegetables are brown and fork-tender, turning every 4 minutes.

To Prepare Vegetables on an Indoor Grill Soak bamboo skewers in water for 30 minutes or more. Remove toothpicks from onion and alternate eggplant, yellow squash, red onion, red pepper, and portobello mushroom on skewers (see note). Place vegetables on a preheated grill over moderately high heat and cook for 20 to 30 minutes or until vegetables are brown and fork-tender, turning vegetables every 8 minutes.

Note If vegetables are uneven in size and shape, thread the vegetables onto two bamboo skewers that are parallel to each other, about 1 inch apart. This will make it easier to turn the skewers and it will keep the vegetables secure.

Grilled Vegetables with Mozzarella

SERVES 4

The smoky flavor from the grill, the savory marinated vegetables, and the melted mozzarella combine to form an epicurean delight! As a side dish, it complements most grilled lamb and beef dishes, but it can be served as a wonderful vegetarian entree as well.

3	tablespoons extra virgin olive oil	1	red bell pepper, seeded and cut into 8 pieces
3	cloves garlic, minced	1	Japanese eggplant, sliced into ¼-inch-thick rounds
1	tablespoon thyme	1	zucchini, sliced into ¼-inch-thick rounds
1	tablespoon oregano		
1	tablespoon basil	1	red onion, cut into 8 pieces, each held together with a toothpick
1	teaspoon freshly ground pepper		
¼	teaspoon salt	4	ounces shredded mozzarella cheese
8	new potatoes		

To Make Marinade Combine olive oil, 1 tablespoon cold water, garlic, thyme, oregano, basil, pepper, and salt in a resealable plastic bag and blend.

Place potatoes in a large saucepan with enough water to cover and bring to a boil over high heat. Turn heat off, cover saucepan, and allow potatoes to come to room temperature. (This method for cooking potatoes can also be used to make hard-boiled eggs.) When potatoes are cool, drain well. Cut potatoes in half.

Place potatoes, red pepper, eggplant, zucchini, and red onion in marinade and turn to coat all over. Marinate for several hours or overnight, turning vegetables at least once.

To Prepare Vegetables on an Outdoor Grill Soak bamboo skewers in water for 30 minutes or more. Remove toothpicks from onion and alternate potatoes, red pepper, eggplant, zucchini, and red onion on skewers (see note). Over moderately hot coals, place vegetables on a grill coated with a nonstick vegetable spray. Cover grill and cook for 8 to 12 minutes or until vegetables are well browned, turning vegetables every 4 minutes.

To Prepare Vegetables on an Indoor Grill Soak bamboo skewers in water for 30 minutes or more. Remove toothpicks from onion and alternate potatoes, red pepper, eggplant, zucchini, and red onion on skewers (see note). Place them on a preheated grill over moderately high heat and cook for 20 to 30 minutes, turning vegetables every 8 minutes.

To Serve Preheat broiler and remove vegetables from skewers. Place the vegetables in a shallow broiler-proof dish and distribute mozzarella cheese over top. Place vegetables under broiler until cheese melts. Serve while hot.

Note If vegetables are uneven in size and shape, thread the vegetables onto two bamboo skewers that are parallel to each other, about 1 inch apart. This will make it easier to turn the skewers and it will keep the vegetables secure.

Grilled Zucchini Soup with Cinnamon Croutons

SERVES 4

When your garden is overflowing with zucchini, you will love the delicious opportunity this recipe provides. The soup has a subtly spicy flavor from the cinnamon stick and the crisp cinnamon croutons sprinkled over the top of each serving. Serve the soup hot or at room temperature.

Cinnamon Croutons

2½ tablespoons butter, melted
2 teaspoons cinnamon
1¼ cups bread cubes
(½-inch cubes)

Zucchini Soup

1 tablespoon extra virgin
olive oil
3 pounds zucchini, cut
horizontally into
¼-inch-thick slices

2 tablespoons butter
1 Vidalia onion or other sweet
onion, coarsely chopped
1 can (14½ ounces)
vegetable broth
1 (3-inch) cinnamon stick
½ teaspoon cinnamon
½ teaspoon thyme
½ teaspoon marjoram
¼ teaspoon salt
1 cup heavy cream

To Make Croutons Preheat oven to 350 degrees. Combine butter and cinnamon in a medium bowl. Add bread cubes and turn to coat all over. Place bread cubes on a baking sheet and bake for 10 to 15 minutes or until croutons are crisp. Cool cinnamon croutons before storing in a covered container.

To Prepare Zucchini on an Outdoor Grill Combine olive oil and zucchini in a plastic bag and turn zucchini to coat all over. Over moderately hot coals, place zucchini on a grilling grid coated with a nonstick vegetable spray. Cover grill and cook for 10 to 12 minutes or until zucchini slices are brown and fork-tender, turning frequently.

To Prepare Zucchini on an Indoor Grill Combine olive oil and zucchini in a plastic bag and turn zucchini to coat all over. Place zucchini on a preheated grill over moderately high heat and cook for 20 to 24 minutes or until zucchini slices are brown and fork-tender, turning frequently.

To Make Soup Melt butter in a large saucepan over moderate heat. Add onion and sauté for 5 minutes, turning occasionally. Add vegetable broth, cinnamon stick, cinnamon, thyme, marjoram, and salt and bring to a boil. Reduce heat, cover, and simmer for 25 minutes. Allow the soup to cool for 10 minutes.

In a large work bowl of a food processor fitted with a metal blade, process grilled zucchini until finely chopped. Add soup and process until smooth. Return soup to saucepan and add heavy cream. Cook over moderate heat until hot, stirring frequently.

To Serve Divide soup among four soup bowls and garnish with cinnamon croutons.

Marinated Tofu Kebabs

SERVES 4

Tofu, made from soybeans, is recognized as one of the most nutritious foods. If you have resisted eating tofu, this is the time to try it! In this recipe, the tofu readily absorbs the multitude of flavors contained in the marinade.

½ cup fresh orange juice
¼ cup soy sauce
½ tablespoon canola oil
1½ teaspoons oriental sesame oil
1 tablespoon packed dark brown sugar
1 tablespoon minced ginger

¼ teaspoon crushed red pepper
1 pound firm tofu, drained
8 shiitake mushrooms
8 red bell pepper, cut into 8 pieces
8 fresh pineapple chunks

To Make Marinade Combine orange juice, soy sauce, canola oil, sesame oil, brown sugar, ginger, and crushed red pepper in a nonmetal dish.

Place tofu between two flat plates and weight the top with a bowl of water or a stack of plates (pressing the tofu makes it firmer and more absorbent). Refrigerate for 1 hour, then pour off any water. Slice the tofu in half horizontally. Place it in the marinade and turn to coat both sides. Allow the tofu to sit at room temperature for 1 hour (see note).

To Prepare Kebabs on an Outdoor Grill Soak bamboo skewers in water for 30 minutes or more. Cut tofu into 1¼-inch squares. Alternate tofu, shiitake mushrooms, red pepper, and pineapple on skewers. Over moderately hot coals, place tofu kebabs on a grill coated with a nonstick vegetable spray. Cover grill and cook for 10 minutes or until kebabs are brown all over, turning tofu kebabs frequently.

To Prepare Kebabs on an Indoor Grill Soak bamboo skewers in water for 30 minutes or more. Cut tofu into 1¼-inch squares. Alternate tofu, shiitake mushrooms, red pepper, and pineapple on skewers. Place them on a preheated grill over moderately high heat and cook for 30 minutes or until kebabs are brown all over, turning tofu kebabs frequently.

Note The tofu can also be prepared by cutting it into two pieces, marinating it, and inserting two skewers parallel to each other lengthwise into the tofu (the cooking time remains the same). After it is grilled, it can be eaten as is or added to a salad made with mixed baby greens and mango slices, laced with an oriental dressing.

Vegetables and Fruit

Pita Bread with Grilled Vegetables

SERVES 4

This is a favorite recipe from my cookbook The Lowfat Grill, *and I have adapted it to use with an indoor grill. Tahini paste, which is frequently used in Middle Eastern cooking, is made from ground, toasted, and hulled sesame seeds. It is fabulous in combination with lemon juice, spices, and yogurt, and it highlights the smoky flavor of grilled vegetables. Serve with Tabbouleh (page 92).*

Tahini Sauce

2	cloves garlic
½	cup coarsely chopped parsley
6	tablespoons plain yogurt
¼	cup fresh lemon juice
3	tablespoons tahini paste
2	tablespoons cumin
⅛	teaspoon salt
⅛	teaspoon freshly ground white pepper

Grilled Vegetables

1	eggplant (12 ounces), peeled and cut horizontally into ¼-inch-thick slices

	Salt
1½	tablespoons extra virgin olive oil
1	zucchini, cut horizontally into ¼-inch-thick slices
2	cloves garlic
1	yellow bell pepper
⅛	teaspoon salt
⅛	teaspoon freshly ground pepper
2	tablespoons chopped parsley
4	pita breads, halved and warmed

To Make Tahini Sauce In the work bowl of a food processor fitted with a metal blade, process garlic and parsley until finely chopped. Add yogurt, lemon juice, tahini paste, cumin, salt, and white pepper and process until blended. Refrigerate tahini sauce in a covered container until ready to serve.

To Prepare Vegetables on an Outdoor Grill Place eggplant in a colander and sprinkle salt all over. Allow to sit for 30 minutes. Combine olive oil, eggplant, zucchini, and garlic in a resealable plastic bag and turn to coat all over.

Over moderately hot coals, place the yellow pepper on a grill. Cover grill and cook for 20 to 24 minutes or until skin is charred all over, turning pepper as skin blackens. Place pepper in a plastic bag and allow to steam for 15 minutes. When the pepper is cool enough to handle, peel away the skins and remove the tops and seeds (do not wash the pepper). Cut the pepper into thin slices and set aside.

Place eggplant and zucchini on a grilling grid coated with a nonstick vegetable spray. Cover grill and cook for 10 to 12 minutes or until vegetables are brown and fork-tender, turning occasionally. Cut the eggplant and zucchini into thin slices.

To Prepare Vegetables on an Indoor Grill Place eggplant in a colander and sprinkle salt all over. Allow to sit for 30 minutes. Combine olive oil, eggplant, zucchini, and garlic in a resealable plastic bag and turn to coat all over.

Place the yellow pepper on a preheated grill over high heat and cook for 30 to 40 minutes or until skin is charred all over, turning the pepper as skin blackens. Place the pepper in a plastic bag and allow to steam for 15 minutes. When the pepper is cool enough to handle, peel away the skins and remove the tops and seeds (do not rinse the pepper). Cut the pepper into thin slices and set aside.

Place eggplant and zucchini on a preheated grill over high heat and cook for 16 to 24 minutes or until vegetables are brown all over, turning occasionally. Cut the eggplant and zucchini into thin slices.

To Serve Combine yellow pepper, eggplant, and zucchini slices in a bowl. Add salt, pepper, and parsley and blend well. Spoon vegetable filling two-thirds full into warmed pita bread halves and spoon some tahini sauce over each.

Pizza with Tomatoes, Basil, and Mozzarella

SERVES 4

Pizza cooked on a grill is a great taste sensation! Although the preparation techniques differ somewhat for an indoor and an outdoor grill, the result is uniformly rewarding.

1	Boboli Italian Pizza Crust (thin crust) or favorite pizza crust	2	tablespoons packed thinly sliced basil
1	tablespoon extra virgin olive oil	1½	cups freshly grated mozzarella cheese
4	plum tomatoes, thinly sliced	¼	cup freshly grated Parmesan cheese

To Prepare Pizza on an Outdoor Grill Prepare the grill by placing charcoal on one half of the fuel grate and a drip pan on the other half. When coals are moderately hot, brush top of pizza crust with olive oil. Place the crust, oiled side down, on a grill coated with a nonstick vegetable spray and set it over the side with the coals. Cover grill and cook for 2 minutes or until grill marks form. Remove pizza crust from grill and turn over so oiled side is facing up. Distribute tomatoes, basil, mozzarella cheese, and Parmesan cheese all over the crust. Place pizza on grill over the side with the aluminum pan. Cover grill and cook for 10 minutes or until cheese has melted, occasionally giving pizza quarter turns.

To Prepare Pizza on an Indoor Grill Preheat both burners of indoor grill. Brush top of pizza crust with olive oil. Place pizza crust, oiled side down, on a pizza grid that has been coated with a nonstick vegetable spray. Place the pizza grid in the center of the two grates over moderate heat for 4 minutes, giving it a quarter turn at 1-minute intervals. Remove pizza grid from grill and turn pizza crust over so the oiled side is facing up on the grid. Distribute tomatoes, basil, mozzarella cheese, and Parmesan cheese all over the crust. Place pizza grid back on grill in the same position and cook for 15 minutes, giving pizza grid a quarter turn every 3 minutes. Remove pizza grid from the grill and place it under a preheated broiler for 2 to 3 minutes or just until cheese starts to bubble.

Note Pizza grids are available in most hardware stores, gourmet shops, or catalogs. Although relatively inexpensive, they are an invaluable tool for making perfect pizzas on an indoor grill. They can also be used on an outdoor grill.

Pizza with Zucchini and Red Bell Peppers

SERVES 4

The idea for this pizza occurred to me when I received a call from a neighbor imploring me to take some zucchini and red peppers from her overflowing garden. It's a great way to utilize your garden bounty.

2 red bell peppers
3 tablespoons extra virgin olive oil
1 small zucchini, cut horizontally into ¼-inch-thick slices
1 Boboli Italian Pizza Crust (thin crust) or favorite pizza crust

¼ cup freshly grated Parmesan cheese
¼ teaspoon salt
¼ teaspoon freshly ground pepper
1½ cups freshly grated mozzarella cheese

To Prepare Peppers and Zucchini on an Outdoor Grill
Over moderately hot coals, place the red peppers on a grill coated with a nonstick vegetable spray. Cover and cook for 20 to 24 minutes or until skins are charred all over, turning the peppers as skins blacken. Once grilled, place the peppers in a plastic bag and allow to steam for 15 minutes. When they are cool enough to handle, peel away the skins and remove tops and seeds (do not rinse the peppers). Cut the red peppers into slivers.

Combine 2 tablespoons olive oil and zucchini in a resealable plastic bag and turn to coat zucchini all over. Place zucchini on a grilling grid coated with a nonstick vegetable spray and place over moderately hot coals. Cover grill and cook for 10 to 12 minutes or until zucchini slices are brown and fork-tender, turning frequently. Cut the zucchini into slivers.

To Prepare Peppers and Zucchini on an Indoor Grill
Place the red peppers on a preheated grill over high heat and cook for 30 to 40 minutes or until skins are charred all over, turning the peppers as skins blacken. Once grilled, place the peppers in a plastic bag and allow to steam for 15 minutes. When they are cool enough to handle, peel away the skins and remove the tops and seeds (do not rinse the peppers). Cut the red peppers into slivers.

Combine 2 tablespoons olive oil and zucchini in a resealable plastic bag and turn to coat zucchini all over. Place zucchini on a preheated grill over high heat and cook for 16 to 24 minutes or until zucchini slices are brown and fork-tender, turning frequently. Cut the zucchini into slivers.

To Prepare Pizza on an Outdoor Grill Using barbecue tongs, carefully move hot coals so they are all concentrated on one half of the fuel grate and place a drip pan on the empty half. Brush top of pizza crust with remaining 1 tablespoon olive oil. Place the crust, oiled side down, on a grill coated with a nonstick vegetable spray and set it over the side with coals. Cover grill and cook for 2 minutes or until grill marks form. Remove pizza crust from grill and turn over so oiled side is facing up. Distribute Parmesan cheese, grilled zucchini and red peppers, salt, pepper, and mozzarella cheese all over the crust. Place pizza on grill over the side with the aluminum pan. Cover grill and cook for 10 minutes or until cheese has melted, occasionally giving pizza quarter turns.

To Prepare Pizza on an Indoor Grill Preheat both burners of indoor grill. Brush top of pizza crust with remaining 1 tablespoon olive oil. Place pizza crust, oiled side down, on a pizza grid that has been coated with a nonstick vegetable spray. Place the pizza grid in the center of the two grates over moderate heat for 4 minutes, giving it a quarter turn at 1-minute intervals. Remove pizza grid from grill and turn pizza crust over so the oiled side is facing up on the grid. Distribute Parmesan cheese, grilled zucchini and red peppers, salt, pepper, and mozzarella cheese all over the crust. Place pizza grid back on grill in the same position and cook for 15 minutes, giving pizza grid a quarter turn every 3 minutes. Remove pizza grid from the grill and place it under a preheated broiler for 2 to 3 minutes or just until cheese starts to bubble.

Glossary

Aioli is a garlic mayonnaise that originated in France. It is an excellent condiment for seafood, meats, or vegetables.

Basmati rice is an aromatic long-grain rice. The most prized basmati is from northern India, especially Dehra Dun basmati, which derives its name from the Indian town in which it grows.

Boletus (cepe in French and **porcini** in Italian) is a wild mushroom with a firm cap that can grow up to seven inches across. It has a very rich flavor, which is intensified when the Boletus is cooked.

Bulgur is made from wheat berries. The berries are steamed, crushed, and then dried or dehydrated. When cooked, bulgur has a nutty flavor and is somewhat crunchy. It is available in health food stores.

Capers are the unopened flower buds of the caper bush. Typically they are pickled in vinegar and therefore should be rinsed before being used. As a garnish or condiment, they add piquancy to any dish. Capers are found in the olive section of most supermarkets.

Chanterelle (girolle) is a wild mushroom that is vase- or trumpet-shaped and yellow-orange in color. Because its meaty flesh has such an exceptionally sweet and delicious flavor and it has an appealing apricot-like aroma, it is highly prized by culinary experts.

CHILES:

Jalapeño is about one and a half inches long and one inch across. It is medium to dark green in color but is sometimes red. Regardless of color, jalapeños are very hot.

Pasilla is a dark mahogany, long and narrow, wrinkled chile that is sold dried. It has a very intense flavor.

Poblano is dark green and about four to five inches long and three to four inches around. Although it is medium to hot on the heat scale, grilling a poblano tends to make it sweeter.

Serrano is a bright green or red chile about two inches in length and a quarter inch across. It is one of the hottest chiles.

Chinese Five Spice powder is a mixture of cloves, cinnamon, fennel, star anise, and Szechwan peppercorns.

Cilantro is also known as Chinese parsley or fresh coriander. It is a member of the carrot/parsley family and has a very intense and pungent flavor. Look for fresh, undamaged leaves that are flat, crisp, and green. Cilantro is found in the produce section of supermarkets.

Coconut cream is the congealed coconut fat that rises to the surface when coconut milk is made. Coconut cream is found in Asian food stores.

Coconut milk is made by chopping or grating fresh coconut and soaking it in hot water, milk, or coconut water. This mixture is then mashed and strained. The strained liquid is coconut milk, which is an essential ingredient in Thai cooking. Coconut milk is found in Asian food stores.

Feta cheese is a soft, white Greek cheese that is made from goat or sheep's milk and is cured in a salt brine. It is crumbly and has a slightly sour, salty taste.

Ginger is a rhizome, or root, that originated in India but is now found throughout Asia. It is light brown and knotty on the outside and golden and juicy on the inside. Its flavor is both sweet and spicy. Ginger is found in Asian food stores or the produce section of supermarkets.

Gorgonzola cheese is a blue-veined cheese that was first made in the ninth century in Gorgonzola, a small Italian village near Milan. It is now made around the world, including in the U.S. It has a strong flavor and an exceptionally creamy texture.

Greek olives (kalamatas) are glossy black, almond-shaped olives that are cured in red wine vinegar and packed in jars. These rich and meaty olives are frequently used in salads. Kalamatas can be purchased by the pound at most specialty food stores or delis. They also can be found in the gourmet or olive section of supermarkets.

Green peppercorns (black, green, and white) are from the *Pipern nigrum,* a clinging vine that bears clusters of berries, or peppercorns. The berries that are picked before they ripen are still green and less pungent in taste. These berries, or green peppercorns, are frequently pickled, although some are also dehydrated and freeze-dried. Pickled green peppercorns can be sprinkled over food, combined in a sauce, or used to add color, texture, or flavor. They can also be mashed into a paste and combined with other ingredients.

Hearts of palm are the tender buds found at the top of certain palm trees grown in Florida and the Caribbean. The ivory-colored hearts of palm can be purchased canned and are found in the gourmet department or canned vegetable section of supermarkets.

Jasmine rice is a fragrant long-grain rice from Thailand. It can be found in Asian food stores.

Kecap manis is an Indonesian condiment. It is a sweet soy sauce made with palm sugar. Kecap manis is denser than the variety of soy sauce available in most supermarkets. It can be found in Asian food stores.

Kiwi fruit is about the size of a plum and grows on a vine. It has a brown fuzzy skin and a luscious emerald green pulp that surrounds a cluster of black seeds. The kiwi fruit was originally grown in the Far East and was known as the Chinese gooseberry. However, there are some who believe this fruit originated in New Zealand, and in keeping with this belief, it was renamed "kiwi" in honor of the famous bird native to this island republic.

Lemongrass is a Southeast Asian herb. Its fibrous outer layer is removed to reveal the inner stalk, which is the culinary heart of the plant. It contains a delicate lemony flavor that seems to embrace food with a subtle, citrus perfume. Look for fresh lemongrass stalks in the produce section of a market.

Mirin (rice wine) is a golden, sweet, syrupy cooking wine made from sake (a Japanese rice wine), sweet rice, and rice malt. The alcohol content evaporates during the cooking process, leaving a distinct sweetness. Mirin is found in Asian food stores and in the Asian section of most supermarkets.

Miso is a fermented soybean paste produced by salting and fermenting soybeans and rice. It can be found in a range of colors, from dark brown to golden, each variety having its own characteristic taste and texture. It is found in Asian food stores.

Morels (sponge mushrooms) are wild mushrooms that have a honeycomb cap resembling a sponge. They are considered to be one of the most delicious wild mushrooms. Morels must be cooked before they are eaten.

Mushroom soy sauce is a variety of soy sauce that is richer in flavor and is denser than ordinary soy sauce. It is available in Asian food stores.

Pecorino cheese   is a pungent-tasting Italian cheese made from sheep's milk.

Pepperoncinis   are peppers that are green at first, then turn red when allowed to ripen. After the peppers are harvested in the green stage, they are usually pickled. These crunchy and spicy pickled pepperoncinis are ideal as a garnish, as additions to salads, or as an ingredient on an antipasto platter.

Pesto   is an Italian sauce that is a specialty of Genoa. The traditional ingredients in pesto are basil, pecorino cheese, pine nuts, and olive oil, all of which are blended together until the consistency of creamy butter is reached. Pesto is excellent on pasta, added to sauces, or made into a delicious pesto tart.

Pine nuts (pignolias or **pinon nuts)**   are the small, edible seeds found in the cones of the stone pine. They can be eaten raw or toasted; when they are ground into a flour, they are used to make desserts. Pine nuts can be found in health food stores or in the gourmet section of supermarkets.

Polenta   is known to have originated in Italy in the sixteenth century. It is an Italian porridge or mush that is made from cornmeal. Polenta placed in a pan and refrigerated for several hours becomes firm and is suitable for grilling, baking, or frying. Prepared this way, it acquires a consistency similar to that of corn bread.

Portobello mushrooms   are giant, cultivated mushrooms with open caps that measure from four to ten inches across and are dark brown in color. They are found in the produce section of supermarkets.

Quinoa   (pronounced keen-wa) is a South American grain that is an excellent source of protein and other nutrients. In fact, it is higher in protein than any other grain. It is used as a substitute for rice or couscous and makes a delicious salad ingredient. Quinoa is available in health food stores.

Ricotta   is an Italian white cheese made from milk whey that is left over from the production of other cheeses.

Sake   is an Asian rice wine. The most recognized variety is Japanese sake, which is very potent and somewhat sweet. It is used in cooking or served warm to drink.

Sesame oil   is an aromatic, amber-colored oil made from roasted sesame seeds. It has a distinctive nutty flavor. Oriental sesame oils have the most flavor.

Sesame paste   is made from ground toasted sesame seeds and has a distinct, nutty taste. It can be found in most Asian or Middle Eastern food stores.

Shallots   like onions and garlic, are a bulbous member of the lily family. Shallots are milder in taste than onions and less pungent than garlic.

Shiitake mushrooms (oak, Chinese, or **Black Forest mushrooms)**   are tan to dark brown in color with a white veil on their underside between the cap and stem. Only the cap of the mushroom, with its smoky flavor, is eaten. Shiitake mushrooms are frequently used in Asian cuisine. They can be found in the produce section of supermarkets.

Shoyu sauce   is a Japanese variety of soy sauce. It is somewhat sweeter and less salty than Chinese soy sauce.

Sriracha hot chili sauce   is a smooth, red sauce made from serrano chiles. It is milder and thicker than other hot pepper sauces.

Star fruit (carambola)   is a juicy fruit that is both sweet and tart. It has a smooth, waxy yellow-orange skin with five distinct ridges. When the star fruit is sliced, its outline resembles that of a star. The star fruit is native to the Malay Archipelago, but it is now grown commercially in southern Florida.

Szechwan peppercorns   are reddish brown berries that are very aromatic. They are found in Asian food stores.

Tabbouleh   is a Middle Eastern salad made with bulgur.

Tandoori paste   is a blend of ground Indian spices. The paste can be mixed with yogurt to create a marinade for poultry, meat, or fish before grilling. Tandoori paste is found in Asian or Indian food stores.

Tobiko caviar   is the roe of the orange-red flying fish, tobiko. The roe has a mild, sweet flavor and is slightly crunchy.

Tofu (bean curd)   is a high-protein soybean food that is eaten throughout Asia. It is white and resembles soft cheese in texture. Tofu has a very bland taste, although it readily absorbs other flavors. The versatility of tofu allows it to be used in soups and salads, in baking, and as a substitute for meat. It is found in Asian food stores or in the produce section of supermarkets.

Tomatillos   are Mexican green tomatoes that resemble cherry tomatoes but are firmer, juicier, and more tart. They will turn yellow if allowed to ripen; however, the preferred way to use them is when they are green. Before using tomatillos, remove the papery, brown husk that covers them and the resinous material under the husk by boiling them in water and then peeling. Tomatillos are found in the produce section of supermarkets.

Watercress   is a popular salad green that has a peppery taste. It is often used to add a kick to sandwiches, soups, and salads.

Wild rice   is a North American aquatic grass, not a rice. Its small black seeds are the same size and shape as rice, so the early European explorers of the Americas named it "wild rice." Most wild rice is cultivated in Minnesota, Wisconsin, and Michigan, with some now being grown in California as well. It is used as an ingredient for salads and stuffing or served as a grain side dish. Wild rice is found in boxes and bags in the rice section of the supermarket.

Index

INTERNATIONAL CONVERSION CHART

These are not exact equivalents: they have been slightly rounded to make measuring easier.

LIQUID MEASUREMENTS

American	Imperial	Metric	Australian
2 tablespoons (1 oz.)	1 fl. oz.	30 ml	1 tablespoon
¼ cup (2 oz.)	2 fl. oz.	60 ml	2 tablespoons
⅓ cup (3 oz.)	3 fl. oz.	80 ml	¼ cup
½ cup (4 oz.)	4 fl. oz.	125 ml	⅓ cup
⅔ cup (5 oz.)	5 fl. oz.	165 ml	½ cup
¾ cup (6 oz.)	6 fl. oz.	185 ml	⅔ cup
1 cup (8 oz.)	8 fl. oz.	250 ml	¾ cup

SPOON MEASUREMENTS

American	Metric
¼ teaspoon	1 ml
½ teaspoon	2 ml
1 teaspoon	5 ml
1 tablespoon	15 ml

OVEN TEMPERATURES

Fahrenheit	Centigrade	Gas
250	120	½
300	150	2
325	160	3
350	180	4
375	190	5
400	200	6
450	230	8

WEIGHTS

U.S./UK	Metric
1 oz.	30 grams (g)
2 oz.	60 g
4 oz. (¼ lb)	125 g
5 oz. (⅓ lb)	155 g
6 oz.	185 g
7 oz.	220 g
8 oz. (½ lb)	250 g
10 oz.	315 g
12 oz. (¾ lb)	375 g
14 oz.	440 g
16 oz. (1 lb)	500 g
2 lbs.	1 kg

The Lowfat Grill

Donna Rodnitzky

U.S. $18.00
Can. $24.95
ISBN: 0-7615-0265-3
Comb bound / 336 pages

We all love to grill—it's a great way to spend time with friends and family, enjoy the outdoors, and prepare foods with a delicious smoky flavor. However, the foods typically prepared on the grill are frequently high in fat. *The Lowfat Grill* solves this grilling dilemma by providing simple techniques for taking leaner, traditionally less tender cuts of meat and making them juicy, succulent, and delicious through marinating.

175 Surprisingly Succulent Recipes for Meats, Marinades, Vegetables, Sauces, and More!

THE LOWFAT GRILL

DONNA RODNITZKY

To order, call (800) 632-8676 or visit us online at www.primapublishing.com

Bread Baking with Herbs

Mimi Luebbermann

U.S. $15.00
Can. $19.95
ISBN: 0-7615-0245-9
Hardcover / 224 pages

From the herb gardens of Windrush Farm, cookbook author Mimi Luebbermann has been creating and baking heavenly herb treats—shortbreads, muffins, foccacia breads, herbed pizza dough, sandwich bread, tarts, and more! This cookbook offers recipes for both sweet and savory breads, and instructions for growing your own herbs. Mimi also demonstrates how to dry and blend herbs, plus create and use herb-infused oils for baking.

To order, call (800) 632-8676 or visit us online at www.primapublishing.com

To Order Books

Please send me the following items:

Quantity	Title	Unit Price	Total
_____	**The Lowfat Grill**	$ **18.00**	$ _____
_____	**Bread Baking with Herbs**	$ **15.00**	$ _____
_____	_____	$ _____	$ _____
_____	_____	$ _____	$ _____
_____	_____	$ _____	$ _____

Subtotal $ _____

Deduct 10% when ordering 3–5 books $ _____

7.25% Sales Tax (CA only) $ _____

8.25% Sales Tax (TN only) $ _____

5.0% Sales Tax (MD and IN only) $ _____

7.0% G.S.T. Tax (Canada only) $ _____

Shipping and Handling* $ _____

Total Order $ _____

*Shipping and Handling depend on Subtotal.

Subtotal	Shipping/Handling
$0.00–$14.99	$3.00
$15.00–$29.99	$4.00
$30.00–$49.99	$6.00
$50.00–$99.99	$10.00
$100.00–$199.99	$13.50
$200.00+	Call for Quote

Foreign and all Priority Request orders:
Call Order Entry department
for price quote at 916-632-4400

This chart represents the total retail price of books only
(before applicable discounts are taken).

By Telephone: With MC or Visa, call 800-632-8676 or 916-632-4400. Mon–Fri, 8:30-4:30.

WWW: http://www.primapublishing.com

By Internet E-mail: sales@primapub.com

By Mail: Just fill out the information below and send with your remittance to:

Prima Publishing
P.O. Box 1260BK
Rocklin, CA 95677

Name _____

Address _____

City _____ State _____ ZIP _____

MC/Visa# _____ Exp. _____

Check/money order enclosed for $ _____ Payable to Prima Publishing

Daytime telephone _____

Signature _____